The Creation of Modern Buenos Aires

The Creation of Modern
BUENOS AIRES

Football, Civic Associations,
Barrios, and Politics, 1912-1943

Joel Horowitz

University of New Mexico Press | Albuquerque

© 2024 by University of New Mexico Press
All rights reserved. Published 2024
Printed in the United States of America

ISBN 978-0-8263-6574-3 (cloth)
ISBN 978-0-8263-6887-4 (paper)
ISBN 978-0-8263-6575-0 (pdf)

Library of Congress Control Number: 2024933654

Founded in 1889, the University of New Mexico sits on the traditional homelands of the Pueblo of Sandia. The original peoples of New Mexico—Pueblo, Navajo, and Apache—since time immemorial have deep connections to the land and have made significant contributions to the broader community statewide. We honor the land itself and those who remain stewards of this land throughout the generations and also acknowledge our committed relationship to Indigenous peoples. We gratefully recognize our history.

Cover illustration: cover of *River Plate* magazine #1
Designed by Felicia Cedillos
Composed in Alegreya and Tropiline

To Carol, Sarah, and Rachel
with love and gratitude

Contents

Acknowledgments ix

Introduction 1
CHAPTER ONE. The Barrio's Place in a Growing City 11
CHAPTER TWO. Political Capital and Civic Associations 28
CHAPTER THREE. Football: Politics and Barrios 41
CHAPTER FOUR. Popular Libraries as Civic Associations and Anchors of the Community 68
CHAPTER FIVE. Development Societies as Lobbyists and Centers of Sociability 94
CHAPTER SIX. The Search for More Education: Universidades Populares 119
Conclusion 143

Notes 151
Bibliography 177
Index 193

Acknowledgments

Over the many years that it took to write this book I have incurred many debts, both intellectual and personal. I am immensely grateful for the help and friendship I have received. It has made the effort even more fulfilling. If I have forgotten to mention someone, it has been an oversight and not an intended slight.

St. Bonaventure University helped fund a portion of the research. It also granted me several sabbaticals. Sandra Gayol invited me to make a presentation at a conference sponsored by the Universidad Nacional de General Sarmiento, which also allowed me to spend additional time in Argentina.

No historian can function without the assistance of librarians and archivists; they make research possible and frequently much more enjoyable. I thank the staff of Friedsam Library at St. Bonaventure University, especially Theresa Shaffer, who was the interlibrary loan librarian extraordinaire. I am also grateful to the staff of Widener Library at Harvard University. In Buenos Aires I owe a great debt to the staffs of the Biblioteca Nacional, the Biblioteca Pública Esteban Echeverría, the Archivo General de la Nación, and the Archivo Intermedio de la Nación and to the librarians of the Instituto Ravignani. I am extremely thankful to Leandro de Sagastizábal, Esteban Gutiérrez, Sebastián Ricardi, and Mariana Feyling for taking time from their busy schedules to arrange for me to consult the historical archive of the Comisión Nacional de Bibliotecas Populares (CONABIP), which is usually not available to scholars, and making my time at their important institution useful and pleasant. I would also like to thank the David Rockefeller Center for Latin American Studies at Harvard University.

I thank Jonathan Abelard, the late Joseph Arbena, Steven Brown, Lila Caimari, Alejandro Cattaruzza, Bridget María Chesterton, Juan Corradi, Sandra Gayol, Mark Healey, Roy Hora, Ruth Horowitz, Nils Jacobsen, Juan Carlos

Korol, Steven Levitsky, Johanna Liander, Sergio Lodise, Rory Miller, Jorge Nállim, Silvana Palermo, Phillip Payne, Mariano Plotkin, Fernando Rocchi, Hilda Sabato, the late Thomas Schaeper, Sergio Serulnikov, Melina Tobias, Juan Carlos Torre, and Gardenia Vidal for their help. I also thank the participants in conferences and workshops in both Argentina and North America who made excellent comments on my presentations. Lila Caimari, Nils Jacobsen, and Gardenia Vidal read an earlier version of significant portions of this work. Their comments were invariably useful and helpful. Mariano Plotkin not only read several chapters just after they were first composed but also read a complete version of the work. His comments were, as usual, intelligent, to the point, and scholarly.

I offer a special thanks to two readers for the press, Diego Armus and Rory Miller, who offered extremely useful suggestions to improve the work. I am also grateful to Michael Millman, senior acquisitions editor, at the press. I thank my copyeditor, Merryl Sloane, for her skillful and thoughtful work. I am extremely thankful to all who have aided me. I, of course, am responsible for all opinions and errors in the text.

I owe a special debt to my friend and mentor for decades, the late Tulio Halperín Donghi. He passed away while the project was still in its early stages. He only read a preliminary draft of an early chapter, but he displayed, in some ways not surprisingly, tremendous knowledge about a subject that one would assume that he knew little about. His influence lingers—if only in my head. I still wonder, when I am uncertain, what he would suggest. I know that my answer is different than what his would have been, but it does help me to think much more broadly.

The writing of history is much more than the time spent in libraries and archives. I thank Piroska Csurí, Estela Domínguez, Elsa Pintow, the late Mauricio Schaikevich, Juan Carlos Korol, Silvana Ablin, Mariano Plotkin, and Graciela Garone for sharing their city of Buenos Aires with me and Carol.

In Olean, New York, I thank Steven Brown for more shared lunches and conversations than I would like to contemplate. I also thank Paul Spaeth for many discussions and those lunches in the Lakeview Chinese Restaurant.

Finally, there is my family. Sarah and Rachel have both helped my intellectual pursuits in their own ways. More important, they have been a source of great joy. Carol read the manuscript many times and made suggestions. She has listened to my chattering on Argentine history and accompanied me on many of my research trips. Most of all, she has been my dream companion for almost half a century.

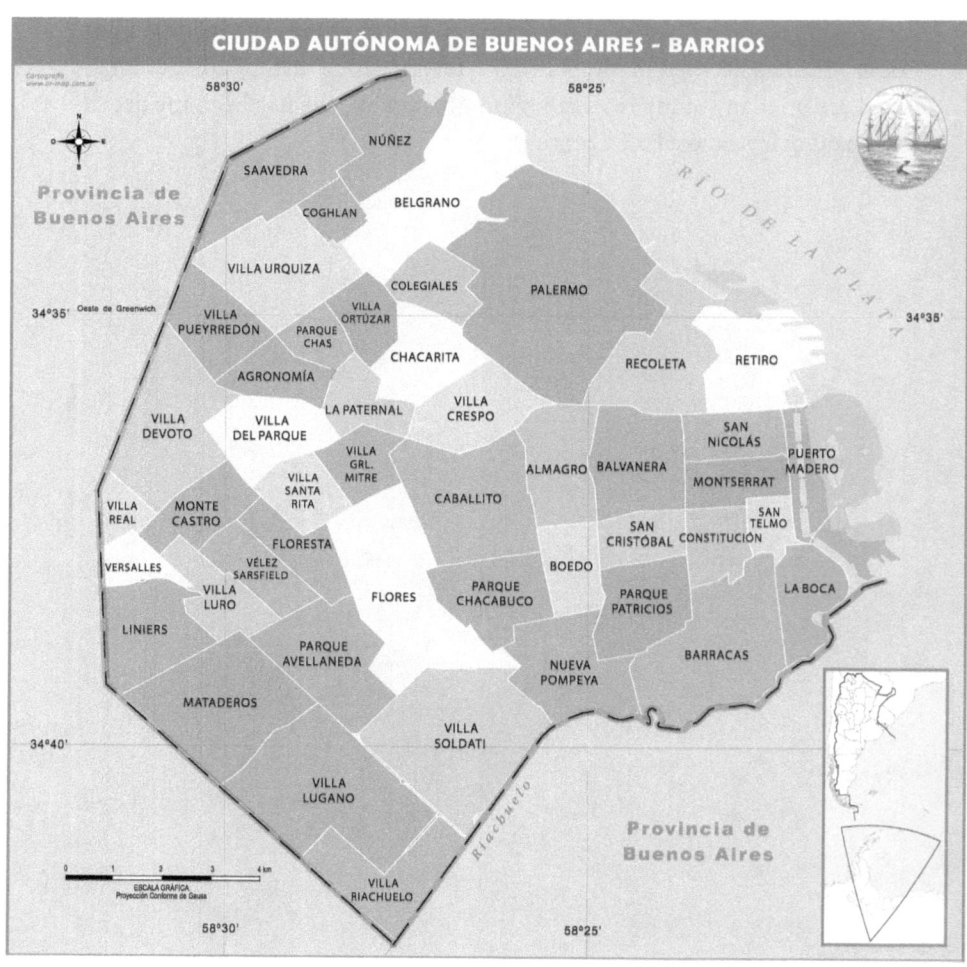

FIGURE 1. The Current Legally Established Barrios of the City of Buenos Aires.
Source: Sagape68, CC BY-SA 4.0, via Wikimedia Commons.

Introduction

Marco Polo describes a bridge, stone by stone.
"But which is the stone that supports the bridge?" Kublai Khan asks.
"The bridge is not supported by one stone or another," Marco answers, "but by the line of the arch that they form."
Kublai Khan remains silent, reflecting. Then he adds: "Why do you speak to me of the stones? It is only the arch that matters to me."
Polo answers: "Without stones there is no arch."

—ITALO CALVINO, *INVISIBLE CITIES*

WHEN IN DECEMBER 2015 Mauricio Macri, who first had become known to the general public as a president of the football club Boca Juniors, was sworn in as president of Argentina, the link between football and politics became most obvious. However, ties have existed since the first days of the sport in the country. Argentine football clubs were and are organized as civic associations, and they and many other types of civic associations became linked to the political world in the first decades of the twentieth century. The thousands of civic associations were much more than just political vehicles. They provided things that the inhabitants of Buenos Aires needed or wanted. They became centers of neighborhoods (barrios), places for social interchange and pride. They helped create the sense of barrio that became ingrained in the life of Buenos Aires. The barrio also was romanticized in tangos, the popular urban music of the first half of the twentieth century in Buenos Aires.

This book examines the impact of civic associations on the culture and the society of Buenos Aires and their ties to politics in the first decades of the twentieth century. The period saw the emergence of the modern political system with true appeals to the voters, tremendous urban growth, and the solidification of a barrio identity. The role of the civic associations in the making of modern Buenos Aires was critical. I make my arguments by examining four types of organizations: football clubs, *bibliotecas populares* (popular libraries), *sociedades de fomento* (development societies that pushed for barrio improvements), and *universidades populares* (popular universities that provided practical training beyond the primary school level). The decision to examine football clubs, which in Argentina are governed by, at least on paper, democratic rules, was the easiest to make, as I was first drawn to this subject by looking at them. They also had the most conspicuous ties to neighborhoods and politics. The other three types of association were chosen because they represent the inhabitants' abilities to step into the gaps left by the society. They provided education, libraries, or improvements in urban conditions; in other words, they were not the more common social or recreational civic associations.

All four types of organization became important social centers and were connected to the political world. The book focuses on the period from the passage of a voting reform law in 1912, which made male citizens' voting obligatory and fraud more difficult, to the military coup of 1943. The voting reform marked an important shift in the nature of politics, because for the first time politicians needed to obtain widespread support among voters. The military take-over led to the coming to power of Juan Perón and major changes in politics, an enlarged state, and an altered role for civic associations.

This book examines how civic associations helped create the social world of the city, especially the part they played in the development of the sense of barrio. It also shows how civic associations became vital links in the system of politics that emerged. Civic associations became places for politicians to build connections to different communities. However, despite being created by inhabitants to fulfill some of their needs and despite generally being run according to rules that prescribed democratic procedures, civic associations did not function as schools for democracy.

This volume is both an examination of the nature of urban politics and a study of the ever-changing urban and social world in which politics was embedded in the early twentieth century. It examines how politicians built bases of support in neighborhoods through forging ties to the civic associations. The intervention of politicians and other important people frequently meant obtaining desired services or goods. A system of clientelism developed, which politicians used to create support. The quid pro quo was not always visible, but successful politicians did not continue to help organizations without getting something in return, whether organizational support or votes. The clientelism examined here is not politicians doing favors for individual voters but rather politicians tying voters to themselves by helping their civic association or their neighborhood. This is essentially what Rebecca Weitz-Shapiro has referred to as an "earlier definition of clientelism"; in other words, "the practice was embedded in social ties and accompanied the exchange of a broad range of services and support between patrons and clients."[1]

Civic associations were not, at least in the written records, major centers of job patronage, although some political figures who played key roles in them did offer such patronage. Similarly, this book does not look at the distribution of food and other necessities common in the era, the so-called *pan radical* (Radical Party bread), although some civic associations did distribute goods.[2]

What I do examine is why politicians played key roles in so many civic associations. Leadership roles gave them local publicity and, in a few cases, particularly in the larger football clubs, citywide fame. In other civic associations, politicians provided assistance or neighborhood improvements and thus built ties to a neighborhood and its voters. As a political broker in greater Buenos Aires said in the twenty-first century, "You must help the poor but be careful not to make it look like clientelism. Nobody likes being used."[3]

While political changes demarcate the beginning and ending dates for this study, the nature of politics does not suddenly and completely alter in a specific year. The social life of the inhabitants or the nature of urban infrastructure does not abruptly change. However, the period from 1912 to 1943 saw the intensification of several critical changes: the rapid expansion of the city into new areas; the solidification of neighborhood identification; and the increase in the amount of leisure time, which allowed for the creation of many more civic associations.

My work on the book began with the idea of transforming into a quick article some material about football clubs and politics that was left over from previous work. I soon realized that I had become fascinated with the complex cultural, social, and political ideas that I had uncovered. I had gone down the rabbit hole, and I have yet to fully emerge. I also realized that if I were going to understand what was going on, I needed to compare the football clubs to other civic associations, which did not receive as much publicity but played crucial parts in the lives of many inhabitants of Buenos Aires. I had to include organizations that represented something more complex than recreation or social clubs. I also concluded that examining one or two examples of any type of civic association would not be helpful, since a representative example does not exist. A more complete picture needed to be painted. The individual stones make up the arch.

The Role of Civic Associations

The discussion of civic associations has become commonplace in examinations of the establishment and maintenance of democratic norms in much of the world. However, a close look at civic associations in Buenos Aires in the first decades of the twentieth century shows that the tie between civic associations and democracy does not work there. Despite a complex web of such societies, run by democratic norms, the path to democracy in Argentina has been rocky and difficult. In this case the existence of civic associations cannot be tied to the practice of democracy.

Examining the role of civic associations in democracies dates to the nineteenth-century writings of Alexis de Tocqueville about the United States. In the United States, Robert Putnam's work has renewed attention to civic associations. The emphasis on the ties between civic associations and democracy has led to a belief that interest and participation in government needs to be placed within a network of social and mutual relationships. Formal and informal associations teach the skills and attitudes necessary for the development of democracy. Associations can also mediate between the world of politics and the larger society.[4] Although some commentators have placed more importance on the design of institutions or socioeconomic factors, the existence of civic organizations has been given a critical role in creating strong democracies.[5]

In Argentina, the study of such organizations and their perceived ties to democratic politics comes from the work of a group of young scholars who, as the last military dictatorship came to its end in the early 1980s, began a search for the recoverable roots of a democratic tradition. As Hilda Sabato, Luis Alberto Romero, Leandro Gutiérrez, their students, and others have amply demonstrated, the inhabitants of greater Buenos Aires (*porteños*) built a dense web of civic associations starting in the mid-nineteenth century. These scholars' initial studies linked civic associations to the creation of democratic traditions and practices. These organizations were seen as transformative places.[6]

In many ways reflecting trends in other regions of the world, in the late twentieth century and early twenty-first, some of the initiators of the study of civic associations in Argentina have grown much less sanguine about their role.[7] In Argentina this less optimistic vision also reflects the rocky history of Argentine democracy, despite the impressive creation of organizations run by its inhabitants. Argentina from 1930 to 1983 was beset by military coups and dictatorships, and the path of the restored democracy since then has not been smooth.

My analysis supports the less than optimistic vision of civic associations and the observations made about Europe in the volume edited by Nancy Bermeo and Philip Nord: the long-range impact of civic associations depends on the societies in which they develop.[8] This observation, while not in itself surprising, allows us to move beyond seeing civic associations in simple terms. Argentine civic associations were shaped by the political system that emerged in the twentieth century while simultaneously helping to shape that system.

The challenges to achieving a stable democracy occurred despite porteños creating a vigorous system of civic associations that filled many of the holes left by the state. Porteños did not react politically that differently than the inhabitants of other regions of the country. The civic associations helped shape many aspects of life in the city, including its cultural and social world and its politics. Even the physical world of the city was partially transformed by them. Civic associations created a sense of belonging in a city that was growing rapidly. They became neighborhood centers of sociability and thus helped foster identifications beyond the self and especially with a barrio. Barrios in the first decades of the twentieth century developed distinct identities. People were from Mataderos or Almagro or another barrio. These identifications remained fluid since the expansion of the city was rapid. Key to developing a sense of belonging to a portion of the city were the civic associations, which became nexuses of sociability, creating formal and informal connections while simultaneously providing needed services.

In the Buenos Aires of the early twentieth century, many politicians sought connections that would permit them to develop relationships in a barrio in order to forge bases of support. They were creating political capital. This was not a new idea as clientelism and patronage had existed for a long time, but a political system that required much more mobilization of support changed the parameters. Civic associations were ideal places for politicians to look for support since they had become crucial neighborhood institutions, and their leaders and members frequently were locally influential. At the same time, civic associations often needed monetary and other assistance from the state, which connections to politicians and other important individuals could provide. These needs became intertwined, creating a symbiotic relationship but clearly not one between equals. Several politicians who make an appearance in these pages because of their ties to civic associations had long careers. Active in the period covered by the book, they emerged again in the late 1950s and early 1960s as successful politicians after the overthrow of Perón. Clearly their ties were effective.[9]

The founding of civic associations in greater Buenos Aires follows a pattern that was seen in many countries in the Atlantic world roughly simultaneously. As societies became more literate and the inhabitants had a greater amount of free time, they formed civic associations to provide places for socializing and for solving problems that they faced as a group. In other Latin American countries civic associations, like those in Argentina, emerged. However, unsurprisingly, their trajectories differed because of the varied political, economic, and social conditions. Whether porteños were more or less successful in creating civic associations than people in other societies is difficult to assess. However, the sheer number is impressive and demonstrates a remarkable ability to establish and maintain organizations.[10]

To examine the role of civic associations I have looked at four different types of organization. The goal is to portray how these associations functioned, interacted with their members and the political world, and became key to barrio identities. I have made no attempt to give detailed information on a set number of institutions in each category, but by examining a handful of different associations in each category a fuller impression can be gained. Obviously, like any historical work, I made choices about which institutions to include, based partially on the availability of sources. The paper trail of many civic associations is scant. I have also chosen to look at organizations that had different trajectories and orientations.

The type of information I was able to obtain in each category is different. For football clubs and popular libraries, the sources are more diverse, and so I have included information from greater Buenos Aires. Football leagues from the very beginning made no distinction between the city and the other centers of population in greater Buenos Aires. Also, the difference in the politics between the city of Buenos Aires and the surrounding province seems to have made less difference than in the other two types of civic association. There was little difference in the social composition of the city's neighborhoods and the neighborhoods just outside of the city in the province. Politics, however, did have an impact on such important questions as urban infrastructure and the funding of much else. The popular libraries depended to a large extent on support from a national government agency.

The football clubs attracted a great deal of attention from contemporary newspapers and sporting magazines, as well as producing their own publications. In addition, the continuing fascination with football has generated an interest in club history from both social scientists and passionate amateurs. The Biblioteca Nacional in Buenos Aires is often full of football enthusiasts doing research, and academics have begun to examine football carefully. The vast quantity of information permits an analysis of the conflicts and activities that in-house publications avoided.

The other institutions I studied did not receive intense scrutiny from the press because of their small size nor did they receive the same level of interest from later generations. However, in the case of bibliotecas populares, the use of publications generated by the institutions is supplemented by government sources, which demonstrate some of the weaknesses of small membership organizations: lack of money, problems with leadership, and so on. My examination of the other two types of civic association depends heavily on the publications of the institutions or other material generated by them, which reveal a great deal but also conceal much.

Scope of the Book

The book begins with the large-scale creation of civic associations in the first decades of the twentieth century, starting with the opening up of the political system in 1912. Conveniently, this coincided with a massive surge in the creation of relatively enduring civic associations and with the emergence of new barrios on the outskirts of the city. Together they created a new world for civic associations and politics.

The military coup that removed the government in 1943 is a good place to halt this study. The government that emerged led to the election of Perón in 1946, and the nature of politics was altered. Not only did a new political force emerge that has dominated Argentine politics until the present, but more important from the perspective of this study is that a stronger and larger state arose that took on some of the roles that civic associations had played previously. However, many civic associations have maintained essential roles. Other changes also occurred that compounded the political transformation. Changes in transportation and the growth of industrial plants and other sources of employment far from where people lived weakened some of the barrio loyalties that had existed. Even the increasing attendance at secondary schools and the need to travel to get there created an awareness of the wider city. The growth in the number of union members created other allegiances and ties beyond the barrio. As Anahí Ballent has perceptively observed, in some ways the basic social order began to shift in the city.[11] All of this makes 1943 a good ending date for this book.

Structure of the Book

The first chapter examines the socioeconomic and political context in which the civic associations existed. I focus particular attention on the changes in the city of Buenos Aires and explore the nature of the developing loyalty to the barrio, especially the role of civic associations in establishing that identity through becoming places of sociability.

In chapter 2, I look at the relationship between politicians and civic associations. I discuss how the relationship worked and why it was critical for both the organizations and the politicians. I provide several examples of politicians who built support in part through their connections to different civic associations, as well as an example of one civic association, the football club Almagro, which was both a functioning organization and a vehicle for building a political base.

The next four chapters discuss the four categories of civic association: football clubs, bibliotecas populares, sociedades de fomento, and universidades populares. Each chapter focuses on how the associations functioned, how they provided social opportunities for the barrio, and how they connected to the political world.

Chapter 3 examines football clubs. Most football clubs were created by groups of young men with the goal of playing the game, but some grew into large institutions that offered a wide range of leisure activities for their members. They thus became centers of barrio pride and socialization. Politics often played a key role in their development.

In chapter 4 I look at bibliotecas populares, which were libraries created by inhabitants and run as civic associations. The state provided few public libraries intended for the average reader, and a very real hunger for books existed. The inhabitants responded by creating hundreds of libraries. Despite a system of government aid to bibliotecas populares, many had few books and were open limited hours, but they slaked some of the thirst for books and became important centers of the social world of the barrios. Their need for funds encouraged them to become connected to the political world. I also discuss what types of books were read and who was reading them.

Chapter 5 examines sociedades de fomento, civic associations created to better the physical conditions of neighborhoods. Rapid growth left many barrios with serious infrastructural deficiencies. Some improvements the development societies could do on their own, but for others they lobbied the state. The need for support made them seek ties to politicians or others with good connections. More than the other civic associations that I studied, their roles were channeled by the state. They also became important social centers, sponsoring libraries, holding classes, and offering social events of all types. As Ariel Gravano has argued, the sociedades de fomento played a crucial role in creating the sense of barrio.[12]

In chapter 6 I deal with the universidades populares. A strong desire for more education existed, but the public school system did not offer sufficient opportunities for practical education, and porteños formed schools to do just that. Like the other institutions I studied, these were barrio-based civic associations that brought to a neighborhood social opportunities as well as education. They were always short of funds and turned to the political system for support. I also discuss the nature of what was taught and who the students were.

Unless otherwise indicated, all translations in this book are mine.

Chapter One

The Barrio's Place in a Growing City

Barrio que nunca te he podido olvidar
Aunque mi ausencia mucho tiempo duró
Barrio, rincón de mi alegría,
Vengo a buscar la gloria
De mis lejanos días.
Quiero que sepas que no puedo vivir
Lejos de tus calles cubiertos de sol
Porque el esplendor
Que siempre hay en ti,
Hace revivir mi amor.

Barrio that I could never forget
Although my absence lasted for a long time.
Barrio, dwelling place of my happiness,
I come to look for the glory
Of my bygone days.
I want you to know that I cannot live
Far from your streets covered with sun
Because the splendor
That always is in you
has rekindled my love.

—EUGENIO CÁRDENAS, "BARRIO VIEJO"

THE EVOCATION OF THE barrio, as in this tango from 1928, was a key component of the popular culture of Buenos Aires in the first decades of the twentieth century. Undoubtedly this was partly a result of commercialism, but the constant repetition demonstrates that it had resonance. A sense of belonging to a neighborhood developed as Buenos Aires grew rapidly and as the inhabitants of the city created civic associations to fill the lacunae of their needs produced by urban expansion and rising expectations. To a large extent, civic associations produced that sense of belonging. The world of barrios and civic associations cannot be separated from politics. This was true both in the city itself and in the surrounding suburbs.

The city's geography and its street network helped determine the nature of barrios. Buenos Aires is largely built on a flat plain and is laid out almost entirely in a grid pattern; with few exceptions, there are no natural physical features that differentiate one barrio from another. The French politician Georges Clemenceau, who visited the city in the early twentieth century, said: "One of the peculiarities of Buenos Ayres is that you can see no end to it. Since on the side of the Pampas there is no obstacle to building operations, small colonial houses . . . make a fringe on the city that extends ever farther and farther into the plains."[1] In this period barrios lacked legal status, and no official lines divided them. Even their inhabitants had a difficult time drawing exact boundaries between barrios.[2] Barrios were imagined communities that developed around commercial centers or places of employment, and their sense of identity grew out of civic associations. The imagined nature of the barrios did not make their existence or their identities any less real to their inhabitants.

The growth of civic associations in greater Buenos Aires in the first decades of the twentieth century occurred during a swift transformation of the urban world. The city expanded quickly in population but, perhaps much more important, in area. Inhabitants settled in previously lightly populated sectors when landowners subdivided parcels, developing centers of settlement along transportation routes and near nodes of employment. The expansion was propelled in part by high rates of immigration until 1930, with a pause during World War I, and in the late 1930s by large-scale internal migration. People's need to adjust to a new environment meant that civic associations played critical roles in attaching inhabitants to their barrio.

The political world altered also. With the passage in 1912 of the Sáenz Peña voting reform law, which made male citizens' voting both secret and obligatory, and fraud more difficult, politicians needed to actively pursue voter support for the first time. The search for voters intensified after the creation in 1917 of a popularly elected city council in Buenos Aires.[3] The competition for voters created a symbiotic relationship between civic associations and politicians of almost all political orientations. The former needed financial and other types of assistance from the state, and politicians wanted bases of support, which some found in the neighborhood-based civic associations.

In the first decades of the twentieth century Argentina was a wealthy country with a standard of living comparable to, if not better than, many European countries. Immigrants from Southern and Eastern Europe poured in until 1930. In 1914 the per capita income of Argentines was tenth in the world. Obviously, such a number says nothing about regional disparities, as Buenos Aires was much wealthier than much of the country, nor does it indicate the scale of the class differentiations. The economy rested on the relatively free movement of goods, services, and labor, and Argentina was a major exporter of agricultural goods. Buenos Aires was the hub of the nation. It was the principal port and the center of the railroad network. It was the national capital and the site of its most prestigious university. Research has shown that before the Great Depression Buenos Aires had a sizeable manufacturing sector. The Depression initially hit Argentina hard, as nations ruptured long-standing practices and retreated behind trade barriers and used other protective devices. The inability to continue to import because of a decline in the value of exports forced a turn to import-substitution industrialization, and by the mid-1930s the urban economy had recovered, and employment levels had increased, though rural areas continued to suffer. Both World War I and World War II produced inflation and serious problems for certain sectors.[4]

The Importance of Civic Associations and Their Creation

The rapid expansion of the city, plus a state that lacked the capacity or perhaps at times the desire to provide services, pushed the inhabitants to create civic associations to fulfill what they perceived as their needs. Whether it was the young men who established football clubs so that they could play the game or the porteños who organized bibliotecas populares to have libraries to partially satiate the desire to read, people created institutions to fulfill their longings. Striking examples of inhabitants taking on what the state failed to provide were the sociedades de fomento, which labored to improve neighborhood conditions, and the universidades populares, which provided adult education, especially vocational training. Buenos Aires saw the establishment of literally thousands of civic associations.

Porteños founded a vast array of mutual aid societies, popular libraries, development associations, unions, ethnic societies, and football and social clubs. Almost all followed democratic procedures, at least on paper. They had dues-paying members and written regulations, and they were governed by general assemblies and elected boards. Like any such organizations, they were at times plagued by monetary problems, disinterest of the general membership, and the desire of some individuals to use the organization for their own ends. These and a myriad of other problems should in no way be surprising. In all parts of the world, membership organizations suffer similarly. The political situation in Argentina, especially in the 1930s when even the political parties that pushed for a more democratic society had internal problems, undoubtedly contributed.[5]

Politicians sought to create neighborhood bases of support, and civic associations became ideal locations to extend their influence. Since the institutions needed financial and political assistance, their needs coincided. They depended on each other. The associations demonstrated the ability of porteños to create organizations to deal with their problems. However, although they helped shape the political and social world of the city, they also reflected the milieu in which they arose. It is clear that in the years from 1912 to 1943 the powerful came to colonize many of them. By "colonize," I mean the politicians came to influence the civic associations because of what they offered in real terms. A similar process occurred in other cities in Argentina.[6]

Given the nature of Buenos Aires society in this era, it is unsurprising that most of the civic associations examined were dominated by males, although women did play roles both formally and informally. It is at times difficult to see women's roles, but frequently, with little publicity, they organized many of the social activities of the civic associations. These activities helped connect porteños to their institutions and to a barrio.

One reason for the porteños' ability to create so many civic associations was the increasing amount of time they spent away from work. By the beginning of the twentieth century, the inhabitants of Buenos Aires had more free time than previously, and they wanted to be entertained and educated. Free time increased over the next several decades as the eight-hour workday and the half-day Saturday were legally mandated.

The increase in leisure time coincided with a growth in literacy, which reached impressive heights, especially in the city of Buenos Aires. In 1914 literacy in Buenos Aires for those over seven years old was 82.2 percent, while for the native-born population it stood at 91.6 percent. By 1936 the literacy rate had risen to 93.3 percent and for the native-born to 97.6 percent. The figures for greater Buenos Aires were not that far behind. Beginning in the 1880s schooling was required until children were fourteen years old, and in urban areas the state did a good job in providing elementary schools where children learned to read and do arithmetic and developed a sense of nationalism. However, many young porteños needed to work, and few opportunities existed for further education, especially vocational training. Traditional secondary education was academically focused and charged fees.[7]

The nature of Buenos Aires neighborhoods also aided the establishment of civic associations. Although there were wealthy barrios and working-class ones, they were never solidly so.[8] The barrios of the "rich" contained many who were far from that, and working-class barrios contained store owners and professionals (lawyers, doctors, and so on). These often functioned as barrio elites, even if the true elites would never have recognized them as such. Unlike many other countries that received heavy waves of immigration, nothing that can be truly labeled ghetto-like neighborhoods arose. Barrios tended to be ethnically diverse. Even stereotyped neighborhoods, such as La Boca (Italian) or Once (Jewish), although containing large numbers of one ethnicity had residents of quite varied origin.[9]

Growth of the City

Buenos Aires's population surged in the first decades of the twentieth century. In 1910 the city had slightly over 1.3 million people and reached over 1.7 million by 1920. The growth continued, and by 1930 the population had reached 2.3 million, and it was over 2.7 million by 1940. In other words, the population had doubled in thirty years. The inhabitants tended to be young and therefore of the age to want to play football or take advantage of the bibliotecas populares and the universidades populares.[10] Peripheral barrios expanded even faster than the overall growth rate and much more rapidly than the urban infrastructure. As Tulio Halperín Donghi pointed out, in 1910 all the city's barrios had an unfinished air since so much construction was going on. For example, multistory buildings were becoming more common.[11]

The rising population and better public transit encouraged the spread of porteños away from the traditional core on the eastern edge of the city near the Río de la Plata. The desire to escape the center of the city was to a large extent fed by the expensive and poor-quality housing available there, especially the *conventillos* or slum-like multifamily dwellings where many poorer porteños lived. The subdivision and sale of large properties, frequently before the provision of urban amenities, allowed the creation of areas of settlement where few had lived previously. Plots were frequently sold on installment plans ranging from 40 to 120 months of payments. Often the buyers built their houses in stages, with enlargements occurring when owners could afford to do so.[12]

At the end of the first decade of the twentieth century, the *Revista Municipal* noted the sharp difference in the urbanization of the richest barrio, Barrio Norte, and barrios in the poorer southern half of the city.[13] The difference between barrios increased, at least temporarily, as the city spread. The scope of the problems that the municipality faced can be seen by looking at two of the census tracts farthest from the center, Vélez Sarsfield and San Bernardo. In Vélez between 1904 and 1909 the population climbed from 17,275 to 47,917 while in San Bernardo it went from 16,176 to 48,381. In 1914 Vélez had a population of 103,358; in 1936 it was 330,982; and it reached 444,719 in 1947. San Bernardo followed a similar pattern of explosive growth. In terms of infrastructure, in 1909 in Vélez only 4.84 percent of the 7,599 households had piped-in running water, and none had connections to sewer pipes; in San Bernardo only 29 of the 7,151 houses had running water while none had sewer connections. These were the fastest growing areas of the city but far from the only ones that lacked services.[14]

The national government did respond, since by the mid-1920s most city inhabitants had water, though fewer had sewer connections. Water and sewage systems are just two examples of settlement outpacing infrastructure; barrios also frequently lacked paved and illuminated streets and faced periodic flooding caused by inadequate stormwater drainage. A Spanish visitor claimed in the early 1920s that Buenos Aires was even cleaner than Berlin, but frequently residents had to take matters into their own hands.[15]

In addition, the city lacked green spaces. According to one study in the 1940s, only 4.5 percent of the city's overall area was composed of parks or gardens. These were concentrated on the wealthier north side of the city. There were, however, plazas, and many more were equipped with facilities, especially for children, than previously. Still, often the playing of football was discouraged. Many of the improvements resulted from pressure by sociedades de fomento, which sometimes raised funds to equip plazas. In 1929, forty-five sociedades de fomento petitioned the city council for improvements to plazas,[16] and the authorities did address many of the problems, partially due to this pressure.

The population growth was a product of the birth rate but also of immigration and then internal migration. Until the Great Depression, Buenos Aires and Argentina in general were major recipients of European migration. The flow was particularly intense right before the start of World War I in 1914. That year, 49 percent of the population of Buenos Aires was foreign-born.[17] The largest group of immigrants was Italians followed by Spaniards. In some years over 200,000 more migrants came to Argentina than left, and a significant percentage stayed in Buenos Aires. During World War I, the migration pattern reversed but immigration became important again in the 1920s, with the sources of the incomers diversifying, many arriving from Eastern Europe and the eastern Mediterranean. However, the numbers remained lower than previously. With the onset of the Depression, large-scale immigration ceased due to economic problems and government policies.[18] However, a continuing rural crisis and the recovery of the urban economy after the mid-1930s led to tens of thousands of internal migrants coming to greater Buenos Aires, especially from the provinces of the nearby Pampas.[19]

An additional source for the increasing population was a rapidly falling mortality rate. This began in the late nineteenth century with some fluctuations until 1910 and then continued to decline almost without pause. By 1936 the average person in the city lived until almost sixty. This indicates both improved living conditions and better control of infectious diseases, although the city still felt the impact of illnesses such as tuberculosis.[20]

The large number of newcomers to the city, whether from abroad or from the interior of the country, meant that civic associations played a critical role in helping people's acculturation to new ways of life. However, the civic associations I studied tended to be dominated by the native-born. Probably this is due to the acculturation of the Argentinian-born to the society and their fluency in Spanish. The increase of the native-born as a percentage of the city's population after the end of mass immigration may partially account for the strengthening of civic associations in the 1930s, despite the Depression and a more complex political situation. Unfortunately, the existing data do not permit a distinction between those who were locally born and those who were internal migrants.

The key to the movement of people inside the city in the early years of the twentieth century was the trolley system. In 1909 it had 609 kilometers of tracks, and it reached 851 in 1930. By that year, the trolleys had a host of competitors, including the commuter railroad system. According to government statistics, in 1914 the brand-new subway carried 7 percent of the passengers, and the rest went by trolley. (The railroad users are not included in the statistics.) By 1930 trolley riders comprised 56 percent of total commuters, while the subway carried 7 percent and buses 32 percent; the new system of *colectivos* (jitneys) served 5 percent. The latter were taxis that ran fixed routes; over time the vehicles were enlarged.

By 1938 the form of transportation carrying the most passengers was buses with 32 percent of the total, followed by trolleys with 31, jitneys with 28, and the subway with 9. The total number of passengers increased more than three times between 1914 and 1938. In 1939 the trolley network had gone down to 734 kilometers, but there were 51 kilometers of subway tracks, 1,963 of bus routes, and 1,633 of colectivo routes. Commuter trains played an important role, especially bringing people from the suburbs into the city. The number and speed of trips also increased over time.[21] The expansion of the transportation system, especially the much more agile buses and jitneys, allowed porteños to move around the city more rapidly because the trolleys' progress through the streets was frequently impeded. People could thus live farther from places of employment and seek diversion and shopping away from their barrio. Neighborhoods became less of an enclosed world.

An additional reason for the movement away from the traditional areas was a desire for social mobility. In the academic world there has been discussion about whether such mobility really existed, but more important for this study was the belief that it did.[22] The improving conditions for many workers has been stressed by several authors, as has the lessening of sharp distinctions between classes.[23] Many inhabitants believed that through hard work and education they could better their position in the world and, if not for themselves, then for their children. They wanted to become something. An important politician in the 1920s, Leopoldo Bard, who migrated to Argentina as a child, displayed this clearly in the subtitle of an autobiographical account written years later, *La fe puesta en un ideal "llegar a ser algo"* (Faith placed in an ideal "to become something"). The writer had fulfilled the dream of many immigrant parents; he became a doctor.[24] Similar sentiments were discussed in a popular book published in 1931, *Como se llega: Nuestros self-made men* (How they arrived: Our self-made men), which is a series of short biographies of men who made a fortune. The book was based on interviews that originally appeared in a popular magazine.[25] Social mobility seemed possible.

Barrios

Belonging to a barrio is part of the mythical ethos of the city, prominent in tangos and fiction, but for many porteños it is real. Although it has lessened since the mid-twentieth century, that connection still survives. Some barrios have a stronger identity than others, but there is still a tendency to ask someone whom you have just met what barrio they are from, just as it is common to ask what football club they support. The responses to both questions allow a recent acquaintance to make a rough assessment of who the person is.

Cultural identification with a geographic entity, much more than simply geography or economics, determined the nature of barrios. Civic associations and other places of encounter helped create a mental world that led many to identify with a neighborhood. The largely undifferentiated nature of the terrain and the grid pattern of the streets made neighborhoods blend into each other, and therefore the identification had to be based on something more than geography. Adrián Gorelik has argued that around 1910 the clusters where people lived began to become barrios because of institutions, including civic associations, schools, and church parishes. I would add cafés and other commercial places of socialization. This role of civic associations was not unique to Buenos Aires.[26]

The nature of the territorial grouping with which residents identify has long been a matter of debate. Did barrio identity focus on larger areas like those that have been legally recognized since 1972 (there are forty-eight such barrios shown on the map included in this book), or did residents give loyalty to smaller areas?[27] Since barrios in this era had no fixed boundaries, their limits were established by residents, who did not always agree, and resulted from their inhabitants' identification with a set of institutions. At times, this connection was to a very small area.

In his 1974 classic examination of the urban development of Buenos Aires between 1870 and 1910, James Scobie adopted the idea of a smaller barrio, what we can call the micro barrio, as the basis of life in the outlying sections of the city. In the late 1930s in the contest for the presidency of the large football club Boca Juniors, Camilo Cichero was backed by a group of people who had lived on one street and had gone to a particular café even though many had moved away after becoming economically successful.[28] Mario Aiscurri in discussing the barrio of Mataderos claims that there are really five barrios within the bigger district. Angel Prignano made similar comments about other barrios. These types of observation are not unique to Buenos Aires. For example, in his memoir Mario Vargas Llosa describes his youthful attachment to a small area inside the Lima, Peru, suburb of Miraflores.[29] One can hypothesize that identification with a small geographical area and with a larger barrio are not mutually exclusive. A person could identify with both; the primary identity might be with the smaller area but acknowledgment of the larger one could also exist. In response to an outsider's question of where someone lived, the answer likely would be the larger area. Further, the sense of identity probably altered over time; as transportation improved, increased mobility made the micro barrio identity less important.

Barrio identities in the early twentieth century remained far from permanent or fixed. The best example of a changing sense of identification is the emergence of the barrio of Boedo in the 1930s in a previously settled area in which other identifications had existed. The sense of being from Boedo lasted and became one of the more intensely felt identifications in the city.[30]

Civic associations helped create the sense of belonging to a neighborhood by providing places of sociability. By "sociability," I mean the creation of locations where people got together and formed informal or formal relationships, which therefore helped shape ideas and identities.[31] Many people built much of their nonfamilial connections through these associations. At times they even became acquainted with their future spouse there. Headquarters of the associations served as places to talk or play cards. Those in leadership positions spent a hefty portion of their "leisure" time involved in them. Civic associations provided diversions of all types, from picnics and lectures to plays, movies, carnival celebrations, and dances. Some of these activities also took place in commercial venues such as cafés, cinemas, or theaters. The ubiquitous cafés especially provided places for men to gather. In 1914 there were over a thousand of them. However, civic associations could be seen as safe spaces where young people could mingle under the eyes of respectable members of the community. This was unlike the supposedly dangerous world of downtown portrayed in tangos.[32]

Civic associations also offered other types of diversion. They provided athletic activities, and it was not just the football clubs that had a plethora of such opportunities. The civic associations sponsored classes and libraries. The sociedades de fomento improved the conditions of the neighborhoods. Many civic associations provided social services, such as cheaper medical care or legal advice. Football clubs gave barrios a sense of pride and a common identification. However, it was not just football clubs that became "theirs." People took pride in their library or sociedad de fomento. Over time people developed a special relationship with their neighborhood in large part through institutions. This was particularly important for a city composed so heavily of immigrants and their children. The barrio provided a sense of rootedness. Even after the Depression limited the inflow of people from abroad, this need for a sense of identification continued. By the mid-1930s the inflow of migrants from the interior meant that there was a new group of people who had left behind the world that they had known. Civic associations and barrio identity provided for many a sense of belonging.

Barrio identities were not exclusive, since people frequently identified with things that were not restricted to one barrio, including class, political parties, unions, religions, and ethnic organizations. Someone could identify with the barrio of Mataderos, be a fan and member of the football club Nueva Chicago, be a committed Socialist, and also be a fervent union member.

The 1930s did see a gradual lessening of barrio identities. The decline came for many reasons. The improvements in transportation allowed people to move more quickly to the city center or other neighborhoods. Larger circulations for the national newspapers and the growth of the radio broke down barriers. Because its appeal had transcended a barrio, one football club, River Plate, could open a new stadium in 1938 in a distant suburban district just inside the city of Buenos Aires, Núñez, which lacked good transportation. Several other large football clubs opened branch centers far from their barrio base. Media coverage had allowed the bigger clubs to widen their appeal beyond their barrio boundaries, though most retained a barrio identity (see chapter 3). Even the act of going to secondary school, which was still far from universal in the 1920s and 1930s, widened the world of barrio inhabitants as they forged relations with people from other neighborhoods.[33]

Politics

When Argentina achieved independence in the early nineteenth century, it was torn by political violence, and only after almost half a century did peace begin to emerge. After the victory of Julio Roca in a civil conflict and his assumption of the presidency in 1880, a system of government developed that followed the constitution on paper but depended on voter fraud and political deal making to ensure the ruling clique's control. As studies have shown, it was a political elite more than an economic one that dominated. Peace and the propitious economic moment allowed for an export-driven economy, which permitted Argentina to become a rich country by most measures. The system of governance depended greatly on the political skills of Roca, and after his death, increasing pressure from excluded groups and those who wanted change came to the fore. In 1912 they managed to pass the Sáenz Peña voting reform law, which opened up the political system.[34]

That enactment marks the beginning of the modern era of Argentine politics because for the first time attracting mass voter support became essential. Although the break with past practices was less sharp than some have posited, by making voting obligatory for male citizens from the age of eighteen and by making fraud more difficult, the reform opened the way for a true participatory electoral system, especially in the city of Buenos Aires. It is important to point out that in Argentina immigrants rarely became citizens because of or despite their large numbers. This limited the reasons to appeal to the working class, of which immigrants composed a sizeable proportion.[35] Women were excluded from voting, though of course not from politics. Social tensions, especially labor strife, were particularly high right after the reform, ebbed in the 1920s, and intensified again in the 1930s.

The Radical Party dominated the years from 1916 to 1930 with Hipólito Yrigoyen as the key force. In 1916 in the first presidential election under the new rules, Yrigoyen won the presidency and pursued a policy of attempting to continually expand his popularity both through concrete measures to better the lives of the average inhabitant and perhaps as importantly through symbolic recognition of their importance. Yrigoyen was a dominant figure, and the party propaganda sang his praises. The Radical Party saw other parties as being antipatriotic, and they were unable to match its popularity.

Yrigoyen imposed his personal choice, Marcelo T. de Alvear, as his party's candidate in 1922, and he easily won election. Although a longtime friend of

Yrigoyen and a man who appeared to lack political drive, Alvear partially broke with Yrigoyen, and the Radical Party divided in two. The principal cause of the split is demonstrated by the names by which people referred to the two branches: Personalists (the supporters of Yrigoyen) and Antipersonalists (who supported Alvear but whose unifying element was their dislike of the power of Yrigoyen within the party). Although traditionally it has been assumed that the Antipersonalists were the more conservative faction, some Antipersonalists were far from conservative and were motivated by their distaste for Yrigoyen's dominance.

Both factions maintained many features of the parent party. The Antipersonalists continued many of Yrigoyen's policies but were hamstrung by a lack of clear ideas and strategies. Alvear proved less than decisive. The Antipersonalists failed to undermine Yrigoyen's popularity and never gathered much traction. In the 1928 presidential election the key contenders were Yrigoyen and an Antipersonalist. Yrigoyen won handily. However, in September 1930 a military coup overthrew him. His second term in office was limited by the impact of the Depression, by the fear of many of the political and social elites of total Radical Party dominance, and by Yrigoyen's decline, probably due to age.[36]

The military coup had the support of most of the political parties that opposed Yrigoyen. The establishment of military rule under General José F. Uriburu brought much more intense repression against anarchists, Communists, Radicals, and others than many had expected, and the jockeying for control by factions within the military led to the victory of a group led by General Agustín Justo. The victors wanted a return to the constitution with the Radicals excluded from power. Elections were reinstated. After the government's veto of Alvear as the Radical Party candidate (he had returned to the dominant faction with the blessing of Yrigoyen), the Radicals, the majority party, boycotted the presidential election of late 1931 and continued to boycott electoral politics until 1935.

A coalition of Antipersonalists, Conservatives, and Independent Socialists, which would politically dominate the subsequent era, nominated Justo as their candidate. The opposition was composed of the Socialists and the Progressive Democrats (a relatively conservative party that believed in democracy). Justo won decisively. The governing coalition in large part represented key elements of the landed elite and was truly conservative in orientation. Its members are often referred to as neoconservatives. However, the reality of the Depression forced the government to take measures that favored import-substitution industrialization.

Because the Radicals remained outside the electoral competition, the governing coalition could win elections relatively easily, except in the capital, where the Socialists were well established, and in the province of Santa Fe, where the Progressive Democrats had their base. The governing coalition did not hesitate to use voter fraud, which it saw as increasingly necessary after the Radicals returned to the electoral fray. Although not fully democratic, the government tended to function with the trappings of a democracy—regular elections, a relatively free press, and so on—though Communists and anarchists faced periodic repression, and the electoral results did not reflect the will of the populace. The voting was always fair in the city of Buenos Aires, however.

The increased use of fraud after the return of the Radicals to electoral participation plus the divisions in the society produced by the ideological impacts of the Spanish Civil War led to ever-wider fissures. In 1938, in a largely fraudulent contest, the governing coalition's candidate, Roberto M. Ortiz, won election as Justo's successor. Despite the origins of his presidency, Ortiz attempted to end voter fraud, but his efforts were undermined by the failure of his health, which forced him to cede power and then the presidency to his vice president, Ramón Castillo, who held vastly different views. From 1940 repression increased, reflecting the divisions produced by World War II and the growing difficulty of maintaining the political model. The military again seized power in June 1943, and a new trajectory in politics began, marked by the rise of Perón and a larger state apparatus.[37]

THE CITY OF BUENOS AIRES

The city of Buenos Aires held a unique position in the Argentine political system. Since 1880 it had been a federal district, with the nation's executive wielding a tremendous amount of power. The president appointed the *intendente* (mayor), and the national government directly controlled the schools, the provision of water, the major drainage systems, and the police. Various types of appointed city councils or ones elected by limited suffrage had existed, but only in 1917 was a popularly elected city council created, which allowed voters to pressure the city government. The move from a council chosen by restricted suffrage to one in which all male adult citizens could cast ballots increased the number of voters ten times in the first post-reform election.[38] Voting was done by list, and candidates ran citywide, but the awarding of seats was proportional to the vote totals, and small parties could win seats. The council never had a great deal of power, but it could bring pressure to bear on issues. Intendentes needed to have their budgets approved, and the council could legislate on specific problems. Also important was the councilors' ability to call attention to issues through debates. Intendentes who faced hostile councils had a hard time. In general, the president and the intendente needed to worry about popular support in the city since it had an oversized political impact.[39]

Buenos Aires, like the rest of the country, elected members of Congress with a system of lists, and unlike in the provinces, voters directly elected the city's senators. Unlike most other regions, the city remained competitive politically, and the city council was divided among the different parties. The Radicals and the Socialists were the most important, but smaller parties played significant roles.[40] The selection of candidates in a relatively open manner and the low totals needed to win seats, especially on the city council, meant that those with support in certain barrios could become key players.

THE PROVINCIAL SUBURBS

The boundary between the capital city of Buenos Aires and the surrounding province of Buenos Aires is artificial since outlying barrios frequently resemble those on the other side of the border, but it is still a legal barrier. In the early twentieth century, the provincial suburbs were connected to the city by commuter rail and other means of transport, and people came into the city to work, to buy, to study, or in search of entertainment. As Gorelik has mentioned, until late in the twentieth century maps of the city of Buenos Aires frequently included Avellaneda, a suburban industrial city, and the social composition of Avellaneda mirrored that of the barrio directly adjacent in the capital, Barracas.[41] In general, the suburbs to the south, especially Avellaneda, were places where much of the dirty industry was situated. The other provincial suburbs were more diverse, and some contained many wealthy residents. The major difference between the two jurisdictions was politics, which had an impact on social conditions and some types of civic associations. For example, the sociedades de fomento operated in very different political worlds, and therefore I don't discuss those in the province.

In the province the governor was elected and led a far larger (in territory) governmental unit, but these were not the only differences. The province had a legislature with two houses. Politics was also less democratic in the province. From 1914 to 1930 elections were fiercely contested, and old ways were not immediately discarded. In addition, presidents used the right to intervene (the legal take-over of a provincial government) to change the basis of power. After the 1930 coup, the province of Buenos Aires was dominated by the Conservative Party through fraud.[42]

The situation of Avellaneda was unique. It was a large industrial city with over 160,000 inhabitants in 1920, lying due south of the city of Buenos Aires, just across the Riachuelo River.[43] During the entire period covered by this book, Alberto Barceló loomed large in Avellaneda since he had created a Conservative Party machine that dispensed patronage, encouraged the establishment of big industry, and favored public works. He regularly received friends, followers, and favor seekers in his home. He permitted, or perhaps encouraged, prostitution and gambling, which undoubtedly paid the costs of his political machine, and he reputedly had ties to gangsters. The large football club Racing was identified with Barceló, and he had a close relationship with the legendary tango singer Carlos Gardel, who was a fan of Racing. Although Barceló was unable to totally control the district during the era of Radical dominance, he remained a critical figure. During the 1930s his machine proved capable of winning elections honestly, and Barceló became a national figure.[44]

Greater Buenos Aires expanded quickly from 1912 to 1943. Its population grew rapidly with many living in new barrios. The porteños created a series of institutions that helped them fulfill some of their desires, including recreational opportunities and improving their own or their children's education. These institutions gave barrios their identities, although they became intimately tied to politics.

CHAPTER TWO

Political Capital and Civic Associations

POLITICS IN GREATER BUENOS Aires in the first decades of the twentieth century was not just centered on ideas. Like in many other areas of the world, political success frequently depended on the development of a network of people to whom personal ties had been forged. The 1912 voting reforms created a need to build a wide base of appeal. It was not that the old ways were suddenly discarded but rather that practices needed to evolve. Local bosses had traditionally delivered votes, but how they did so altered. Bosses no longer could march a limited number of voters to the polls and know how they voted. Politicians needed to find support in a political party, and that party had to mount campaigns that could attract votes across wide areas.[1] They needed to build political capital, that is, a network of friends, followers, and acquaintances that could provide a base of support.

The opening of the political system roughly coincided with a dramatic surge in the formation of civic associations. Although civic associations had existed previously, the new political situation combined with increased prosperity, growing free time, and the desire to fulfill some of the inhabitants perceived needs contributed to the increase, as did the political ambitions of some of their founders and leaders. For some, civic associations were stepping-stones for personal advancement, but they were also more than that. Ideology and the personal combined into something much larger.

The civic associations faced shortages of funds or the inability to obtain goods, such as land, so they sought help from the state, and they needed the intercession of powerful figures to succeed. Politicians needed to build bases of support, and relationships established with barrio-based civic associations became a useful tool to forge a network of people who saw them as benefactors and frequently as one of them. This was a type of clientelism, a mutually beneficial relationship, although the politicians held most of the cards. From the politicians' perspective it was a crucial way of building political capital, but if they failed to deliver what they promised, they could lose that support.

At times businessmen assumed roles like those of politicians, using connections and their money to aid civic associations. Besides their personal reasons, aiding civic associations enabled businessmen to expand their influence in the political system. They widened their contacts and gained publicity and prestige. Janet Lever in her examination of football clubs in Brazil argues that the holding of club posts was part of a career pattern of holding more than one job. The additional jobs served as springboards to more lucrative opportunities, and alliance building was crucial for advancement. James Brennan and Marcelo Rougier make a similar observation about Argentine business associations.[2] In other words, holding positions in civic associations could allow businesspeople to further their careers. The importance of the identification between barrio residents and their civic associations should not be underestimated. Local business owners might feel a great love for local organizations and their barrio, but a leadership role could engender barrio residents' loyalty to their business as well as gratitude for their support.

Police *comisarios* (commissioners) also played a role in the leadership of some civic associations. The police in the city of Buenos Aires were controlled by the president and tightly tied to politics. Police involvement in politics has its roots in the early nineteenth century. The police chiefs of Buenos Aires were frequently men of political importance. For example, Elpidio González, a close political confidant of Yrigoyen, went almost directly from police chief to serving as vice president (1922–1928). According to crime statistics, the city was a relatively safe place, safer than comparable cities in the United States or Europe. Still, especially in the outer reaches of the city in the 1930s, many felt insecure and complained about the low number of police officers. The police had a wide set of roles besides attempting to control crime, since they monitored morals, behavior, and noise and had a great deal of discretion in doing so.

The city was divided into some forty police precincts with the number increasing slightly during the period discussed in this book. Each district was overseen by a comisario, who frequently had been given the job as patronage, often after serving as a justice of the peace (*juez de paz*), also usually a political position. Why would a police official become involved in civic associations? As Lila Caimari argues, the police were trying to build ties to the public to overcome a bad relationship with the average porteño. Certainly, a role in community institutions might help this effort.[3] Also, participation in popular libraries and universidades populares would help ensure that those institutions offered books and courses intended to insulate the young from "dangerous" ideas, such as Communism.

How Civic Associations Fit into the Political Landscape

The most successful political party during the period after 1912, the Radical Party, was nonprogrammatic. This is not to agree with its enemies, who claimed that the Radicals stood for little, if anything, but ideas were not how its politicians tended to build a following. Even in the Socialist Party, where ideas were important, the party structure helped make other issues crucial. Political parties in Buenos Aires during the interwar period created party organizations in each of the city's twenty voting wards, sometimes more than one. The district party apparatus organized campaign events and other activities. The party ward organizations sent representatives to party conventions, and candidates for office were supposedly selected openly. For new leaders to emerge from these district organizations, they had to build local followings. This was the pattern among the Radicals and is true to a lesser extent among the Socialists. Other parties did not behave very differently.[4]

The party organization in each ward provided the workers for the extensive pre-electoral spectacles of the pre-1943 era. The level of activity depended on the electoral cycle and on the amount of popular excitement. Campaigns were partially entertainment since they offered numerous rallies, parades, and speeches. Volunteers plastered walls with posters. Campaigning was barrio-based until just before the election. By the late 1920s campaigns also incorporated the latest technology, such as movies and radio.[5] Campaigns required a vast quantity of human resources and organization at the neighborhood level. Local leaders who had the connections to mobilize support were at times rewarded with positions on party lists high enough to win elections. This led to the rise of local party bosses, especially in the Radical Party, but similar figures existed in other parties.[6]

How did politicians and parties get that kind of support? Recipients of patronage were expected to reciprocate the help that they had received. Politicians looked elsewhere as well. By involving themselves with civic associations, politicians built political capital or a web of relationships, formal and informal, that gave them the base to mount campaigns. This is parallel to what sociologists call "social capital." As Mario Small has stated:

> Social capital theory argues that people do better when they are connected to others because of the goods inherent in social relationships. These goods—the social capital—include the obligations that people who are connected may feel toward each other, the sense of solidarity they may call upon, the information they are willing to share, and the services they are to perform. People who are socially connected therefore have recourse to a stock of "capital" they can employ when needed.[7]

Politicians developed friends and associates who could help with their political career. People are more likely to vote for someone that they know and that they think of as being like them, sharing basic identities. They could also provide the labor for campaigns. In return, politicians provided patronage jobs or help with the bureaucracy. They could also aid local civic associations and win loyalty in that fashion.

This style of attracting voters borrowed heavily from earlier traditions; clientelism and patronage had been around for decades. Some politicians who began their rise before 1912 survived. Still, the increase in the size of the electorate meant that politicians had to have a wide appeal. The voter mattered.[8] While the dispensing of patronage was common, it was more complex than an exchange of favors for votes since many nonvoters benefited. For example, in 1926 just 42 percent of municipal employees in Buenos Aires were Argentinian-born, while an additional 13.2 percent had been naturalized, despite many being patronage appointments.[9] Most elementary school teachers were women, and their posts were often obtained through patronage.[10] Personal connections mattered, and both noncitizens and women could work for political campaigns and had relatives who could vote.

As I have argued elsewhere, patronage alone could not make a leader or a political party popular. Both the Antipersonalists in the 1920s and the governing coalition during the 1930s handed out a great amount of patronage but never became popular.[11] Patronage was useful in mobilizing campaign workers, but it does not explain political popularity. On the local level the doling out of jobs would be even less reason for popularity since the number that could be provided was limited. However, identification with and leadership of beloved neighborhood organizations cemented ties, as did aid provided to them. Personal relationships could be created. Politicians could develop links to influential local elites respected in their barrio. A politician could become one of "us" even if he were not similar at all.

Leadership in or assistance to civic associations tied politicians to a neighborhood. They helped lead an organization or obtained from the city government streetlights or a paved street. They made the lives of a portion of a barrio's population slightly better and raised the hopes of others. Thus, they created a sense of reciprocal obligation, though obviously people were not always grateful. At times political figures worked to forge connections to voters across wide areas through their relationship to civic associations.

It is in football clubs that the role of politicians in civic associations can be observed most easily. Politicians frequently played conspicuous roles. Leaving aside love of the game and loyalty to the club, prominence in a football club brought a great deal of publicity, since press and radio coverage was extensive. Some clubs became quite large, and porteños were extremely passionate about the game. Politicians could hope that some of that fervor would be transferred to their campaigns. Football was a passion, and leading a club and dealing with players was attractive in a way that helping run a library would not be for many. In addition, other types of civic associations received little publicity beyond their home barrio, and government regulations forbade municipal officials from holding office in sociedades de fomento.

Although participation in smaller, less conspicuous civic associations could not make a person well known throughout the city, it could make someone famous in a barrio or several adjoining barrios. They could win the respect and interest of residents. The politicians' need for local bases and the civic associations' need for assistance helped shape both the associations and the nature of politics. The intervention of politicians and other powerful figures was particularly important because the bureaucracy was on the whole weak.[12]

Politicians who did not hold leadership roles in civic organizations could gain political capital through using their connections to aid the organizations. A good example is Florencio Arias, an activist in the Radical Party in an outlying portion of the city where he had lived since 1909 when it was still largely undeveloped. A physician, Arias cared for many poor patients. He served as president of the local school board (*concejo escolar*), an appointed position that was usually a political reward and presented opportunities to engage in patronage by appointing teachers, and as president of the equivalent of a local parent-teacher association (intended to help schools and their students). He sat on the honorary commission of the football club Nueva Chicago. In addition, he aided the local sociedades de fomento. For example, he was honorary president of the Sociedad de Fomento José Enrique Rodó. According to its periodical, the sociedades de fomento "always received the ardor of his wise advice, the knowledge of his constant and effective cooperation, and the gracious contribution of his influence and goodness." Arias won election to the city council in 1922.[13] He was far from unique as my examination of the civic associations makes clear.

The convergence of the need to create popular support and the rapid expansion of civic associations desiring government aid led to a mutual if unequal relationship—with the politicians holding the upper hand. However, loyalty could be given to political rivals, and there were numerous sources of employment, even though government jobs sometimes provided more stability.[14] Still, personal contacts were important. If you knew a city councilor, he might help you or your civic association; therefore, it would pay to help him win an election.

A Socialist Barrio Activist, Fernando Ghio

Fernando Ghio was an activist in the largely working-class barrio of Nueva Chicago, also known as Mataderos. He built his base in the Socialist Party by being president of a soccer club and by intense participation in the life of his barrio. His role in the football club Nueva Chicago not only made him better known in his barrio but spread his name across the city. The popular newspaper *Crítica* frequently referred to football clubs by the name of their president. For example, in an article in 1922 it said, "Nueva Chicago or better said the club of don Ghio."[15]

Ghio's family had emigrated in 1885 from Italy to the portside barrio of La Boca when he was five. Shortly thereafter they moved to Nueva Chicago, where they were among the early inhabitants of the new barrio. Ghio became active in the Centro Social Nueva Chicago and other social clubs. The most important football club in the barrio was Nueva Chicago, and Ghio played a crucial role from its earliest days, was elected president three times in the 1920s, and served as its representative to the football federation. He also was among the founders and a longtime member of a sociedad de fomento in Nueva Chicago. In the 1930s, when he sat on the city council and could not legally serve on the society's directing board, his brother Atilio served in that capacity. (Atilio was also a Socialist Party activist.) In 1917 Fernando was elected president of a congress of sociedades de fomento. He founded the first barrio newspaper and later edited another.

Fernando Ghio was a crucial figure in the local Socialist apparatus. He helped form the party's first local committee, and as early as 1914 was elected to a party congress. He continued to attend party congresses and participate in the party's internal affairs. He won election to the city council on the Socialist slate in 1932. He used his seat on the council to try to obtain benefits for the barrio. For example, he pushed legislation that would have required that all meat sold in the city come from the municipal slaughterhouse, which was in his barrio.

Ghio's role in the community was also personal. After 1910 he owned a bar, which was famous for its traditional gaucho singers, as well as for cultural discussions attended by intellectuals close to the Socialist Party. Ghio reputedly taught people to read and lent books from his large private library. Ghio's activities clearly built a coterie of people who liked and respected him, and his leadership of the football club Nueva Chicago made him known citywide.[16] Other politicians followed paths that were not dissimilar.

Reinaldo Elena and La Boca

Reinaldo Elena also built a political base in a barrio, in his case La Boca, in part because of his support of local civic associations. His father owned a marine hardware store in the barrio, and in 1919, at the age of twenty, Reinaldo helped start a pro-Radical newspaper, *La Pluma*, which covered La Boca and the adjacent barrio of Barracas. In the 1920s he dispensed patronage as a boss of the Antipersonalist Radicals in La Boca and was appointed to the school board that covered La Boca and Barracas. He sought patronage appointments for people in the 1930s as well.[17] In 1938 two newspapers, *La Razón* and *La República*, claimed that the Antipersonalists' good showing in elections in La Boca was due to Elena.[18] He won election to the city council twice in the 1930s and to Congress three times after the overthrow of Perón in 1955.

Besides dispensing patronage, how did he attract support? Elena positioned himself to seem close to barrio inhabitants and obtained benefits for them. He frequently appeared in the neighborhood cantinas, and he was intimately linked to key people in the barrio, especially its artistic elite, such as the painter Benito Quinquela Martín. He belonged to several local development associations. He played a key role in a small football club, Boca Alumni, which had 252 members in 1926 and ceased to exist in 1935. Most of its supporters lived in a particularly poor segment of the barrio. Representing the club, Elena played an important role on the council of the Asociación Argentina de Football, one of two competing confederations of football clubs. He also belonged to the most popular football club in the barrio, if not the city, Boca Juniors. In 1927 Boca Juniors had two competing factions, and both offered to make him president, but he refused. When Boca Juniors needed something and Elena sat on the city council, he always helped. For example, in 1932 the club wanted to build a stadium, but it needed the city's permission to use the land, and it wanted the complex to be tax-exempt for ten years. Elena presented the proposal to the council, which ultimately passed it. In 1938 when representatives of Boca went to the intendente to invite him to the laying of the cornerstone of their new stadium, they brought Elena along. Earlier, the club had made Elena an honorary member simultaneously with president-elect Roberto M. Ortiz. River Plate, the Boca Juniors' bitter rival, which also had been founded in La Boca, named him an honorary member as well. In 1936 Elena was under consideration for the presidency of the national football confederation but met opposition from at least one important club for political reasons. Elena's activities gave him widespread visibility. For example, in 1936 he organized a banquet in honor of the intendente, Mariano de Vedia y Mitre, at the locale of the Boca Juniors, which 1,800 people attended and which received major press coverage. As late as 1965, Elena retained influence in his barrio's football club because his political right-hand man was Boca Juniors' vice president.[19]

Remigio Iriondo and a Career Begun before the Voting Reform

Remigio Iriondo developed political capital through involvement in local organizations, but he began prior to the creation of the modern political system. Born in 1872, he moved to the predominantly working-class Villa Crespo neighborhood in 1896 and started a career in education. When he established a school in 1897, he called it Colegio Salvador after Salvador Benedit, who is considered the founder of the barrio and was an important businessman and politician. Iriondo also was involved with several local periodicals.

From the last years of the nineteenth century, he played an active role in civic associations. These include a local development society, Asociación de Fomento Defensa Vecinal, founded shortly after the beginning of the new century, which he served as president for many years and which was later named after him. He was also active for over thirty years in the Biblioteca Popular Alberdi (see chapter 4), which he presided over from 1934 to 1940. When the Universidad Popular Florentino Ameghino was established in Villa Crespo, its first rector was Iriondo, and its classes met in his school. He also played a critical role in the creation of the Universidad Popular Salvador, which was started by Defensa Vecinal. A boxing club was founded in his house and was subsequently named for him. He was president of a local social club and an honorary meritorious member of another.

Iriondo served in municipal posts before the political reform, and in 1921 he won election to the city council on the list of the Progressive Democrats.

During his time on the council, he did not hesitate to help the institutions with which he was connected. In 1931 he was appointed as a juez de paz, and he was appointed to serve on two local school boards after that.[20] Clearly political capital could be accumulated by being active in civic associations.

Luis Boffi and a Different Model of Creating Support

Not all politicians active in civic associations developed a base in the barrio where they lived. According to his own account, Luis L. Boffi followed an unusual path into politics. Despite joining the Radical Party in 1923 at the age of eighteen, Boffi dedicated himself mostly to the medical profession until 1932, when he published an attack on the postcoup government's treatment of the University of Buenos Aires. After the personal intervention of Colonel José María Sarobe, the secretary of the presidency, Boffi was fired from his post in a municipal hospital. Efforts by the city council to restore his position failed, even after the return of the Radical Party to the council. This sparked in him an intense focus on politics, which led to Boffi being elected to the city council on the Radical Party list in 1938 and to Congress twice in the 1960s. His hospital position was restored only after he won election to the council.[21]

In part, Boffi built support by expanding his connections through civic associations. In addition to serving as a doctor for several types of institutions, he played important roles in sports clubs and popular universities. In addition to being the doctor for the Club Social y Deportivo Buenos Aires (Social and Sporting Club of Buenos Aires), Boffi served on its governing board and as its president. He was the doctor for the key football club River Plate in 1935 and held the same position with another of the so-called Big Five, San Lorenzo de Almagro, in 1937 and 1938 while he also served on its governing board. He helped San Lorenzo while on the city council as he, along with another councilor who had held office in the club, were among the three councilors to propose legislation exempting it from certain taxes. He was also active in the national football association.[22]

Boffi also played a large role in universidades populares. He served as vice president of the Universidad Popular de Bernardino Rivadavia from 1935 until at least 1943. He used his connections along with those of a police commissioner to help the institution receive the aid that it was supposed to. He also served on the governing board of the Universidad Popular Mariano Moreno from 1938 until at least 1943 and was honorary president of Universidad Popular La Argentina from 1940 on.[23] Clearly Boffi had a political strategy that included creating political capital through connections to civic associations, and he seems to differ only in that the institutions were scattered around the city.

Civic Associations as Political Organizations

Entire civic associations could be tied to a political party. There were organizations whose sole purpose was politics, but others that had a dual function, acting as a base of political power but also having another role. If we examine the football club Almagro (not to be confused with the much larger club San Lorenzo de Almagro), the latter phenomenon is clear. Almagro was of considerable size, claiming some 400 members in 1924 and 1,053 in 1926. In 1930 it possessed the sixth largest stadium in Buenos Aires. In 1936 it had some 2,600 members. Still, Almagro had spent much of its trajectory not in the first division. It had ties to the Radical Party from its creation and especially in its early days to the political ambitions of Miguel Ortiz de Zárate. Initially founded in 1911, it like many other clubs failed after several founders left. Almagro was definitively refounded in 1916 after Ortiz de Zárate returned to Almagro after a club that he had joined splintered between Radical and Conservative Party members. Two early club presidents, José M. Paglieri and Arturo G. Costa were Radical Party activists. However, the dominant figure was Ortiz de Zárate, who was establishing himself as the Radical political boss of the Seventh Ward.[24]

Ortiz de Zárate became the public face of the club. The newspaper *Crítica* referred to Almagro as "the sympathetic institution of which Ortiz de Zárate is alma mater." In 1924 the sports magazine *El Gráfico* stated that almost all members of Almagro were Radicals at the club's founding, and the party's influence was expanding. The magazine claimed that Ortiz de Zárate used club members to control the local party machinery.²⁵ Ortiz de Zárate was noted for tying the loyalty of Buenos Aires's newspaper vendors (*canillitas*) to the club, partly through sponsoring a football championship for teams of canillitas. The club, like the Radical Party, distributed clothes and toys to children on New Year's and Three Kings Day. Ortiz de Zárate won a seat in Congress in 1928 and 1938.

Ortiz de Zárate was not the only prominent Radical to be a conspicuous member of the club. Rómulo Trucco was the first official member of the club and served as president. He won one term as a city councilor and one as a congressman. Raúl H. Colombo, who also was president of Almagro during this era, was an active Radical; although not terribly successful in city or national politics, he was in football politics, since he was president of the national football confederation between 1956 and 1965. His good friend Arturo Frondizi, a Radical, won election as Argentina's president in the late 1950s. Frondizi played in the youth divisions of the club in the 1920s and was nominated by Almagro for a position with the football federation in 1940.²⁶

What did the club obtain from its political connections? In 1921 Almagro leveled its playing field using city workers and oxen and the municipality's only road-grading machine. A Socialist city councilor requested information from the executive branch, and it became clear that the city had approved the project with a promise of a later reimbursement based only on the word of Trucco. Trucco was then sitting on the city council. From the discussions in the council, it is apparent that political influence had been critical, since not all clubs could have the use of such equipment. Almagro never paid the money, as the council voted to waive the fee with no discussion. The five-man committee that presented the motion included Trucco. (At least two other sitting council members at some point served as presidents of football clubs.) Trucco also sat on the committee that successfully recommended the city grant the club a 2,000-peso subsidy for building playing fields and other improvements. The next year he helped bring forward a bill granting a tax exemption to the club; it passed. When Almagro sought a subsidy from the national government, one of the two deputies who proposed it was Ortiz de Zárate.²⁷

In 1980 Raúl Colombo in an interview said: "At least for me, Almagro was always more than a simple sporting institution. But what I want to talk about is the community plan that the club gave to the neighborhood. It was always an essentially Radical barrio. To say it better, it was always the great Yrigoyenist bastion of the capital. . . . The club in some form always made the connection between the idea and its followers."[28] Although a football club like many others, Almagro was part of a political apparatus. It differed from other clubs in which politicians played a crucial role because in Almagro politics was more central. Other football clubs had political ties that were more complex. Still, Ortiz de Zárate used Almagro as a barrio base, and in that way it resembles other civic associations.

Civic associations cannot be separated from the politics of the time. They needed assistance from the government, which politicians could facilitate. However, it is important to remember that politicians benefited from the connections provided by the organizations. They needed political capital to organize campaigns and gain positions high enough on party slates to win elections.

CHAPTER THREE

Football

Politics and Barrios

FOOTBALL CLUBS HAVE PLAYED an important role in both politics and barrio identity in greater Buenos Aires almost from their initial founding to the present. They became important just as the electoral system was reformed and as, in many cases, barrio identity became manifest. Football, politics, and neighborhoods became intertwined and remain so. For example, club elections have remained important into the twenty-first century. Mauricio Macri rode his reputation, which was built as president of Boca Juniors, to victory as the chief executive of the city of Buenos Aires and then as the Argentine president from 2015 to 2019.

The passion of fans for their barrio and their club has had a statutory impact as well. In late 2012, under pressure from the supporters of the football club San Lorenzo de Almagro, the legislature of the city of Buenos Aires voted to allow the expropriation of a parcel of land so that the team could build a stadium in the exact location of its former one in the neighborhood of Boedo, a site with which the club had long been identified but had been forced to abandon. Acquiring the land was just the first step in erecting a stadium; steps along the way were greeted with ebullient demonstrations of joy.[1]

Football clubs developed in the first decades of the twentieth century as part of the burgeoning creation of civic associations. But football clubs have largely been ignored in this context. For decades Argentine football was based primarily in greater Buenos Aires, and for many years most fan support for almost all teams was barrio-based.[2] Although young men created football clubs in order to play the game, they needed to turn to outsiders to have their clubs flourish. Many clubs emerged shortly before the voting reform, and since they were the focus of interest of thousands of young men, many of whom were eligible to vote, politicians saw them as potential bastions of support. Many clubs, despite being theoretically controlled by its members, became dominated by powerful men, many of whom were barrio-based.

Campaigns for the control of clubs came to resemble political elections. In 1935 the popular magazine *Caras y Caretas* observed that the election in the football club San Lorenzo de Almagro made the barrio of Boedo look as if it were undergoing a congressional campaign. For almost twenty days Boedo was inundated with propaganda, both oral and written, including leaflets, wall posters, and the like. On election day, all types of motor vehicles brought supporters to the polls.[3] At times, club elections reflected the tensions that existed at both local and national levels. However, both clubs and politicians frequently benefited from the latter's interest in football.

The Beginnings of Football

Football was brought to Argentina by British citizens. By the last decades of the nineteenth century, Britons and their Argentine descendants had established a number of clubs that played football. However, the superiority of British-dominated teams did not last long. By halfway through the second decade of the twentieth century, teams with British ties were surpassed by those composed predominantly of native-born Argentines or those coming from other immigrant communities.[4] It is important to remember that football in its first years was not the dominant sport in Argentina. Horse racing was extraordinarily popular and, Roy Hora has argued, probably more so than football.[5] Boxing also enjoyed popular favor.

Football clubs were created to play the game, although over time the game became more and more a spectator sport.[6] The initial wave of interest in football came from the example of the British-dominated clubs and instruction in some private high schools. Although the state schools stressed physical education, they tended to discourage football. Boys and young men mostly learned to play football in parks, plazas, and the empty lots that became a key part of the myth of Argentine football.[7] The demand for places to play, including stadiums, and other expenses forced successful clubs to turn to men who could provide access to the state or to other sources of wealth.

Football teams are fielded by clubs governed by elected boards, making establishing ties to politicians relatively simple. For example, the statutes that governed River Plate—both before and after a reform of them in 1931—gave administrative power to a board of directors (*comisión directiva*), which was elected by a general assembly of members that met each December. Each board member served for two years with half the members elected each year. The board was supposed to meet at least once a week, and it could also call for a special general assembly. General assemblies also could be convoked by 5 percent of the general membership.[8] Although details varied, other clubs had similar rules.

In the early twentieth century, boys or young men who wanted to play football would found a club in their barrio. Most existed for a short time and then disappeared. A club's success depended on prowess on the field and an ability to lure good players to join it. However, it was not enough to win games; clubs needed organizational stability. Expenses had to be met; a field on which to play had to be found; and if a team climbed the ladder of success, a stadium needed to be built. A characteristic of Argentine football leagues, which they share with most of the world, is that teams are not permanently in the first division. Teams ascend to a higher level by winning or descend to a lower level after doing badly. The clubs in Argentina were designed to be nonprofit, unlike in many other regions of the world. Membership dues and ticket sales frequently could not match expenses, so successful clubs needed to attract patronage. Most of the clubs founded in the early twentieth century disappeared long ago, and we know little about them. Those whose history is recoverable were successful both on the field and organizationally.

Numerous barrio football and social clubs continue to exist, and they have a crucial role in the city by providing places of sociability and the possibility of playing the game.[9] Almost all the important clubs and many of the minor ones in greater Buenos Aires were formed in the first decades of the twentieth century. As early as 1907, 350 clubs existed in greater Buenos Aires, and by 1912 there were 482 clubs.[10] Early record keeping was vague, and much that we know is based on club mythology. Almost all have tales of a group of young males gathering to start a football club in a public space, someone's house, or a café. In 1976 one of the founders of the Club Atlético Atlanta, Emilio Bolinches, recounted how a group of friends who wanted to play football got together to start a club, meeting in the house of a local businessman; when they did not have enough chairs, they moved to a nearby plaza.[11] Although stories exist about difficulties raising even small sums, frequently the founders came from the middle class. For example, many original members of Boca Juniors and River Plate, both of which started in the predominantly working-class barrio of La Boca, were middle class since they were attending or had attended secondary school where some had been exposed to football.[12]

By the 1920s, football had become an integral element of porteño life and fired the imagination of much of the population. Club memberships climbed sharply as they became places to watch rather than just play football. In 1916 Boca Juniors had 1,500 members; in 1922, it had 1,757; in 1929, 6,740; in 1931, 8,565; and in 1935, 22,456. Even a small club like Temperley had 354 members in 1923; 997 in 1930; and 1,860 in 1939.[13] In the wake of professionalization in 1931, game attendance increased significantly.[14] Football had become a mass spectacle. Its growing popularity was stoked by increased coverage in newspapers and sports magazines, such as *El Gráfico*. The use of lighting permitted night games, and radio stations broadcast matches and information on major clubs. More fans enjoyed longer weekends with the legal mandate of Saturday afternoons off, which took effect in the capital in 1932 and in the province in 1938.

The popularity of football in the 1920s pushed both the Communist and the Socialist parties to create their own football leagues, despite the Communists' expressed disdain for what they called "bourgeois" sports. But party-controlled leagues could attract sympathizers or at least help the parties hold on to members and protect them from the bourgeois world. These efforts were extensive but began late, compared to the creation of barrio football clubs. The Communist federation started in 1924 and the Socialist effort later than that. Hernán Camarero counted fifty-seven teams belonging to the Communist sports organization in greater Buenos Aires between 1923 and 1930. According to Cristina Mateu more than seventy such clubs existed. The Socialist efforts were somewhat less successful. However, the political climate after the 1930 coup limited the possibilities of Communist efforts in this arena, and the Socialists were somewhat ambiguous about football.[15]

In addition, unlike the situation so well described by Brenda Elsey in Chile where political parties began organizing politically based football clubs very early and the working class had clear ties to left-wing parties, Argentine football clubs of all sizes remained largely barrio-based, and many were founded before the voting reform of 1912. In the 1920s, the era directly before professionalization, Eduardo Archetti argues, almost every barrio had at least one club in the first or second division, and these were relatively competitive.[16] Barrios tended to be mixed in class terms, and no party or ideology had hegemony among the working class. Political influence in football clubs tended to be individual and frequently contested (see below). In some ways, the role that politics played in the football clubs of Buenos Aires was parallel to what was occurring in neighboring Uruguay, but the nature of that nation's politics—with its two traditional parties, one of which had hegemony—made things somewhat different.[17] It is important to note that even when the Buenos Aires clubs were controlled by politicians or wealthy men, rarely were they members of the traditional elite, probably because elites embraced rugby, field hockey, and equestrian sports.

The Buenos Aires clubs reflected the mixed ethnicity of the city's neighborhoods. As Julio Frydenberg has demonstrated, the names of Buenos Aires clubs do not reference foreign nations, indicating the mixed nature of their founders or at least a desire not to be identified with a foreign community. This stands in sharp contrast to the situation in other Latin American countries where some clubs were composed predominantly of an ethnic or national group, such as Vasco da Gama in Rio de Janeiro; Palestra Itália (today called Palmeiras) in São Paulo; Alianza Lima in Peru; or Audax Italiano and Palestino, both of Santiago, Chile. Unlike in Santiago, in Buenos Aires unions played an insignificant role because teams were created prior to the formation of solid unions. Unlike in Brazil, Peru, and to a lesser extent Chile, Argentine clubs developed in a political system in which politicians needed to search for support. The football clubs in Córdoba, Argentina, resembled those of Buenos Aires, but elites, companies, and institutions played a larger role.[18]

By the 1920s new clubs found it practically impossible to meet the increasingly stringent league requirements for fields and stadiums, and independent leagues that were outside formal football structures had begun to disappear. Football as a spectator sport meant that some clubs drew large paying crowds. In 1928 the team in the first division with the largest gate proceeds took in 23.5 times more money than the team that received the least. In 1931 professional football began, and while a few important teams tried to remain amateur, they quickly lost much of their fan base. The Big Five (Boca Juniors, River Plate, San Lorenzo de Almagro, Racing, and Independiente) dominated the first division because their popularity gave them higher revenues, and therefore they could acquire the best players. By 1942 the gap in game revenues had shrunk compared to 1928, but the largest receiver of game revenue still had 3.7 times that of the smallest.[19] The popular clubs had more members, which meant more dues plus more income from social activities.

Embedded in the Population

Football clubs became crucial to the identity of many barrios. The importance of football clubs for barrio identification is a trait shared with at least Santiago and Lima.[20] In Buenos Aires, football clubs along with other civic associations played a key role in forming that identification. This quote makes the link between clubs and neighborhoods clear: "Atlanta is not Villa Crespo [a barrio] but Villa Crespo would not be Villa Crespo without Atlanta."[21] Historically only two teams developed citywide and national popularity, Boca Juniors and River Plate. After its move out of La Boca to the wealthier northern sector of Buenos Aires, River Plate became identified with the more comfortable sectors and Boca with those that were poorer.

A barrio's identification with a club does not mean that the neighborhood was where the organization was formed. Because of difficulties in locating playing fields, many clubs played away from where their founders lived or worked, at least for a time. Some came to be identified with different neighborhoods than that of their creation, but the connection between a team and a barrio was often very strong.[22] Clubs came to be more than just a place to play or watch football. They became crucial centers of sociability. They provided a respectable location for entertainment, where dances were held and carnivals celebrated.[23]

As clubs got larger, they offered a wide array of programs and activities and bound the community to them. An example is Atlanta, which was founded in 1904. As early as 1910, it had a library, which received a donation of numerous books from the newspaper *La Nación*. In 1936 it built a basketball court and one for tennis. In 1937 the income from festivals and carnival celebrations was a little more than 25 percent of the revenue from football. In 1942, when it opened its new headquarters, it had a roller-skating rink, which it also used for dances. Before 1943 members enjoyed boxing, basketball, tennis, track, bocce (the Italian form of lawn bowling), handball, chess, and ping-pong.[24]

Even a small club like Chacarita Juniors, which spent time in the second division, had programs that tied it to its community. Festivals were important sources of funding. In 1930 such revenue was slightly over 14 percent of the club's total income. In 1936 it held thirty-three dances with attendance of almost 7,000. In 1940 an outside organization based in its headquarters offered art classes to members and their families. In addition, in the early 1940s the club provided its members with free legal consultations and low-cost medical and dental services.[25] Both small and large clubs had places to eat and drink in their facilities.[26] Club headquarters became spaces in which members could talk and share other simple diversions.

The bigger clubs provided members with numerous social activities. Boca Juniors in a short period in mid-1935 held a series of events. On April 11, to celebrate the anniversary of the club's founding, it showed movies on its field. On May 25, Independence Day, a sports tournament for young people was held; and on July 5, the third anniversary of its library, the club staged a festival at a nearby theater in which movies were shown and artistic acts performed. The library was open for three hours a day from Monday through Friday, which equaled the availability of most bibliotecas populares. An internal football championship was also organized. The club offered classes in English, French, math, telegraphy, and literacy. This period in 1935 was not unique; between April and November 1942 the committee on fiestas raised slightly over 19,000 pesos. The end of 1942 was celebrated with performances by music students and gymnasts, and the opening of a new handball court was commemorated with a lunch. The club held a dance on December 26, 1942, with six separate orchestras and additional dances on January 8 and February 6, 1943. In March, the club celebrated carnival with six events with music provided by two notable tango orchestras, including the iconic group led by Aníbal Troilo.[27] The large clubs also offered a wide range of sporting activities for their members in addition to football.

Although football clubs became important places for barrio inhabitants to gather, football remained a largely masculine domain. Women did not play it in the clubs, at least officially, and photographs indicate the predominance of male spectators. Other activities did include women. For example, in 1932 women in River Plate participated in at least track, basketball, tennis, and swimming. Women's track was governed by a committee of women.[28] Women did have roles in several clubs, but they were usually on minor committees. In 1941 the subcommittee of "ladies" in the Chacarita Juniors was praised for organizing social and cultural events. In 1936 for the first time there was a contested election for the women's committee of Independiente. In 1941 in the same club América E. Cal de Casazza ran for the post of auditor of accounts on one of the lists competing for the board of directors. Her list lost, but she was the first woman to compete for a place in the governance structure.[29]

Women tend to appear in the printed records of clubs as dues-payers in a separate category in the 1930s. If women were counted as just members, they are invisible. In River Plate, the pre-1931 governing statutes made no mention of women. The revised guidelines stated that women paid the same dues as youths, and youths had no right to vote or to a voice in the general assembly, which implies that women fell in the same category. However, in some clubs, women could vote. In River, no women were listed as members in 1922, but in 1925 they were 5 percent of the membership; this dropped to 3 percent in 1927. By the late 1930s women were between 14 and 16 percent of members.[30] In Lanús, no women were listed in 1930 as members, but the following year they were 2 percent of the membership, rising to 3 percent in 1937 and almost 4 percent in 1942.[31] In other clubs the percentage of women was higher. For example, in Racing in 1935, 14 percent of the members were women, while in

Estudiantes de La Plata at three separate dates between 1930 and 1942 women comprised either 28 or 29 percent of the membership.[32] So women were a presence in the clubs, but their role stayed clearly secondary. Although women's membership increased over time, the clubs remained predominantly masculine spheres.

The sense of community that clubs generated can be seen through tangos. As early as 1916 Boca Juniors had a tango dedicated to it, which was then recorded. In the next decades, other clubs received similar songs. For example, after San Lorenzo de Almagro's 1927 championship season, a tango was composed celebrating its victory; it was dedicated to Eduardo Larrandart and Pedro Bidegain, the club's president and vice president, who were active politicians. This tango, entitled "San Lorenzo," makes clear the connection between a barrio and its club: "The boys of Boedo [the barrio] celebrated the victory / That the 'tin' [team] of San Lorenzo won this year / Arriving with its triumph at the pedestal of glory / And was the only strong desire that the barrio coveted." Ernesto Ziperstein lists twenty-five tangos connected to San Lorenzo. Other large clubs also had numerous songs dedicated to them.[33]

Successful clubs began attracting members who lived outside the barrio. According to *El Gráfico*, in 1927 the presidential election of Boca Juniors was between two factions; one was composed of older members from the neighborhood, and the other represented newer members and those from outside the barrio. By the mid-1930s, campaign offices in neighborhoods far from La Boca played a critical role in elections. However, what we have called the micro barrio still mattered. In 1937 Boca's president, Camilo Cichero, was questioned about why he ran for office and replied that he had been asked to do so by the opposition group known either as Ayalos or as those of the Café Torre, because many lived on Ayalos Street or went regularly to that café. These were his childhood friends, who now worked in professions that ranged from masons to merchants to professionals. He had grown up there and gone regularly to the café until 1927, when he moved away after receiving his medical degree. From 1927 until 1936, he had been one of Boca's team doctors and served on its governing board. His successor, Eduardo Sánchez Terrero, the son-in-law of Argentina's ex-president Justo, was the first president not from the barrio, and he was chosen for his connections.[34]

The Role of Notable Individuals

Politicians and wealthy individuals have played a critical role in football clubs. That politicians wanted to be identified with football clubs or provide them with favors is not surprising. Leaving aside interest in the game, the clubs provided a way for politicians to become better known and to create a group of supporters. A former leader of the Racing club, Carlos Boloque, said in 1965: "A football club has a tremendous social importance. If we measure only from the point of view of politics, the members and sympathizers used to mean hundreds of thousands of votes that no party is in the position to disdain."[35] This was also true in the 1920s and 1930s. The needs were not unidirectional. The well-connected politicians helped clubs acquire locations to play and could aid them in receiving subsidies or other help.

The use by politicians of young men who formed football clubs as the basis for establishing a local political committee—the heart of a political organization—was featured in a short story by Bernardo Verbitsky. Although the story is set just after the period discussed in this book, it nicely illustrates the argument. A group of young men create a club, Estrella del Sur, to play football. They are approached by a young dentist, who offers to finance a clubhouse for them. The offer is not altruistic, but rather the dentist wants to use the club as a political committee, which will allow him to run for the city council.[36] Fiction appears close to reality.

The desire to be identified with a team started early. In 1914 Defensores de Belgrano reached the first division, and a triumphant march took place. Among the participants was José P. Tamborini, who became an important Radical politician. Tamborini was born and built his political base in the barrio of Belgrano; elected to Congress in 1918, he later became the minister of interior, a senator, and in 1946 a presidential candidate.[37]

Prior to the establishment of professional football in 1931, a system of sham amateurism existed in which players were paid or given jobs that in some cases they were not expected to do. Those who could obtain jobs for players became crucial to the success of teams. As early as 1911 charges of professionalism arose, and in 1916 the Socialist Party paper lamented the paying of players or their being given employment. In 1922 the newspaper *Crítica* listed the amounts that several players of the Boca Juniors received. In 1928, according to *El Gráfico*, River paid its players fifteen pesos for a loss, thirty for a tie, and fifty for a victory. Ludovico Bidoglio, an outstanding defender, transferred to Boca Juniors instead of San Lorenzo because the former got him a job as an electrician in the Ministry of Public Works. In 1930 *El Gráfico* noted sarcastically that a player for Chacarita Juniors, Juan Gil, went regularly to his job at the Department of National Hygiene. Six of his teammates also were employed by that agency, whose secretary-general was Tiburcio Padilla, the president of the club and a Radical politician.[38]

As mentioned in the discussion of Reinaldo Elena in chapter 2, a barrio politician could help local football clubs without assuming a conspicuous role. Such activities could win friendships or alliances with influential men that could help a politician achieve his primary goal: the winning of votes. The importance for the clubs of even minor political figures therefore should not be underestimated. In 1921 Boca Juniors had a shrunken membership and deep debts. The governing council resigned, and a group of older members intervened, raised money, and increased the number of members. The club still needed a new place to play, however. A list of candidates proposed by an emergency committee was elected in 1922 with Manlio Anastasi as president. Anastasi was an active Radical Party member and belonged to a family well entrenched in the barrio. By late 1926 he was the city's director of sanitation. He used his connections to help the club obtain a new field from the railroad Ferrocarril Sud by having Arturo Goyeneche and Federico Guerrico intercede with the railroad company. Goyeneche was a key Radical politician with an interest in La Boca who served in the Chamber of Deputies from 1916 to 1922 and was intendente in the 1930s. Guerrico was a lawyer for the railroad. In the club elections in 1926 two slates faced each other. According to an author in *El Gráfico*, the slate backed by Anastasi won because of his links to the government.[39]

Politically ambitious men forged ties to football clubs to enhance their image. An example is General Justo, who served as minister of war in the 1920s and as president beginning in 1932. Although Justo was an excellent politician, he owed his election more to the coup of 1930 than to his popularity. According to a biographer, it is unclear whether Justo was a football fan, but he regularly attended games and was a member of both River Plate and Boca Juniors. Justo played a role in the running of Boca, serving on its finance committee. After his election as president of the country, he was made honorary president of that committee. His son-in-law Sánchez Terrero was later elected president of Boca, serving from 1939 to 1946. Also, Justo obtained public recognition for his role with Boca; in 1938 when the cornerstone of the new stadium was laid, Justo and his daughter were the patrons. Boca bestowed an honorary membership on Justo, a recognition that he shared with barrio elites and presidents Ortiz and Castillo. What did the club get from Justo? During Justo's presidency, Boca Juniors received a million-peso loan from the government to help with a new stadium. River received an even larger loan.[40]

Wealthy individuals had connections, and they sometimes used their own funds to aid clubs. For businessmen, ties to clubs bestowed publicity and prestige in addition to creating new personal connections. For a barrio business owner, club leadership could engender loyalty to his business. What happened to the football club Vélez Sarsfield illustrates well the role of wealthy men. In 1941 the club owed over 39,000 pesos, had lost its field, and had descended to the second division. José Amalfitani became the president and paid the debt himself after mortgaging his house. The amount owed was sizeable; according to a 1938 government study, the average monthly income of an industrial blue-collar worker was 109 pesos. The club returned to the first division in 1944, and Amalfitani remained president until his death in 1969.[41] Something similar happened to the club Argentinos Juniors in the 1930s. It failed to meet its financial obligations, causing it to lose its playing field. It was also relegated to the second division. An outsider was elected president, and using his own money, he paid the club's debts and obtained a new place to play.[42]

Who could enlarge his influence by a role in a football club varied with the location. For example, the small club Talleres de Remedios de Escalada was based in a suburb south of the city where a major workshop of the railroad company Ferrocarril Sud was located. A railroad union leader, Francisco Agnelli, played a key role in the club between 1928 and 1941 and served as president in 1938 and 1939. Agnelli was a train engineer and important in the engineers union La Fraternidad, including being secretary-general and coauthoring its official history.[43]

The Need for a Place to Play

Buenos Aires had few parks, and stands could not be erected in them without government permission, which was difficult to obtain. In a barrio such as La Boca, the only vacant land was in the port area, which was controlled by the state or large companies, and clubs could only gain access through influential intermediaries. Obtaining a field or building a stadium was not a one-time event. River Plate played in six sites before building its current stadium in 1938. Boca played in five locations before securing its present home. In central portions of the city, finding a field was nearly impossible. For example, Independiente had been formed by young men who worked in a downtown department store, Ciudad de Londres, and employees from other downtown stores. In its first three years, Independiente moved three times inside the city of Buenos Aires before finding a home in the city of Avellaneda. In their early years, Boca, River, and San Lorenzo de Almagro all played briefly outside of the city proper. When Boca played in suburban Wilde, it lost almost all its members.[44]

Clubs based in not fully developed neighborhoods frequently also needed the assistance of politicians or influential individuals to obtain places to play. When clubs advanced to the first division, the football authorities forced them to build stands and other facilities. As clubs increased in size and complexity, obtaining leadership became difficult because presidents were not paid.[45] Only wealthy individuals or those whose efforts were compensated in other areas, such as politicians, had the time to preside over large clubs.

From early in football's development, influence was important. In 1911, three years after its founding and one year before the voting reform, Huracán needed a field that was properly equipped if it was to be admitted to the official football league. Through the intervention of the well-known sportsman Jorge Newbery, who had adopted the club after it began to use a picture of his hot air balloon as the team's symbol, Huracán received the loan of a field from the city government. It still needed to build the required facilities, for which it lacked funds. According to legend, Conservative Party boss Eliseo Cantón gave Huracán the money to buy wood to build the facilities in return for 200 voting documents, many more than the eighty members possessed. These would allow Cantón to control 200 votes. Huracán collected the documents and built the facilities.⁴⁶

Nueva Chicago and a Web of Community

One of the more cohesive barrios in the city in the early twentieth century was Mataderos, which was frequently called Nueva Chicago. Located on the far edge of Buenos Aires and formed around the municipal slaughterhouse and the market where cattle were sold, which opened in 1901, Mataderos rapidly developed a web of civic associations. The location of the barrio and the types of industry around which it grew made for a relatively tight-knit community. In a 1999 study of the neighborhood, María Teresa Sirvent located twenty-five still-existing neighborhood organizations founded prior to 1940. The first real social organization, Centro Social Nueva Chicago, was founded in 1902 with the help of the second director of the national stockyards (who served in that role from 1904 to 1917), the Conservative politician Alejandro Mohr. Mohr won election to the city council in the first open contest in 1918 and was reelected in 1922. He also served on the local school board.

The most important athletic club in the barrio was the Club Atlético Nueva Chicago, which a group of young men, most of whom worked in the stockyards, founded in 1911 to play football. Nueva Chicago rapidly became a key local institution and remains so, though it has rarely played in the first division. Mohr played a crucial role in its establishment. One of its first fields was obtained with his help, as was the wood for the first goalposts. The club's second president, Roberto Grillo, came to the club at Mohr's suggestion. In 1913 when an honorary commission was created, its president was Mohr. Honorary commissions were influential, as at least three future club presidents served on them. In 1932 Mohr's son José served a term as the club's president.⁴⁷

The other crucial political connection was to the Socialist Party through Fernando Ghio who, as already mentioned, played a major role in barrio civic associations. He aided the football club from its earliest days and served three terms as president in the 1920s while being an active politician.

Cooperation between the two political tendencies was possible because of the club's importance to the community and Mataderos's sense of identity. In addition, as Luis Alberto Romero has noted, in this period people with different ideologies coexisted in civic associations. In the city council after Mohr's death, Ghio's speech was unusually complimentary. He stated, "As Director of the Livestock Market and of the Old Slaughterhouse [Mohr] was the best of functionaries and the best of bosses; as an inhabitant of the zone of Nueva Chicago he was the best of its citizens. . . . The neighborhood of Nueva Chicago owes much to Alejandro Mohr; in reality it owes all that it has come to be." Ghio added that for more than fifteen years they had interacted daily for the good of the community and without conflict, despite their differences in political beliefs.[48] It is not hard to image such cooperation within a football club.

Many other presidents of Nueva Chicago were important local figures. Fernando Gacio Mastache owned a food store, published a local newspaper intended to "defend the interests, moral and material, of Nueva Chicago [the barrio]," and was active in the Centro Social Nueva Chicago. Amadeo Cozza had served pro bono as the team doctor.[49]

The barrio's loyalty to the club partially explains the local elites' participation. When a store owner went to a match against Huracán and rooted for that team, he faced a boycott that forced him to leave the neighborhood. Simón Bruchstein, who opened the barrio's second pharmacy in 1921, donated the club's first bocce court. The pharmacy advertised regularly in the periodicals of local sociedades de fomento, and Bruchstein served on several of their honorary commissions.[50] Although his motivations are unknowable, such actions would build ties to potential customers and aid the development of the barrio where his business operated.

In the late 1930s a crisis arose that demonstrates the need for the intervention of important people. The field that Nueva Chicago had used since 1920 was requisitioned for a hospital. After Edmundo Kelly, the longtime director of the national stockyards, interceded, the intendente gave Nueva Chicago a new site, which received the approval of the city council. At the field's inauguration, Kelly gave the ceremonial first kick in front of 5,000 spectators. At the time the club had 800 members, a tempting target for a politician.[51]

Community and Politics

The history of San Lorenzo de Almagro is a great example of the roles of important figures and politics in football clubs. Its history is unique in that a priest played a critical part in its early days, but during the 1920s it was dominated by a family of Radical Party militants who quarreled because of fissures in the party. The club's barrio was dominated by political bosses, and their power came in part because of ties to the community.

Legend has San Lorenzo being founded by boys who were playing football in the street when one was almost hit by a trolley car. A Salesian priest, Father Lorenzo Massa, offered them a place to play and became their advisor and benefactor, helping pick the team name and buying their first shirts.

Like many other clubs, its early history was beset with difficulties. For two years the club ceased to exist, and when it was reconstituted it played far from its home barrio in the northern suburb of Martínez; players walked eighteen blocks from the train station. When the club rented a field closer to Almagro, the league maintained that it was inadequate. The club needed to pay what it owed, and a sizeable contribution came from Massa. In addition, he located a rental property that could be developed as a football field. Massa and several others contributed relatively large sums to make it playable. After this period, Massa was sent to other parts of the country.[52]

Pedro Bidegain became the dominant Radical operative in the Sixth Ward, the home of San Lorenzo. Bidegain was born, married, and lived in the ward. As early as 1906 Bidegain held a position in the party's ward structure, and by 1920 he headed it. He won election to the city council in 1921 and to Congress in 1926. In 1923, *Crítica* used him as an example of the local party barons. Bidegain possessed charisma. In 1935 a female fan was asked why she rooted for San Lorenzo. She replied that she was religious and knew that Massa had founded the club, and she was honoring "the sympathy that was inspired in me by don Pedro Bidegain who I always remember." Bidegain had died in 1933.[53]

Earlier, in 1918, Bidegain became vice president of San Lorenzo. Bidegain's brother José served on the board of directors, while his nephew Eduardo Larrandart was secretary. Both José Bidegain and Larrandart were Radical Party activists. Between 1920 and 1928 Larrandart served as president with Pedro Bidegain as vice president. Bidegain also helped found the Universidad Popular de Boedo and a social club that survived until 2003, of which he was first president. Larrandart served as president of that club in the 1930s.[54]

San Lorenzo became an integral part of the community. Bidegain and Larrandart spent considerable time in the Café Dante speaking with the club's players and members of the community, including many literary figures who identified with that section of the city, Boedo. Reputedly, fans of Huracán, a rival based in an adjacent barrio, were barred from the Dante; similarly, followers of San Lorenzo were not allowed in the café frequented by Huracán. A tango composed in 1933 after San Lorenzo won a championship makes clear the connection to the Café Dante: "Because San Lorenzo won on Sunday, / The habitués of the Dante put on their party clothes." The rivalry between San Lorenzo and Huracán was intense. In 1933 the newspaper *La Nación* referred to a game between the two teams as a competition for the sporting supremacy of the neighborhood. The barrio's attachment to San Lorenzo was deep. *Caras y Caretas* headlined an article in 1937, "The Heart of Boedo Beats to the Rhythm of the Multitude That Follows San Lorenzo." The article includes phrases like "This is Boedo! The constant anxiety for the state of the score!" In 1937 the president of San Lorenzo claimed that his club was no longer just of the barrio because it had fans and members all over the city, but the identification with the barrio still exists.[55]

The splintering of the Radical Party during the presidency of Alvear led to conflict in San Lorenzo in 1924, despite the familial ties of the leaders of the two factions. Larrandart was an Antipersonalist, while Bidegain supported Yrigoyen. Larrandart's hold on the presidency may not reflect approval of his politics, but rather that San Lorenzo won league titles in 1923, 1924, and 1927.

Despite his faction's failure to dominate the club, in March 1926 Bidegain used San Lorenzo's rolls to ask for support for his candidacy for Congress. The flyer that was distributed said in part, "If until now San Lorenzo de Almagro had in Mr. Bidegain one of its best collaborators, what cannot be hoped for if the porteño electorate sends him to occupy a seat in the Chamber of Deputies?" The Socialist newspaper claimed that some members were displeased that their addresses were obtained from club records, but Bidegain retorted that it was not a major issue and that he had obtained a subsidy for the club, among other things. According to one story, his influence helped force Huracán from a stadium just blocks from San Lorenzo's, thus aiding his club to consolidate its base.

Tensions heightened in 1928, purportedly over who should have represented the football federation on a trip to Europe. However, the likely cause of the intensification was that 1928 witnessed a heated national presidential election with the Radical factions as prime contenders. Friction led to Bidegain's resignation from the club's vice presidency.

After Yrigoyen won the presidential election, in early 1929 Bidegain faced his nephew in a club election. According to *La Vanguardia*, Bidegain threatened the government employment of players and board members. The players openly supported Bidegain, and his opponents charged that the players were intentionally losing games to discredit Larrandart. Rumors circulated that San Lorenzo was going to receive a congressional subsidy and that several important footballers wanted to play for San Lorenzo if Bidegain won the election. Two bus companies had posters in their vehicles' windows supporting Bidegain. The newspaper *Última Hora* also backed him; for example, a headline said: "San Lorenzo without Bidegain Is Not San Lorenzo: Never will the club San Lorenzo de Almagro be in better hands than those of señor Pedro Bidegain." Despite the presence of police and government officials, the election assembly was marred by several fights. Bidegain won 597–482.[56]

Bidegain's presidency was extremely active. Membership rose from 3,612 to 13,638, a sharp increase but not totally out of line with other clubs. The playing of basketball and tennis began. Bidegain recruited football players and convinced them to suit up for San Lorenzo. The stadium was enlarged and became the biggest in the capital—seating 73,400. According to one account, municipal workers were used. Bidegain also had political help. In 1930 the club's vice president was the Radical Party politician Pedro Villemur, an Almagro resident who was president of the city council. Villemur had been on the club's executive board for most of the 1920s.[57]

After the September 1930 coup, Bidegain went into exile, and on his return, he was jailed. Other Radicals were driven from the club's leadership, and an interim president was put in charge. In early 1931, elections took place with the factions from 1929 competing. Larrandart's supporters proclaimed that they would remove politics from the club and restore good administration to an organization that was in bad financial shape. Larrandart won 2,052–1,411, a turnout much higher than two years before. His election was unsurprising given the Antipersonalist support for the coup. The players were upset, and some left the club. Bidegain's followers remained out of power.[58]

The Radicals still retained influence in the club. When in the late 1930s it sought help from the city to build a social center, which would include a gym and a library, two Radical city councilors, Villemur and Boffi, who had been on the governing council of San Lorenzo, presented the project. It did not pass.[59]

A Suburb and the Role of Its Key Football Clubs

In Avellaneda, two clubs—Racing and Independiente—embedded themselves, becoming two of the largest and most popular clubs in the country. They became centers of sociability for members and sometimes for other local inhabitants, offering athletic and cultural activities and educational opportunities. The two clubs developed into fierce rivals on the playing field, and they also came to represent opposing political positions.

From its inception, Racing was tightly tied to the Conservative political boss Alberto Barceló, who dominated Avellaneda during almost the entire interwar period. Therefore, Racing was usually run by men connected to the local Conservative political elite. Barceló's initial support for Racing came when football had not yet become important and before the voting reform of 1912, and therefore he was not looking for popular support. Barceló carried out a more traditional type of patronage, aiding his friends and relatives in something they wanted to do.

Racing's initial supporters came from Avellaneda's middle class. One direct predecessor was created by Argentine employees of the Ferrocarril Sud while another was formed after a meeting at the home of two of Barceló's brothers. A member of that club, Alberto's brother-in-law Leandro Boloque, later would lead Racing for three years.[60]

After several twists and turns, in 1903 Racing was founded by Argentine males who were mostly under twenty. By January 1909, the club had 251 members and received economic assistance from the Barceló family. Opposition to the Barcelós caused some founding members to leave Racing and play for Independiente. Independiente had just moved to Avellaneda,[61] and it became identified with Barceló's opponents. Racing's connection to Barceló had many other consequences. For example, in 1915 and 1916 the opposition paper in Avellaneda claimed that the local police favored fans of Racing over those of Independiente. In 1917, after President Yrigoyen intervened in the province of Buenos Aires, replacing a Conservative governor and charging a Radical with organizing new elections, at least three Racing players lost their city employment.[62]

Racing dominated Argentine football from 1913 to 1919, and according to some, its manner of play began the start of a distinctive Argentine style. In 1920 Racing was the largest club in the country with 1,413 members. As it grew, Racing increasingly became a center for many types of activities, which increased its attractiveness. At the beginning of the 1920s members could participate in basketball, swimming, track, and Basque paddle ball. In 1926 Racing had 2,624 members, making it the third largest club—just ahead of Independiente. By 1931 it claimed slightly over 7,000 members, while Independiente had over 5,000. In 1935 Racing had 21,500 members, and its rival had 14,500. In 1941 the former claimed 17,053 members and the latter 17,454. Racing had continued to add sports. By the end of 1935, members enjoyed football, tennis, bocce, basketball, paddle ball, roller skating, field hockey, track, gymnastics, swimming, ping-pong, fencing, and Greco-Roman wrestling. Some sports were played by both men and women.[63]

Racing also celebrated carnival; for example, in 1936 it scheduled six dances, each with two bands, one that played tango and one that played jazz. The club also held dances at other times, frequently with the same musical lineup. It established a beach for its members along the coast. For its young members it had a summer camp, offered excursions, and created a chorus and a theater. During the summer, Racing showed free movies, which nonmembers could attend. The club offered lectures by diverse speakers, including the Communist militant and historian Rodolfo Puiggrós, the educator Pablo Pizzurno, the physician and Socialist Alicia Moreau de Justo, and the Radical Party politician and historian Emilio Ravignani. It hung art in its facility and sponsored concerts of works by famous composers. The club organized classes, including cooking instruction by Petrona de Gandulfo (known as doña Petrona), the author of Argentina's iconic cookbook. Racing also organized a football tournament in 1933 in which twenty-eight schools participated. It gave milk to 500 children three times a week. In other words, it was part of the community and a critical center of sociability.[64]

Barceló's influence over the club was extremely large. According to Juan Corradi, Barceló discussed Racing's affairs with club leaders at his home. The club's political connections are revealed by the indictment in 1916 of Barceló and several followers for using their official positions to influence elections. Three of the accused, Leopoldo Siri, Luis Carbone, and Pedro Groppo, had been or would be presidents of Racing; together, they held that post for thirteen years. All were absolved.[65] In a study of the twenty-eight most influential followers of Barceló, ten belonged to Racing and one to Independiente.[66] However, elections were often contested, and the close allies of Barceló were not always victorious.

Many club leaders were important men. The president of Racing in 1922–1923 and in 1925, Groppo, was a physician who became director of the Hospital Fiorito, which was built by Barceló. He presided over Avellaneda's city council in 1919–1920 and from 1922 through 1927. In 1930 the military government selected him to run the city. At various times Groppo held seats in both houses of the provincial legislature and in the lower house of the national Congress. Between 1938 and 1940 he was the national finance minister. When Groppo got married in 1934, Barceló served as a witness at the civil ceremony.[67] Luis Carbone held the presidency of Racing for nine years and was a municipal functionary.[68]

As football's popularity increased, especially after professionalization, Racing, like other large clubs, attracted members who could not use the club's facilities because they lived some distance away. This produced friction and for a time helped members who were not close to Barceló to control the club. Roughly simultaneously, both Racing and Independiente confronted internal problems, including charges of electoral manipulation. In many ways the internal conflicts mirrored the political problems of the society at large.

By 1932 unhappiness existed in Racing about the direction of the club. The lack of success of the football team, the emphasis on social activities, its financial situation, and the failure to create a branch in the capital contributed as did the role of politics in the club. That year two electoral lists were presented: one consisted of the traditional leaders, and the other was composed of newer members, especially from the capital. The latter's presidential candidate and the easy victor was Ernesto Malbec, a former player for Racing and a distinguished plastic surgeon. Shortly after Malbec took office, a branch of the club was opened in the capital, and soon after, one was created south of Avellaneda in Bernal.[69]

Despite Malbec becoming head of the national football association, which created a vacancy in the club presidency, the election of 1934 did not generate much tension.[70] The next year saw a vastly different scenario with two lists competing fiercely. One was headed by Luis Carbone, an early member of the club and a fixture in its leadership. The other faction was headed by Malbec; his vice presidential candidate, Jerónimo Della Latta, was a congressman who had a long history of involvement in politics and civic associations in Avellaneda. Della Latta is an anomaly in that he was a Socialist. The issues paralleled those of the previous few years, but the campaign assumed the air of a national election. Newspapers took sides. Carbone appeared on the radio. The factions had election offices in the capital as well as in Avellaneda. Charges of electoral manipulation arose. Malbec won decisively.[71]

The following election generated little interest, despite Malbec stepping aside for a member of his faction, Antonio Salustio. This apathy did not continue in the next election, however, as economic problems had worsened because the football team's poor performance had lowered revenues, and past alliances splintered. At the last moment, the opposition withdrew from the election, and Salustio remained in office.[72]

Although Malbec and Salustio may not have been close to Barceló, they were not necessarily political opponents. Salustio, when he was president of Racing, joined the presidents of Boca, River, San Lorenzo, and Vélez Sarsfield in a banquet in honor of presidential candidate Roberto M. Ortiz, whom Barceló supported.[73] Still, in 1938 the Conservative governor of Buenos Aires province took over Racing and handed it to Boloque, Barceló's brother-in-law, alleging misuse of power by those in charge and financial problems, which certainly existed. When new elections were held, the opposition led by Della Latta charged that there was fraud and withdrew from the contest, and Carbone became president again.[74]

Independiente gave its members and the community many of the same opportunities that Racing offered, though on a slightly smaller scale; it was still a significant club, however. For example, in 1928 it inaugurated with the presence of the Radical governor of the province the first cement stadium in South America, which sat 60,000.[75] Although its members could enjoy a variety of sports, the opportunities were fewer than those at Racing. Fewer cultural opportunities existed as well. However, it too was a center of sociability. Independiente sponsored lectures and classes of music, singing, and various needle-working skills. It hosted carnival celebrations and dances that paralleled its rival. Club members also created a theater company. In early 1936 Independiente opened a site for camping at a beach in the nearby community of Quilmes. The club also involved itself in the community and helped provide physical education for local schools. In 1935 it gave a year's pass to its field to the two best students in each local school, and it held a celebration for the graduates of local elementary schools. When Independiente, as part of its expansion into the capital, purchased a preexisting facility, members could participate in dances and several sports there.[76]

The larger scope of Racing is not surprising in a city dominated by Barceló, and to a large extent his opponents ran Independiente. Its first dominant figure was Juan R. Mignaburu, a lawyer, who had been intendente of what became Avellaneda in 1899 and served on the city council in 1902. In 1894 he had founded a newspaper that defended the political positions of Bartolomé Mitre (an opponent of the Conservatives). Mignaburu served as president of the club in 1911–1912, 1917–1918, and 1920–1921 and was active in the club for many other years. His successor as the dominant figure was Pedro Canaveri, a Radical who was president in 1919 and from 1922 through 1933 and from 1942 to 1945. During two of those years, he served on the city council of Avellaneda. Miguel Martinicorena, who was club president from 1938 to 1941, was also a Radical Party militant.[77]

Like at Racing, the 1930s at Independiente were a time of upheaval.

Unhappiness had existed for some time over Independiente's financial situation plus the less than stellar performance of the football team. Still, elections had often remained uncontested until in 1933 Canaveri stepped aside for health reasons. Two factions competed for control with the victory going to a candidate backed by Canaveri.

The following year saw a reemergence of Canaveri, but he lost the election to Alfredo Roche, who had traditionally held positions in the club. The winning faction dominated for three years, emphasizing the creation of more social opportunities, the building of new physical structures, and the addition of other sports. An opposition faction argued that the club needed better governance, such as the publication of monthly balances and giving female members the vote, as well as a more powerful football team. This faction was led by Dante Tortonese, a doctor, writer of tangos, and Radical politician, who after the fall of Perón won three elections to Congress. In the elections in December 1937, a dissident slate led by Martinicorena won. The campaign bore similarities to intense elections in other large clubs with appeals made in Avellaneda and many barrios of the capital.

The next three years were complex. The Independiente football team won the league championship in 1938 and 1939 and finished second the following year. Game attendance and membership surged, producing an increase in income. Still, tensions reigned with charges of electoral fraud and problems at meetings. More shocking was the throwing of a game at the end of the 1940 season so that Vélez Sarsfield would be relegated to the second division instead of Atlanta. Atlanta sent a player to Independiente in exchange for the latter taking a dive. In 1941 in a three-sided electoral contest, the opposition slates called for honesty and more open decision making. Canaveri returned to power with a resounding 73 percent of the vote.[78]

The two clubs created deep loyalty in Avellaneda, and even funeral homes got involved. Two funeral homes existed in the city: one owned by the Peruihl family, who were fans of Independiente, while the other was owned by the Corradi family, who supported Racing and not incidentally Barceló. When the two teams played, the victor's followers would go to "their" funeral parlor, borrow coffins, and parade them past their opponents.[79]

Escaping the Barrio

River Plate has the reputation of being a team of the wealthy but was founded in predominantly working-class La Boca. Its image developed partly because it moved to the wealthier northern sector of the city. The move away from its barrio was made possible by the improved transportation networks in Buenos Aires, by the increased media coverage of football, and by the club's success on the field.

River Plate was formed from the merger of two clubs. One, La Rosales, was considered middle class since its direct predecessor had been formed by high school students. The other, Santa Rosa, was created by young men who met at the house of a Mr. Jacobs, a vice manager of the Wilson Coal Yards, to have tea, dance, and practice English. One attendee, Isodoro Kitzler, had been born in Mumbai and attended the school of Alejandro Watson Hutton, who is considered the founder of football in Argentina. Two others, Leopoldo Bard and Livio Ratto, both future presidents of River and players on the team, became medical students and Radicals. Despite being born in the Austro-Hungarian Empire and having anti-Semitism directed at him, Bard became an important politician, serving as majority leader in the Chamber of Deputies. Bard's presidency of River occurred before he and the club became important.[80] His ties to River undoubtedly helped his political career. Many of River's founders clearly came from the middle sectors of society.

In 1916, five clubs in La Boca belonged to the major football association, making the search for support difficult. A newspaper held a popularity contest, and Boca Juniors with 2,067 votes was the most popular. River followed with 1,629 votes, and the others lagged far behind.[81] River was tightly tied to La Boca; a café in the barrio, Las Camelias, acted as its unofficial headquarters.[82]

Like many other clubs, River had difficulty locating places to play, and that search lays bare the role of politics and influential men. River first played on land near the docks in La Boca. In 1906 the Ministry of Agriculture forced the club off that field, and River played in the southern suburb of Sarandí on land offered to the club by José Bernasconi, an executive of the naval store company Dresco. Bernasconi became president of River in 1909.[83]

One year later, the team returned to its previous location in La Boca and remained until 1913 when the government again threw it off that field. This occurred despite in 1912 the president of River, Antonio Zolezzi, having obtained 3,000 pesos from the municipal government to build stands. Zolezzi was the Conservative Party boss for La Boca and was a city councilor from 1908 to 1914. Whether Zolezzi was born in Italy or in Buenos Aires is unclear, but he owned a store that did very well, supported mutual aid societies and popular education, and founded several institutions for orphans. He made the motion in favor of the subsidy. When objections were raised, Zolezzi retorted that another club had received 15,000 pesos and that some 3,000 people attended River's games. He was an honorary member of Boca Juniors and served as president of River again from 1925 to 1927.[84] He was not the only La Boca–based politician to be involved in the club. Antonio Zaccagnini, a Socialist labor leader and politician who served both in Congress and on the city council, spent two years as a substitute member of the board of directors.[85]

In 1914 River played on the field of the athletic club Ferrocarril Oeste, which was some distance from La Boca. The following year River relocated to rented land in the port area. In the early 1920s, River moved to rented property in Recoleta, a wealthy barrio in the northern portion of the city. River's president, José Bacigaluppi, explained the move by saying: "River is not a club for a barrio but for a city." This attitude is not surprising, since his family was an important seller of subdivided lots and thus opened new areas for settlement. River built a stadium that could hold 58,000, a basketball court, four tennis courts and three of bocce, a swimming pool, an equipped gymnasium, and a place for children to play.[86] Not only did the club offer opportunities for physical activities for members, but despite the move River was a center of sociability. For example, River held dances on its tennis courts on December 24 and 31, 1931, and January 5, 1932. In 1936 it offered a wide variety of classes, including Spanish, French, Italian, English, musical instruction, cooking, handwork of various types, typing, radio, and telegraphy. The previous year, the end of classes had been celebrated with presentations of student work, musical numbers by outsiders, a master cooking class by doña Petrona, and a talk by Leopoldo Bard on the beauty of the female silhouette. Public lectures were frequent. These activities continued after the club moved farther north.[87]

In the 1930s when River's lease was up, it was forced to relocate. After failing to obtain sites closer to La Boca, it made the great leap to Núñez at the northern fringe of the city, which was then sparsely populated. The club received major assistance with the city ceding a significant portion of the land and the national government lending 2.5 million pesos (over US$800,000 in 1935–1939). The organization in 1938 claimed 33,282 members.[88]

The club's break with La Boca was not sudden. Several years after it moved from La Boca, an official club publication dedicated a page to its glory. Only in 1938 was the headquarters removed from La Boca, but remnants of fan support lingered.[89] Although River cut ties to its barrio of origin, it became more attractive to the wealthier inhabitants of the northern barrios. River still offered to its members many of the same activities, physical and cultural, as its peers.

Conclusions

The founding of football clubs shows the ability of porteños to build the institutions that they felt they needed, including playing football. Most of the clubs have long since disappeared, but others have survived. Those were successful on the field and as institutions and centers of sociability. Politics became intertwined with football when clubs turned to men who could solve their problems. Politicians helped the clubs, and in return they hoped to receive support. Politicians' involvement at times led to divisiveness, as political conflicts in the larger society came to be reflected in the institutions.

Football clubs more than other civic associations became objects of love and pride. They were crucial to barrio identity, which helps explain why many businessmen gave so much of their time and money to these institutions. Over time, attachment to football clubs began to transcend the barrio from which they sprang. They also became part of the political world. The other civic associations discussed in this book were smaller, less conspicuous, and individually much less important, but they followed patterns that were not so different.

CHAPTER FOUR

Popular Libraries as Civic Associations and Anchors of the Community

IN GREATER BUENOS AIRES in the first decades of the twentieth century many porteños hungered to read books. Books provided entertainment, but they were also perceived as a tool for self-improvement. The elites saw books as a way of bettering the society by improving the skills and the character of others, while many from poorer segments of society saw reading as a path toward social and economic advancement. People in the working class felt that learning was a road to moral self-improvement in ways that differed only somewhat from the views of the elites. The desire to read also reflected the high literacy rates and growing leisure time in the city. The civic associations founded to satisfy the desire to read became a focus for politicians from different parties hoping to build neighborhood bases. By becoming centers of sociability and pride, the popular libraries also helped forge a sense of barrio identity.

The Argentine state had failed to develop a minimally acceptable number of libraries. The inhabitants responded by creating their own institutions, bibliotecas populares, which only partially met their needs. Many libraries were too small and open too few hours to satisfy the hunger for books. Despite the desires of many of the founders, the libraries' users preferred fiction to other types of reading. At the same time, the increasing number of students created a demand for books needed for coursework. The failure to build a network of public libraries or to give more support to the private initiatives was due at least partially to the politicians' vested interest in the existing system, in which politicians built personal connections in neighborhoods. Despite the limitations the libraries had, they provided crucial reading matter and became important barrio centers.

The limited early research on popular libraries in Buenos Aires was at first optimistic about their impact on the society and saw them as important features of a bottom-up creation of democracy, but in line with the growing pessimism about the impact of civic associations these impressions have been modified.[1] In this chapter I show that the bibliotecas populares, like the other civic associations studied, became part of the political culture. The libraries needed financial and political assistance, and the politicians wanted to build political capital; their needs coincided.

Background

Although many who helped run bibliotecas populares had political or patriotic goals to improve society or themselves, many readers pursued pleasure. The largest portion of books read was literature, much of it escapist. Readership in the libraries was not evenly spread among the populace. It was heavily male. More surprising was its heavily Argentinian-born nature, even though nearly half of Buenos Aires's residents were foreign-born in 1914. The discrepancy cannot be explained by the books appearing to be almost totally in Spanish, as the second largest immigrant group was Spaniards and the largest Italians, who after a few years in the country could easily have read Spanish, if they so desired. Even a popular library whose almanac was mostly in Yiddish had more books in Spanish than in other languages.[2] The nature of the readership made the libraries an ideal place to pursue political support since few immigrants became citizens. Many libraries catered to students, and male students would likely become voters. Parents of students would also be grateful to politicians who aided the libraries that their children used.

Many Argentines believed in the potential for upward mobility through education and hard work, and books were crucial elements in this trajectory. Libraries were therefore essential, and neighborhood activists of all types created them. For example, in a petition to a government agency for help with its library, the Asociación de Fomento y Biblioteca Popular Cornelio Saavedra wrote: "The youth of this locality called together by noble ideals . . . decided to join forces and channel our energies for the good of the community. . . . With the conviction that a library is called upon to cultivate our minds and create the muscle of the spirit, thus we have dedicated preferentially our attention to it and thus [are] doing everything possible for it."[3]

Books and libraries also supposedly provided moral uplift. A commentary in the newspaper of the telephone workers union said: "Comrade, don't forget that books are one of the great wonders of the world. Reading purifies the soul; reading enlightens the mind." Announcing a series of lectures, the same periodical had commented: "Undoubtedly with these events, with the meritorious labor done by our library . . . the union will go forward rapidly and surely to the higher moral, intellectual, and spiritual state that has been one of the wise and noble objectives that has guided the foundation of our Federation."[4] The idea of uplift was not limited to unions. In 1932 Bernardo Braylan proposed that his local development association, the Asociación de Fomento de Villa Devoto, found a library. He stressed the moral improvement that could come from reading: "The founding of a library should not make us believe that we will attract many readers, as much as that would be ideal; but our duty as an active and progressive entity is to facilitate the cultural activity of the inhabitants. . . . To found a library is to open a furrow for the germination of noble ideas, of altruistic sentiments, of patriotic initiatives, all of which could benefit our youth, tempering their character through contact with knowledge and moral optimism." Braylan also pointed out that almost all outlying neighborhoods had popular libraries based in their development societies.[5] If his neighborhood was going to be the equal of the nearby barrios, it needed a library.

An example of the impact of the libraries comes from the historian Lidia González, who remembers that her grandfather, an Italian-born railroad worker, had been a founder of a biblioteca popular in the barrio Villa Pueyrredón, and it was there that he learned to read and write Spanish. He also brought books home from the library to read at night. González's mother was a librarian for the biblioteca popular while her brother Horacio, a sociologist and public intellectual, was deeply influenced by their grandfather. Clearly the library had a profound influence on the family.[6]

The belief in the transformative nature of libraries can be seen in the names that many received. This is perhaps clearest in the constant use of the names of Domingo Faustino Sarmiento and Juan Bautista Alberdi, intellectual politicians of the nineteenth century who set out to alter the nation. Libraries sometimes had names like Democracia y Progreso (Democracy and Progress), Ciencia y Labor (Science and Labor), Renovación (Renovation), José Enrique Rodó, and Eurindia, which had clear ideological and political connotations. For example, Eurindia was the title of a work by Ricardo Rojas, a nationalistic Radical Party intellectual, that proclaimed a new culture for Latin America. Upon choosing the name Eurindia for its library, the periodical of the sponsoring sociedad de fomento said: "What is Eurindia? It is the new culture, the definitive culture which [Latin] America will have."[7]

While the goal of providing reading material did not vary greatly, the motives of the early leaders of popular libraries did. Some people (usually men) wanted to meet their own and their barrio's hunger for books. Others were barrio elites (also usually men) who wanted to uplift their neighbors. Other motives included the political ambitions of many founders and distinct ideological goals.

Residents of Buenos Aires consumed a lot of written words. Newspapers had high circulations, as well as being available in libraries and cafés. Commercial, political, and foreign-language newspapers vied for readers. In 1928, three Buenos Aires papers each claimed circulations over 180,000, and the number of readers grew during the next decade. By 1936 five different papers claimed to have regular circulations of over 200,000. During this period, some Argentine publishing houses expanded their output with cheaper books and inexpensive pamphlets containing material of all kinds. Frequently a reader could buy a series of pamphlets and thus own an entire book. During the decade 1901–1910 the average number of books published per year in Argentina was 400, but by 1931–1935 it had climbed to 750. At the end of the 1930s the number of books published in Argentina soared, reflecting both a growing market and changes in the international and local book trade caused by the Spanish Civil War. In 1943 the number had reached 4,904.[8]

However, for those with limited incomes, the regular purchase of books remained difficult. In January 1930, a price list of thirty books prepared for a popular library totaled 119.15 pesos with the books costing between 1 peso and 20, although the prices tended toward the lower number.[9] According to a study published in 1937, the head of an average working-class household earned on average 127.26 pesos a month, and family expenses were higher than that.[10] Clearly, they could not afford many books.

Libraries

The municipality of Buenos Aires and other government entities did not provide enough libraries oriented to the average reader. In 1935 there were just four public libraries in the city intended for the general reader plus six kiosks in public spaces.[11] Specialized libraries, such as the Biblioteca Nacional and the Library of Congress, existed. This left a gap that was filled by private initiative.

We can define "popular libraries" to mean libraries oriented to the general public and run by nongovernmental groups. A great majority were civic associations and were open to all, though usually only members could take books home. Membership dues were almost always a chief income source. They may or may not have received some government aid, but they were governed by their members. A typical governance structure was that of the Biblioteca Popular Democracia y Progreso. Its chief governing body was a general assembly of its members, which under ordinary circumstances met once a year. On a daily basis the library was run by a nine-person board elected by the general assembly for two-year terms with half the members renewed each year.[12] An example of another governance structure was the Biblioteca Popular General Juan Martín de Pueyrredón, which was part of the Sociedad de Fomento Flores Sud; the elected body of the latter picked the library's governing board. In the library of the Liga de Fomento de Villa General Mitre, the larger organization's governing board appointed two members to run the library.[13] Libraries tied openly to political or religious organizations had at times different governing structures, but they did serve the general public.

With rare exceptions, men ran popular libraries and comprised most of the readers. The latter did not derive from greater male literacy. Female librarians existed, such as in the popular library connected with the Liga de Fomento de Villa General Mitre.[14] Another library claimed that female readership increased when it had women librarians.[15] One of the few libraries in which women played a significant public role was the Biblioteca Popular Iberoamericana, founded in 1941 through the driving force of Liberia Rovere y Oddino. The library was based in a school, and Rovere y Oddino was an educator who coauthored a book of readings for first-graders.[16] Women also played a sizeable role in the well-stocked biblioteca popular located in the Normal School No. 8, Julio A. Roca. In 1945 the governing board's president, vice president, secretary, and five of the seven board members were women. Probably, the women were normal school teachers.[17] Also, the Hijas de María de Guadalupe ran a library for young women.[18]

A national government agency, Comisión Protectora de Bibliotecas Populares, was created in 1870 at the urging of President Domingo F. Sarmiento to encourage the development of libraries. (Today, it is known as CONABIP, the Comisión Nacional de Bibliotecas Populares). Like many such initiatives it then lapsed and was only reconstituted in 1908. It aided libraries by giving books and/or monetary subsidies. In addition, it purchased books for the libraries based on requests from the institutions and contributed amounts equal to what the library sent. CONABIP also worked to assist the Argentine book industry by buying and giving books to the libraries. At least one library complained that it received Argentine books rather than those written by foreign authors, which it needed to attract readers; it is unclear whether this was a common belief.[19] Like much else that depended on the national budget, CONABIP's generosity varied. The existence of CONABIP does help explain the expansion of popular libraries starting in the second decade of the twentieth century.

In 1910 CONABIP recognized 13 libraries in the capital, and by 1916 there were 59, though it was not a clean upward trajectory. It recognized 125 in 1932 and 131 in 1938. The numbers also climbed dramatically in the province of Buenos Aires.[20] This increase also reflects the expansion of the city, the growth of civic associations of all types, and the expansion of the reading public.

Among the requirements for recognition were free access, being open for twelve hours each week, and that the books should help develop national sentiment, strengthen character, and increase goodwill. Regulations adopted in 1920 under President Yrigoyen said the libraries should refrain from politics and religion. In addition, those in workers centers needed to foster assimilation and teach respect for the laws and institutions of the country.[21] Many more privately run libraries existed, but some did not meet the criteria established for recognition or simply did not apply. Libraries were not spread evenly across the city.

CONABIP's subventions were unreliable, as its own publications indicate. In 1914 it ceased to function for a year after board members resigned and were not replaced. It often paid subventions late because it had not received the funds. The Depression had a major impact on subventions of all types. In 1923, CONABIP gave 313,394 pesos to 241 libraries nationwide, and in 1927, 274 libraries received 460,694 pesos. In 1929, 316 libraries got 471,050 pesos, a decline in the average amount from 1927. Between 1932 and 1934 no subsidies were granted, and in 1935 and 1936, 258 libraries received only 100,000 pesos. As late as August 1935 CONABIP had not received the funds to pass on to the libraries. In 1937, 908 libraries received 490,800 pesos, but even this large sum was a major decline in the average subvention per library.[22]

Subventions sometimes came from the municipal government, but these appear to have depended on support from city council members for a particular library and tended to be sporadic or geared to a specific project. Under the dictatorship instituted after the 1930 coup, thirty-one libraries were purged nationwide from subventions agreed on for 1930, and several of those had names that tied them to the Radical Party, which had been deposed by the military. Congress played a role in deciding which libraries received monetary subventions through CONABIP. For example, in 1934 the senate decided to add three new libraries from the previous list in 1931.[23]

Government support was critical for many libraries because otherwise they depended on income from dues and fundraising or from support from sponsoring organizations, such as sociedades de fomento. Many libraries were financially strapped, especially those in working-class districts where many inhabitants lacked funds for things beyond necessities. A good example is the Biblioteca Popular Nueva Chicago connected with the Asociación Vecinal de Fomento Nueva Chicago. The library remained small and constantly short of funds. Founded in October 1932, it applied for help from CONABIP soon thereafter. The subsequent inspection by the agency showed that it depended on dues and had a total of 240 books. According to the library regulations, members of the sociedad de fomento had full rights to use the library as did neighbors who paid dues of a peso every three months; minors paid twenty centavos a month. By July 1933, the library served 20 readers a month and was going to be recognized by CONABIP. Still, the library grew remarkably slowly, and it temporarily had its recognition suspended. In 1937 it depended on the 286 members of the sociedad de fomento, who paid dues of fifty centavos a month; 8 minors, who paid twenty centavos monthly to belong to the library; and a few adults who still paid a peso per quarter. It had only 560 volumes, and during a three-month period had only 63 readers, because according to the CONABIP inspector potential readers had already read the novels that the library contained, which comprised most of the books.

Despite its small size, in 1938 the library received a national subsidy of 300 pesos. Given the sociedad de fomento's ties to the Socialist Party through the Ghio family (Fernando's brother Atilio played a role in the organization throughout the period, and he also was active in the party), this aid should not be surprising. By September 1942 the library possessed only 1,010 books, though in a trimester it had 850 readers. The library failed to grow quickly in the Perón era or immediately thereafter, since in 1962 it contained 1,800 volumes and 600 pamphlets.[24]

The Place of Bibliotecas Populares

The creation in Argentina of privately run libraries was far from unique, as similar libraries existed in other countries. However, in the North Atlantic world the pattern seemed to have been that such libraries were followed by the founding of public institutions, which presumably were better funded and geographically less maldistributed. In both Western Europe and the United States, the initiatives of private individuals created the first libraries. In Britain in the eighteenth century subscription libraries were established; those who wanted to participate bought a share or paid a monthly fee. These were far too expensive for a worker, however. Roughly simultaneously, circulating libraries were started as commercial enterprises from which readers could rent books at relatively low rates. Similarly, well-to-do people created mechanics libraries so that workers could have books to read, but in many cases, at least initially, fiction and other works considered frivolous were not permitted. The latter were clearly top-down enterprises.[25]

What we would recognize as public libraries only began to be created in the mid-nineteenth century and only became common in the twentieth. The pattern in much of Western Europe and in the United States was not that different, though the timing was. Frequently the process started somewhat later than in Britain, though some places early created a system of public libraries. The Boston Public Library was established in 1848, and by 1900 it had twenty-two branches in addition to the central library for a population of 580,892. The branches had over 168,000 volumes though they were not evenly distributed, and some libraries appear to have been little more than places that readers could order books to be delivered and then borrowed.[26] There seems to have been recognition that to complement a successful school system, a network of libraries needed to be created.

However, the pattern in some Latin American countries is not that different than in Argentina. In Cuba in 1927 many libraries were part of private organizations, especially those of immigrants from Spain, and public libraries remained uncommon prior to 1959. In Uruguay, many public libraries were not founded until the 1940s or after.[27]

Some political leaders in Argentina recognized that providing schools to educate the young but not providing libraries limited the possibility of creating an educated populace; they drew up plans to regularize support for popular libraries though nothing came of them.[28] The reasons for the failure to better fund a system of libraries are not obvious. Argentina had long supported a public school system that at least in urban areas was quite successful, but it made no major effort to establish a network of libraries to adequately satiate the desire to read, which the creation of the schools had helped induce. Public libraries intended for the average reader remained scarce, and there was a continued dependence on private initiatives; the latter had limited access to public funding, which was neither dependable nor sufficient.

Numerous libraries survived with no government support. Many needed to rent space, which consumed much of their income. Some libraries were forced to move frequently, which obviously disrupted the reading public. The Biblioteca Popular Alberdi occupied nine different locations between its founding in 1910 and mid-1943.[29]

No municipal plan existed to provide equal geographic coverage, so that readers in all neighborhoods could have access to books, nor were the collections of most popular libraries adequate in size or open to readers a significant amount of time. Even the small number of books held may not reflect the actual number of books available to be read. In the first decade of the twentieth century, for example, the Biblioteca Popular Bartolomé Mitre had 1,433 books, 75 of which were reports of various branches of the government, and 38 more were publications of the national Congress. These represented almost 8 percent of the total.[30] In addition, not everyone could take books home from bibliotecas populares; that was reserved for members. Wealthier neighborhoods frequently supported larger popular libraries, although that was not always true.

At least in the period prior to the Great Depression, it was not that governmental funds did not exist. The city of Buenos Aires's budget on a per capita basis surged between 1910 and 1930, but an increasing percentage went to salaries and not other items.[31] The key political decision makers clearly did not consider changing the situation of the libraries to be crucial. Probably the politicians who played roles in individual libraries preferred the status quo, where they held a status as intermediaries and thus developed important ties to neighborhoods, or they lacked the power to make serious changes to the budgets. The civil society depended on the nature of the political system.

Bibliotecas Populares as Centers of Sociability

Bibliotecas populares were important in the social world of the barrios in the first decades of the twentieth century, fostering a sense of belonging. In part this sense of identification came from the individuals who provided the unpaid labor that allowed the libraries to function. Members of governing boards spent a great deal of time on the libraries, made the day-to-day decisions, and frequently served as unpaid librarians. Residents literally belonged to a library and organized the many social events that the libraries held.

As key centers of sociability, libraries provided convenient locations for residents to meet and discuss. Popular libraries also organized numerous social functions. For example, in 1933 the Biblioteca Popular Carlos Mauli sponsored a picnic in what was then the bucolic suburb of San Isidro. When the committee of young women of the Biblioteca Popular Alberdi in Gerli (in suburban Buenos Aires) organized a picnic for families at a beach, trucks left Gerli at six in the morning and did not begin their return until seven that evening.[32] Libraries sponsored lectures and other cultural events. One library, for example, planned an excursion to the colonial museum in the nearby city of Luján. CONABIP regulations for recognized libraries required cultural activities. They also held dances and showed movies to raise funds. A library in the southern suburb of Lanús celebrated carnival with seven dances. This kind of activity was not unusual.[33] In addition, popular libraries provided classes of different types, many geared to the practical. These types of activities were common to all barrio-based civic associations.

The Biblioteca Popular General Pueyrredón, located near the edge of the city, offered free or lower-cost medical care to its members. Dr. Jaime Grimblat gave a discount to members for either home or office visits, and if members came to his office on Friday, the consultation was free. At times library publications served to notify the larger community of social events. For example, the periodical of the Biblioteca Popular General Pueyrredón reported on the marriage of Grimblat to Clara Tisminetsky at a downtown synagogue far from the library's barrio, which was followed by a reception at the iconic Confitería del Molino across the street from the building where Congress meets.[34]

North American sociologist Eric Klineberg argues that libraries in New York are important social centers and have become an integral part of the city's social infrastructure. He also sees libraries as vital for furthering the education of many young people.[35] One can hypothesize that in Buenos Aires libraries were even of greater importance to the community since most were founded and run by local inhabitants who put tremendous effort and at times money into their creation and maintenance. Libraries provided places to read but also offered more formal instruction plus entertainment of all types.

The Desire to Read and the Founding of Libraries

Some popular libraries were created by those with ideologies that aspired to change the society and who saw knowledge as crucial. Socialists, Communists, and anarchists perceived books as representing the ideas of progress and enlightenment. In 1918 the Socialist Party began a major push to establish social institutions as part of its electoral strategy, and by 1934 the party had thirty-three libraries in the capital and sixty-nine more in the province of Buenos Aires.[36] After the mid-1920s, the Communist Party founded its own cultural institutions, including libraries. By 1930 it had some thirty libraries in greater Buenos Aires, although they were usually relatively small and contained mostly party literature. Its libraries did not seek recognition from the national government. Some Communists participated in "nonpolitical" popular libraries too. Anarchists also had libraries.[37] The Radical Party sponsored libraries, as did more conservative parties, such as Concentración Nacional and the Progressive Democrats.[38] Some libraries, such as Democracia y Progreso, had ties to political parties but did not have a formal relationship. On the other hand, the Biblioteca Almirante Brown, located in La Boca, functioned as a political club for Ricardo Hermelo, the port prefect, who was attempting to shape the labor movement on the waterfront.[39]

Many unions had libraries. For example, in 1929 locals of the railroad workers unions had three libraries in the city of Buenos Aires and others scattered around the country. The Unión Obrera Municipal had a recognized biblioteca popular with 2,000 books in 1931. The municipal workers library was exceptional only in that it was recognized by the CONABIP and was probably larger than most union libraries.[40]

The founding of libraries and other cultural apparatus by workers and the organizations that claimed to represent them occurred in many parts of the world. They were trying to build a social and cultural world apart from bourgeois society. However, in Argentina, private libraries were founded by people who held varied political beliefs and by some who just wanted to foster the desire to read in their barrio. The sheer number of popular libraries and the amount of people involved in running them indicate that the creation of libraries was truly a popular movement.

There existed in Buenos Aires, as in many other places, tensions between those who saw libraries as potentially transformative of the individual and the society and who had a didactic view of what should be read, and those who held a less utopian perspective. Ricardo González has shown how a popular library in the late 1920s became embroiled in a controversy between those who felt that libraries should just have a didactic function and those who recognized books' entertainment possibilities.[41] Many believed that libraries could shape their users. While those on the left viewed them as a way of creating a new vision of society, others saw libraries as institutions that could help push the working classes closer to the dominant social norms. For example, the Radical government tried to influence workers to conform to more traditional views by setting requirements for popular libraries. However, even some Socialists saw libraries as helping to shape citizens.[42]

The hunger for books can be seen, though it was not necessarily separate from politics. The Biblioteca Popular Juan Bautista Alberdi in Gerli, a section of Avellaneda, was founded in May 1913. The library's strained situation makes clear the tremendous drive some had to create opportunities for themselves and others to read books. When in 1919 the library petitioned CONABIP for books, it proclaimed itself "a nucleus of citizens, youths in the majority, who have made it their moral and material mission to elevate the intellectual level of this town." In response an inspector was dispatched who reported that the library contained 420 publications of all types and was sustained by a membership of fifty-four young workers who paid dues of twenty-one centavos a month, which paid for rent and light.[43] Unfortunately, the biblioteca did not meet the criteria for aid in acquiring books. The library was clearly a labor of love, since after six years its size and membership remained so restricted. It did achieve government recognition somewhat later.

After a period of inactivity of unclear extent, in 1933 the Biblioteca Popular Juan Bautista Alberdi reopened. An inspector reported that the library had a collection of 924 books and 450 pamphlets and was financed by the dues of its members. The governing board staffed it. The report said that during a single month, it had only ninety-six readers, but the library performed an important service for its isolated community, totally composed of workers. The secretary of the directorship was Cándido Gregorio, who in all probability was the same man who later became an important Socialist leader of a textile workers union and almost certainly reflects the political orientation of some of those who ran the library. Gregorio later became president of the library. By 1937 it claimed 420 members and offered a range of practical classes. In the 1938 national budget, the library received a subsidy of 300 pesos and a loan of 15,000 to enlarge it.[44] The continuing effort to provide a library for residents of a working-class neighborhood shows a belief in the benefits of books and perhaps their political importance.

The Biblioteca Popular Alberdi located in Villa Crespo, a largely working-class neighborhood in the city of Buenos Aires, presents a different scenario. Elites dominated the library with their personal and political objectives. The library was founded in 1910 at the suggestion of Joaquin Sánchez, the *subintendente* of the city, who continued to play a role for some time. From 1910 to 1917 its president was Julián Bourdeu, a police comisario. Born in France, Bourdeu came to Argentina with his family at age eighteen. He went to work as a bookkeeper for a company that had established a large shoe factory in Villa Crespo. The manager, Salvador Benedit, was an active politician in the period before the electoral reform of 1912, who attempted to create in Villa Crespo a world shaped by his vision of paternal Catholicism. He also introduced Bourdeu to politics; Bourdeu served as a justice of the peace, a highly political post, and was an elector in several elections. Bourdeu, Benedit, and others helped found a local newspaper, *El Progreso*. In 1905 Bourdeu began work as a police comisario. He helped establish two sociedades de fomento, one in Villa Crespo and the other, of which he was the first president, in the neighboring barrio of Villa Talar. Obviously, he built a career, in part, through his involvement in local organizations.[45]

Subsequent leaders of Biblioteca Popular Alberdi also tended to be local elites. Bourdeu's successor was a justice of the peace. He was followed by a local industrialist, Francisco L. Bavastro, who served as the library's president for eight years in two separate intervals. Bavastro had founded a company in

1889 to manufacture wooden shoe lasts, which became the largest such firm in Buenos Aires. Bavastro was also a Radical Party politician who used both the company and the library as bases for patronage. In 1919 the father of the future famous author Leopoldo Marechal, who worked in Bavastro's factory, died. Bavastro gave the father's job to Leopoldo's younger brother, and slightly later Leopoldo became a paid librarian in the Biblioteca Popular Alberdi. Bavastro was president of the library at the time. Bavastro's actions would certainly have been remembered by the neighborhood.

In the 1930s another police commissioner, Rómulo Magnani, who later wrote a pamphlet entitled *El agitador comunista no debe ser amparado por la ley de despido* (A Communist agitator should not be protected by the law on layoffs) and who became head of the police's special section, which focused on Communists, anarchists, and others considered politically dangerous, was president of this library for two years.

Remigio Iriondo served as president of Biblioteca Popular Alberdi between 1934 and 1940. Iriondo was a major figure in the barrio, and when he sat on the city council in the 1920s, he had helped secure a sizeable subvention for the library. As already mentioned, he also played a crucial role in a wide range of local organizations. What led these men to put their energy into the library beyond the building of a political base can be seen during Iriondo's presidency, when the library petitioned Congress for funds to acquire larger premises in order that its readers, especially students and children, would not use the Communist libraries in the barrio, "since this would put in danger our Argentine cultural work."[46] The later trajectory of Magnani reinforces the sentiment described in the petition. Villa Crespo was a center of Communist activity, and the library's leaders wanted to shield the neighborhood from that influence. So there were ideological reasons as well as personal political desires lying behind the leaders' efforts in the library. Some elites wanted libraries to help steer porteños away from "dangerous" ideas.

The chaotic nature of the founding of libraries and the inconsistency of government support are both demonstrated by the Biblioteca Popular Belgrano. Once again Joaquin Sánchez, the subintendente, had a hand in founding the library. Probably started in 1907, by the beginning of 1914 it had some 15,000 volumes and subscribed to thirty magazines, both local and foreign.

The library was open from 7:30 to 10:30 every night except Sundays and holidays. It had financial support from the municipality, the national government, and the concejo escolar (local school board). The Biblioteca Popular Belgrano's relationship with the city government was murky, though it was run by a commission of residents. According to accusations made in 1922 by a Socialist city councilor, Roberto Giusti, in 1917 the intendente had handed over the library to a committee headed by Adolfo Calvete, who had helped found the Radical Party, then the governing party. In 1923 Calvete started the newspaper *La República*, which supported the Radicals. According to Giusti, the library's operation was so disorganized that it was forced to close for a time. The Socialists wanted the city to take it over. In a request for money in 1924, the library's governing council admitted that its state of abandonment was public and notorious. The city did take it over between 1939 and 1941.[47]

The state's failure to maintain libraries and the need for inhabitants with the aid of individual politicians to assume control over them can be seen in the Sarmiento, located in the barrio of Villa Urquiza. The city played a role in its creation but later abandoned it. Residents reconstituted the library with the name Biblioteca Popular Sarmiento in 1917, which in all library publications is given as the year of its founding. Félix Fouiller, the head of the local ward committee of the Radical Party, served as president for its first six years. The library began to offer free legal consultations, and by mid-1929 it had 320 members and a collection of 6,558 books and 1,432 pamphlets. Courses that year included English, French, bookkeeping, typing, shorthand, drafting, dressmaking, and cooking; in later years, the library offered fewer courses. In April 1930, the library inaugurated a new headquarters with a celebration, and besides holding festivities for the national holidays, it planned to sponsor either a public lecture or a dance each month.

Who were the Sarmiento's 104 average daily readers between March 20 and August 31, 1930? Argentines comprised an extraordinarily large percentage, 96.5. Many were undoubtedly young, a cohort that had a higher percentage of Argentinian-born, but it still seems amazingly large. Also, readership was overwhelmingly male, 81 percent. What did they read? Literature comprised 54.8 percent of the books, applied science and arts 21.4 percent, and history and geography 18.7 percent. By August 1941, the quantity of reading matter had increased significantly to 15,782 books, 4,054 pamphlets, and 10,756 periodicals. Where did they come from? There were gifts, most notably by the family of the famous poet Almafuerte (Pedro B. Palacios) of 1,384 of his books. The library also received support on a regular basis from CONABIP and somewhat less regularly from the municipality, but the most important source of income was members' dues. The size of the subsidies tended to fluctuate from year to year, making it hard for the library to plan.[48]

Ties to the political elite remained important. For example, in 1934 Sarmiento had three honorary members, Pablo Pizzurno, José Luis Cantilo, and Félix O. Fouiller. Pizzurno was an important educator who worked for many years in the Ministry of Education, was interested in culture, and was president of the honorary commission of the Sociedad de Fomento José Enrique Rodó. He had also served as a board member of CONABIP. Cantilo, a Radical politician, served in the Chamber of Deputies and as governor of the province of Buenos Aires. Yrigoyen appointed him twice as Buenos Aires's intendente. Fouiller, as already noted, had been president of the institution, and he acted as Cantilo's secretary during both his terms as intendente.[49] The political connections of the library helped it secure funding and achieve a reasonable size.

Frequently, popular libraries functioned as part of sociedades de fomento, and there too politicians played crucial roles. One such library was the Biblioteca Popular Democracia y Progreso, founded in August 1915 as the Biblioteca Popular de Villa Leandro Alem under the auspices of the Sociedad de Fomento Democracia y Progreso.[50] Given the original name (Alem was a founder of the Radical Party) and its later leader, the library probably had Radical ties from its beginning. The sociedad de fomento had been established four years earlier in the predominantly working-class neighborhood of Liniers, still a remote barrio of the city of Buenos Aires. According to the library's petition to CONABIP for recognition, most of the inhabitants worked in the recently opened shops of the railroad Ferrocarril Oeste. The library claimed that because of the barrio's isolated nature, people had more time to read. An inspector visited and found that the library just used a room in a house lent by its owner. Some neighbors had gotten together to create a place for socializing and reading but had established no rules or regulations. Later in 1915, the library adopted statutes that made its purpose clear: "to tend to the advancement of the intellect of the people, through the diffusion of instructive books, a reading room, etc."[51]

By January 1916, the library had obtained 54 pesos through sponsoring a festival, enough to rent a space and buy the necessary furniture and 40 books. By 1919 its 230 members allowed it to acquire more reading material, but it also received gifts from individuals and institutions. For example, in 1917 the newspaper *La Nación* donated over 200 books, and the Ferrocarril Oeste donated forty liters of kerosene a month, presumably for lighting. In 1919 for unclear reasons the library lost its independence and merged with its sponsoring sociedad de fomento, Democracia y Progreso. It soon moved to a bigger location and began receiving an annual subsidy of 500 pesos per year from CONABIP, which was later increased to 1,000 pesos, a considerable sum.

When Democracia y Progreso decided to acquire its own building, it could not afford to buy a lot, and a member, Juan Guereño, purchased the property and donated it. He served as president of the sociedad de fomento for a total of eight years. Guereño, a Spanish immigrant, had founded a soap company that had its factory in Liniers, which in the 1920s employed more than a hundred people and produced more than 500 metric tons of soap per month. He was also active in the Radical Party. In the early 1940s the company's product Jabón Radical (Radical Soap) sponsored the radio programs of a young actress, Eva Duarte (later of course Eva Duarte de Perón). Guereño was active in several civic associations, including the football club Vélez Sarsfield and a universidad popular.[52]

In 1940 the library had almost 7,000 books. In its first twenty-five years, its 196,880 readers had been 30 percent female and 70 percent male; those less than sixteen years old were 40 percent of the readership. The latter were probably mostly students and not yet fully in the workforce. The readership was overwhelming Argentine (85 percent), a large figure, especially for a poorer barrio.[53] The library had succeeded in leveraging its political connections into becoming a sizeable institution.

The types of books read during those twenty-five years were diverse. The largest portion fell in the vague category of general works, 44 percent. History, geography, and social science comprised 15.9 percent while literature was 14.1, and philology and languages 9.1 percent.[54] The small percentage classified as literature leads one to suppose that most of the general works were novels. The other libraries I examined show that literature was heavily consumed.

In some cases, libraries were successful in building sizeable collections. The Biblioteca Popular Juan N. Madero in San Fernando in the northern suburban fringe of greater Buenos Aires was established in 1873, easily making it one of the oldest such libraries. As early as 1914 with just 150 members it had 27,595 volumes and 32 readers a day on average. It received an exceptionally large subvention from the national government. By 1934 the library had grown to 46,740 volumes and was financed by its members and a subsidy from the municipality of San Fernando. It was housed in a palatial building inaugurated twelve years previously. The acquisition of books decreased in speed, however, and by 1946 there were 50,379 volumes. The library depended on money from members, the municipality, and the national government. Interestingly, the national government's contribution was lower that year than in 1914.[55]

Problems with the Libraries

Some libraries that existed for many years failed to adequately serve their communities. This is sometimes obvious in the records of the CONABIP, but unfortunately it is not always clear why they had major failings. One can surmise that the libraries had problems similar to those faced by any organization that depends on the willingness of a small group of people to push it forward: money, personal conflict, lack of commitment, and so on.

An excellent example of a library with constant problems is the Biblioteca Popular General Juan Martín de Pueyrredón of the Sociedad de Fomento Flores Sud. In January 1919 the newly founded library asked for help from CONABIP, claiming to represent 120 compact blocks inhabited by workers in which no other library existed. Despite the library having only a reported fifty books (there was confusion about how many it had), CONABIP recognized it and sent some volumes. There is no question that money was tight. The sociedad de fomento had some 200 members, and dues were fifty centavos per month. However, during the period between July 1918 and June 1919 only 662.80 pesos were raised through dues; two festivals brought in an additional 190.60. The yearly rent for the building in which the library and the society functioned consumed 265.60 pesos.[56]

In 1923 the inspector for CONABIP stated that no books had been obtained for some time and that the organization's main objective was to better the neighborhood. Later the same year, the library was not open when it should have been. In 1930 the library was suspended by CONABIP. According to the sociedad de fomento, its building was closed because its directing board lacked sufficient members. However, the problems were more severe. The organization had grown for its first twelve years in part because it sponsored sports programs on open lands in the barrio, but when vacant property no longer existed, the programs stopped, and membership fell away. In addition, in 1928 the organization had bought land to build a headquarters and borrowed money to do so. It then operated in a small house on the property. In 1931 the depth of the crisis became apparent (no doubt partly reflecting the impact of the Depression), and a new directing board took over. It faced a daunting task. The institution was severely behind on its payments for the land and taxes and had only seventy members who still paid fifty centavos a month, which brought in just 35 pesos. The new board righted the ship partly through donations and activities that raised some 2,000 pesos.

The library reapplied for recognition in 1935. The subsequent inspection said that the library was flourishing; it was open two hours a day and had 1,800 volumes. However, problems continued, and in both 1938 and 1939 the library was not open when inspectors appeared, despite having received a subsidy of 300 pesos from the national government in the 1938 budget. In 1938 the CONABIP suspended it for a time because of its inconsistent schedule. The library continued to function irregularly despite considerable investment, a sizeable readership, and the increasing size of its book holdings. The sociedad de fomento obviously was not fully committed to running a library and lacked the connections to receive sizeable government aid. The debt that it had assumed to build a headquarters was too large, especially given the unstable membership. Clearly, the library services that it provided was inadequate.[57]

The problems of the Biblioteca Popular General Juan Martín de Pueyrredón were far from unique. For example, the Biblioteca Popular de la Asociación Florencio Sánchez, based in La Paternal, a working-class barrio, while expanding to considerable size through the collecting of books from residents and having a wide membership, continually had problems staying open. It moved several times and frequently had to pay high rents. The moves adversely impacted the number of readers as well as the organization of the books. Even after receiving a national subsidy of 600 pesos in 1938, it continued to be troubled.[58]

Even in more middle-class neighborhoods some libraries failed to deliver adequate services. The library of the Asociación de Fomento y Biblioteca Popular Cornelio Saavedra, founded in 1919, never grew to have an adequate supply of books, hindered by a lack of funds although, at least in its beginnings, it had political connections. The president of its honorary commission was José Tamborini, a Radical Party deputy and future presidential candidate; the vice president was Adolfo Calvete (see above). Both men were based in the nearby barrio of Belgrano, but they seemed not to have helped the Biblioteca Popular Cornelio Saavedra very much. In 1936 it had 1,290 books and 811 pamphlets. Its income principally came from the ninety-eight members of the association and the ten members of the library, who paid one peso a month and thirty centavos, respectively. This was not a drastic decline in income from earlier years. The rent on its building was thirty pesos a month, and the librarian was salaried. The CONABIP inspector complained that the library was not open six hours a week, the physical condition of the library was bad, and it lacked modern books. Not surprisingly it only averaged six readers a day, almost all students. Despite receiving a national subsidy starting in 1938, the situation did not improve greatly.[59]

Readership and Reading

The users of popular libraries tended to read fiction, probably novels, though what types, given the sources, are not totally knowable. Preference for fiction is not unusual compared to other parts of the world.[60] Reading was part of a culture that sought new types of diversion whether it was football, horse racing, or picnics. Fiction can be educational as well.

The readers tended to be male and Argentinian-born, the latter being partially explained by the overrepresentation of students since the young were much more heavily Argentinian-born. Many students used popular libraries to do their homework, reading books that they did not possess. When petitioning Congress for assistance, libraries frequently stressed their service to students.[61] During the 1930s CONABIP inspectors often mentioned that the readership was heavily composed of students from local schools, both primary and secondary, and occasionally university students. In some cases, they mentioned that teachers also used the libraries. It is unclear whether the comments indicate a change in readership or reflect CONABIP's directives to its inspectors.[62] Language barriers may also partially explain the overwhelmingly Argentinian-born readership.

There existed a strong desire for self-advancement, and books and knowledge were perceived as a component. This helps explain the heavily male readership since large limitations existed on female employment, reducing the practical impact of self-education for women. In addition, females might have felt uncomfortable in male-dominated spaces.[63] The hours that libraries stayed open (typically 7 p.m. to 9 or 10 p.m.) may have also played a role, since that was a time that women would be expected to be preparing dinner and doing other chores at home. However, once books were checked out, we cannot know who read them.

Although what exactly people read is unclear, we do possess an analysis of 8,952 books acquired nationwide by popular libraries during a six-month period in 1935, which gives a good indication of readers' preferences. The most popular category, 40 percent, was fiction (defined as novels, short stories, plays, poetry, and so on). The next largest category was children's literature and then secondary school texts. Foreign authors comprised 54 percent of all the authors, 40 percent of the works were by Argentine authors, and the rest were dictionaries and the like. By far the largest number of works by foreign authors purchased were by French writers, distantly followed by Italians and then more distantly by Spanish and English authors. North American cultural appeal had not yet reached the Argentine book world. The most acquired foreigners were the popular novelists Emilio Salgari and Alexandre Dumas. These were followed by the French novelists Delly (a pen name for two brothers) and Jules Verne. Many fewer copies of novels by more serious authors, such as Émile Zola, Anatole France, Victor Hugo, or Maxim Gorky, were obtained. Among the Argentine writers by far the most popular was Hugo Wast (Gustavo Adolfo Martínez Zuviría), an anti-Semitic novelist, followed by the poet, tango lyricist, and playwright Héctor Pedro Blomberg; the novelist, poet, and historian Manuel Gálvez; and the short story writer Benito Lynch. Much less frequently acquired were works by Juan B. Alberdi, Domingo Sarmiento, or Ricardo Rojas, for example.[64] Clearly entertainment was crucial.

On a smaller scale we can see similar preferences at individual libraries. The Biblioteca Popular de Villa Pueyrredón had 3,090 books at the beginning of 1935. During the second half of 1934 it had 626 readers of whom two-thirds were male and 79 percent were Argentinian-born. These readers took 479 books home and consulted an additional 519 at the library. Although these numbers seem small, the library received books worth 100 pesos from CONABIP because of its high readership. The biblioteca got to choose half the books and CONABIP the other. When the library chose the books, it obtained histories and other nonfiction; classics by Victor Hugo, Honoré de Balzac, and Walter Scott, among others; and Argentine authors such as Blomberg. The readership seemed inclined to read novels, since 57.5 percent of the books consulted were "works in general," and there was no category for fiction. History, geography, and social science represented 11.6 percent of the books consulted, while applied and pure sciences were 10.8 percent.[65]

The nature of what was being read in Argentina in the first decades of the twentieth century can also be seen in the Biblioteca Obrera, located in the headquarters of the Socialist Party but recognized as a biblioteca popular by CONABIP. Here we can see the impact of the increasing number of students. Founded in 1897, the library had 5,368 books by the start of 1911. Of these, 32.4 percent were literature, 19.1 social science, 14.6 applied and pure sciences, and 10.4 percent history and geography. The Socialist nature of the organization explains the numerous books classified as social science, since presumably the writings of Karl Marx and many others would have been so labeled. The library grew rapidly; by mid-1919 it had 11,187 volumes. What was being read? During 1918, of the 7,878 works consulted, 53.2 percent were literature, 11.3 percent social sciences, and 17.3 percent applied and pure sciences.[66]

By 1929 the library held 22,590 works, and in a three-month period in the first half of the following year, 53 percent of the books taken home were literature. However, as the library grew to an extremely impressive size for the time and place, usage shifted. At the end of 1943 it held 39,550 works. In 1942 readers took 33,707 books home; the figure for 1943 is much lower due to the impact of the military coup. In 1942 literature represented just 27 percent of the works brought home, while pure science stood at 23 percent and history and geography at 22 percent. The trend toward more academic reading could also be seen throughout the second half of the 1930s. This indicates heavy usage by high school and university students to do classwork.[67]

It appears that in most cases, despite the wishes of founders and leaders, people seemed to prefer diversion to other types of reading. However, the demand for books on science, history, and the social sciences shows a heavy usage by the growing number of students.

Conclusions

Popular libraries allowed many inhabitants of greater Buenos Aires to read books, but crucial limitations existed. Although their establishment demonstrates an ability to build institutions that fulfilled some of the residents' perceived needs, they left large gaps. Not all neighborhoods had libraries, and many of those that existed remained inadequate in size. Almost all had limited hours. The ability of a barrio to support a substantial library depended to some extent on wealth. Wealthier areas could have libraries that charged higher dues and could expect additional monetary or in-kind support. The lack of obvious sources of financial support could be partially overcome by politically connected leadership, and some working-class neighborhoods had substantial libraries. However, government aid was always spotty.

The structure of this private system favored those with higher incomes or with family members willing to make sacrifices, since only dues-payers could check out books, and those unable to afford the dues had to read books in the library. Buenos Aires had a decidedly uneven system of libraries, maldistributed across the city. Even a system of public libraries would have been somewhat unequal in placement, but all would have had equal opportunity to use them, and they would have been open longer hours. A more adequate subsidization of popular libraries would have permitted collections to be larger and for the libraries to be open more hours. However, bibliotecas populares provided important services to the communities that they served. The libraries allowed porteños access to books to read for either pleasure or education that they otherwise would have lacked. The growing number of secondary and university students made the libraries more important than ever. Also, the libraries became essential nodes of sociability.

The nature of the readership, predominantly male Argentines, increased its attractiveness for politicians, since it coincided with those who could vote. Libraries needed resources beyond those that the members could supply, and they therefore depended on connections to the political system. Politicians used their ability to tap the power of the state to aid popular libraries. The lack of adequate funding, however, reflects a larger problem. Although Argentina in the first decades of the twentieth century was a prosperous country, the state did not build the institutions to sustain economic growth over the long run.

The reasons for the failure to create a more developed system of libraries, along the lines of the public school system, are not totally clear. However, it was partially due to the political establishment's stake in the existing system. They used it to create political bases for themselves. By leading or supporting individual libraries, they earned personal loyalties and built a base. A large public library system or a bigger and fairer funding system for private libraries would have undercut the role of the politician as a needed intercessor.

The nature of the school system underlines the dilemma that those with political ambitions faced. By the second decade of the twentieth century the public school system was a well-established institution. Teachers frequently received positions through political connections, but that was not something that could be publicly trumpeted, since such open patronage was frowned upon.[68] On the other hand, politicians could take credit for supporting the private initiatives that were the bibliotecas populares.

The school system helped create a strong desire to read. Books became an important form of entertainment, and students needed places to read essential books. A belief in the possibility of upward mobility, if not for yourself, at least for your children, intensified the demand for books. The ability to advance on a personal level, as a barrio, or even as a society seemed to depend on education, whether through formal channels or through self-education. Books remained too expensive for most people to have large personal collections; the only potential source was libraries. Popular libraries helped fill a vacuum, providing a place to educate oneself, do school assignments, or just find books to read, as well as serving as important social centers.

CHAPTER FIVE

Development Societies as Lobbyists and Centers of Sociability

SOCIEDADES DE FOMENTO (DEVELOPMENT societies) played a unique role among the civic associations in Buenos Aires. In a city that was growing much too fast to provide amenities to all, sociedades de fomento worked to improve conditions in the barrio they served, struggling to make it a more attractive and healthier place to live. Smaller issues they sometimes tackled on their own, through providing labor or using moral suasion. Larger problems could only be dealt with by what in essence was lobbying, pressuring the government to act. They could do this despite being barrio-based and relatively small because of the connections that they forged with politicians and other key figures. More than the other civic associations I studied, the development societies needed the aid of politicians. If they wanted a street paved, street lighting installed, or a myriad of other things, the societies required the assistance of figures with political clout. Politicians wanted to build bases of support, and the sociedades de fomento represented an opportunity to establish connections to important barrio figures. This created a system of mutual, if uneven, dependency. All political parties contained men who attempted to build political capital by cultivating ties to development societies and thus helped shape the nature of politics. In addition, like other civic associations, they provided a place of sociability.

The creation of numerous sociedades de fomento was part of the wave of civic associations established in the first decades of the twentieth century. Inhabitants wanted to improve their living conditions. Property owners were also motivated by a desire to increase the value of their property and store owners by the possibility of enlarged sales to a more prosperous and bigger pool of customers. In some cases there existed a wish for respectability, a desire to live in a community with a certain sense of orderliness and norms.[1] This desire for respectability should not be surprising in an era when many who engaged in manual labor felt the need to go to work wearing ties. In addition, there was a strong yearning for a feeling of community. A certain level of boosterism also existed, a desire to make a specific barrio equal to others.

Organizations that served similar functions as the sociedades de fomento existed in other Latin American countries, usually bearing other names. How they developed and how they fitted into the social and political landscape differed according to the trajectory of the country. In Bolivia, such organizations were largely founded after the Chaco War, but their political influence was limited, since only 7 percent of the population was eligible to vote until 1954. In La Paz many of the societies emerged out of existing lay brotherhoods, making their origins and structures very different from development societies in Argentina. Few academic studies of such associations appear to exist in Uruguay, but the organizations in Montevideo resemble the sociedades de fomento on the other side of the Río de la Plata, acting as centers of sociability and pressuring the government to improve conditions. Due to the local political situation, they only began to emerge in the late 1930s.[2] The existence in other countries of versions of the sociedades de fomento is to be expected, since neighborhoods needed to express their desires to governments and to try to provide some types of services themselves. However, how they functioned and were organized was shaped by the local political and social environment.

In Buenos Aires, sociedades de fomento played an important role in the politics of the city but also in the development of urban amenities. They gave a voice to inhabitants who wanted to improve their barrio. Development societies were founded from the end of the nineteenth century to the 1940s. A large number were created in the 1920s and 1930s, stimulated by rapid urbanization and aided by a relatively open political system. Many development societies did not survive for the same reasons that any small organization fails, but they were often replaced by others. By the 1930s, more of the societies had become better established with the ability to print publications and the like.

The municipal government's assertion of control over certain aspects of the institutional lives of development societies helped shape their nature. By the end of the 1930s only sociedades de fomento recognized by the city were supposed to be acknowledged by municipal authorities. They therefore had to meet certain standards and follow rules. This does not mean that they were subservient, as several issues generated large-scale campaigns against government policies (see below).

Like other civic associations, the development societies were membership organizations and depended on dues for funding. They were governed by boards elected by assemblies of dues-payers.[3] Women and commercial firms could be members of the development societies, but in an analysis of six such organizations at a distinct moment, few belonged. The proportion of women members varied between 1 and 5 percent while commercial firms comprised between 1 and 8 percent. In several cases the women were listed as the widow of someone, which implies that they inherited the membership from their husband. Exceedingly few women served in elected positions.[4] Érica Cubilla in an interesting examination of the barrio Villa Devoto lists the members of the governing board of the Asociación de Fomento de Villa Devoto from 1930 through 1939. In 1934 six women served on it, but in no other year did women hold office, and Cubilla unfortunately offers no explanation.[5] Women were at times librarians in the popular libraries that were frequently part of the development associations and often taught some of the classes that were given. They also, though frequently without a great deal of publicity, played key roles in organizing social activities. For example, in 1928 the Asociación de Fomento y Cultural Unión de Vélez Sarsfield Sud created an auxiliary commission of "señoritas" with the intention of creating friendship between the families of members, organizing social events, and helping run the library. They at least did the two latter tasks.[6]

The Role of Sociedades de Fomento

The organizations' period of greatest influence, the 1920s and 1930s, came as the city of Buenos Aires spread rapidly away from the long-inhabited core and the other centers of population. Basic urban amenities took a while to reach even middle-class areas, and therefore inhabitants established institutions to pressure the government. Better-organized barrios, especially those that had connections to powerful politicians, had advantages over others.

After the voting reform, gathering popular support truly mattered. The purpose of the organizations played to politicians' strengths. The politicians could influence the delivery of municipal services, and frequently barrio elites led the organizations, which meant that the leadership likely had local influence. These were just the type of people with whom politicians would want to form a relationship. Inhabitants needed ways to pressure authorities to provide what they lacked. Successful sociedades de fomento allowed both desires to be partially satisfied.

Despite development societies' large role in creating the urban world of Buenos Aires, it is easy to underestimate their importance. They tended to be small with few members and represented micro barrios with several operating in what is now generally considered a neighborhood. However, the sociedades de fomento tended to have a large amount of influence in relationship to their size. A significant percentage of their leaders and maybe even members belonged to what one could call the local bourgeoisie, that is, doctors, lawyers, and other professionals plus local business owners. Why would they feel compelled to better their neighborhood, and why would the average inhabitant back their attempts? In many cases, interests coincided. In most cases the "elites" also lived in the barrio, and businesses, homeowners, and renters would all benefit from better drainage or more trees and so on.

Although frequent disagreements erupted among members of these organizations, class cannot explain many of them. At times store owners might support things that, judging solely on a class basis, might seem illogical, but frequently it paid to support the position of their customers. This is parallel to store owners who supported strikers. A store was part of the community. If they lived in the same barrio where their store was located, they too suffered from flooding streets, perceptions of dangerousness, and so on. Their business would benefit from a more prosperous community that identified with a specific locale and therefore shopped there.

The total number of development societies is impressive. By end of 1934 there were 95 recognized development societies, and by the end of the following year there were 125. The growth reflected the spread of the city but also the municipality's attempts to channel petitions through development societies and legal restrictions on their size. It is important to note that informal groups of inhabitants could as late as mid-1939 still talk to key administrators on questions of urban amenities.[7] By the early 1940s the number of sociedades de fomento had grown to 151 recognized organizations, which covered almost all sectors of the city except the core area, its traditional center.[8]

The large number of development societies and the small areas that they represented tell a good deal about the nature of identification with the barrio, although the size of each organization in part reflected limitations imposed by the city. Sociedades de fomento helped stabilize barrio identities, but these remained far from permanent or fixed, since some barrios, such as Villa Talar, have essentially disappeared.[9]

FOUNDING, SIZE, AND LEADERS

No common founding story exists for sociedades de fomento, but the Asociación de Fomento y Biblioteca Popular Emilio Mitre de Caballito Sud can stand as an example, though it was more successful during this period than most. It was established at a meeting on February 27, 1916, with the purpose of "asking the municipal and national authorities for public health work, opening of streets, paving, sweeping, and cleaning of the same and other improvements for the inhabitants." A governing board was selected. The subsequently adopted statutes called for furthering "the physical, intellectual, moral, social, and industrial culture of the zone that it embraces through periodicals and libraries." The statutes also called for the organization to act like a mutual aid society and have its own headquarters, create a biblioteca popular, and be independent of all religious, political, and nationality questions.[10]

Through fundraising among its members and income garnered from festivals, in 1926 it purchased land for a headquarters, which was inaugurated in 1929. The society sought to better the physical conditions of the community, including the embellishment of an important local park (Parque Chacabuco). In 1919 it had created a biblioteca popular, which remained small and offered courses such as dressmaking and bookkeeping. In 1931 the organization started offering free medical consultations and subsequently dental ones. Free vaccinations were given. In 1934 the society opened a dispensary for breast milk. It grew to have considerably over 400 members, though the membership fluctuated.[11]

In September 1939, the Radical deputy Julián Sancerni Giménez presented legislation to the Chamber of Deputies that would require the Banco Hipotecario Nacional to loan money to recognized sociedades de fomento in the capital so that they could own their headquarters. The deputy requested that the minister of finance investigate the proposal's viability. At the minister's request the bank undertook a study, which claimed that the legislation was impractical. Although the report is not everything that a historian could desire, it does reveal certain facts. There existed 126 sociedades recognized by the municipality, and only 31 owned their own building, thus 95 did not. Thirty-seven of those without their own building had fewer than 100 members, while the 58 remaining averaged 180. Among all the recognized institutions, only 5 had more than 300 members, and the rest averaged around 200 members. Only 27 had capital exceeding 5,000 pesos, and 48 had no registered capital. The bank argued that since municipal regulations limited membership dues to one peso per month, most development societies could not pay back a loan. Further, membership numbers could fall, and no guarantees existed that an institution would continue.[12]

The volatility of membership can be seen in the Sociedad de Fomento Edilicio y Cultura José Enrique Rodó located in Nueva Chicago, which was founded in 1924. During the last third of that year, it averaged 134 members. Membership had slipped to 54 by 1927 and then climbed to 69 the following year before reaching 137 in 1930; it then fell again but reached 130 by 1933. By the fiscal year 1936–1937 membership was between 220 and 260, though many were behind in their dues, apparently because of economic hard times. The number of members declined slightly until 1940.[13]

The income from dues of the Asociación de Fomento y Biblioteca Popular Emilio Mitre de Caballito Sud was totally inconsistent, despite the high number of members. In the fiscal year 1931–1932 it stood at 2,072 pesos, dropped to 906 the following year, rose slightly before declining in 1936–1937, rose slightly thereafter before hitting a low of 681.50 pesos in 1939–1940, and then grew to

1,912 pesos in 1943–1944.[14] The large number of claimed members and the lack of income indicate that many simply did not pay their dues, showing a lack of commitment to the organization or strapped economic conditions. This was not an uncommon situation.

In most cases it is difficult to ascertain the background of the leaders of sociedades de fomento. However, some information can be gleaned. The August 1939 governing board of the sociedad de fomento of Belgrano R. had fifteen members; it was possible to learn the occupations of seven. Two were professionals while another had a construction contracting business. Two others owned what appeared to be large sales-based businesses (one was machinery while the other sold animal feed, charcoal, and coal). One ran a grocery store while another taught typing at the organization. The association published a list of ninety-seven member merchants with their category of business and their address. These ranged from flower stores and newspaper distributors to jewelry stores, opticians, and garages. Unfortunately, the total number of members was not given, but the list indicates a hefty percentage were local businesspeople.[15]

The Liga de Fomento Federico Lacroze had a board of twenty. It had four members whose businesses dealt with metal working plus an importer and the owners of a mechanical repair business and of a grocery store.[16] In all likelihood the average board member of a sociedad de fomento was part of what one could call the local elite.

SOCIABILITY

In addition to their primary focus on improving neighborhoods, sociedades de fomento served as important centers of sociability. They became key nodes of interaction in a neighborhood just like libraries, football clubs, and cafés. They became a place to meet friends and acquaintances and thus helped generate a sense of belonging to a barrio. The successor organization of the Sociedad de Fomento General Benito Nazar claims that its greatest success in terms of membership came because of the playing of Basque paddle ball, bocce, and cards as well as various social activities.[17]

Some sociedades de fomento provided significant services for their members. In early 1941 in the barrio Colón, a working-class neighborhood, the sociedad de fomento offered its members free dental, obstetrical, and surgical consultations. In early 1942 it added free legal services.[18] The Enrique Rodó, a similarly situated organization, began offering free medical consultations in late 1933. The service was used in a six-month period in 1937 and 1938 by an average of twenty-seven people a month. It had previously arranged cheap medical services plus free legal consultations. Some development societies offered discounted prescriptions at certain pharmacies.[19]

Partly to raise money and partly to provide entertainment, sociedades de fomento sponsored many activities. In 1935 the Asociación de Fomento y Cultura Los Olivos held three events to raise money for a playground, which it desired to erect in a public park. It showed films in a cinema, held a dance, and organized a family picnic on property lent to the organization. These proved extremely successful, raising 923.60 pesos, a considerable sum, and had been organized by a committee of señoritas, presumably the daughters of members. Such events provided a respectable place to meet young men. A year after the opening of the playground, the organization presented a gold medal to the municipal secretary of public works, Amílcar Razori, at a special screening of the movie *Theodora Goes Wild* starring Irene Dunne and Melvyn Douglas.[20]

Regularly, development societies organized events for patriotic holidays, for carnival, for fundraising, and just for entertainment. Some offered members a range of different activities. One held chess tournaments and had billiards, bocce, and basketball. The Liga de Fomento de Villa General Mitre had at various times tennis, bocce, and basketball courts. In addition, under the auspices of the *liga* a group of young people, many of whom were children of members, formed a sporting club.[21] Some societies went further. From 1920 to at least 1940 the Asociación de Fomento Santiago de Liniers had a group that put on theatrical performances.[22] For many, these activities became a critical element of barrio life.

The sociedades de fomento also played a role in providing education. As already discussed, they frequently sponsored bibliotecas populares. They responded to the demand for classes for those over fourteen years old, as did other civic associations. For example, in 1935 the development society Manuel

Belgrano offered primary school and dressmaking classes. Both the teachers and those who made the necessary benches donated their labor. By 1939 the society had sixty students taking primary school classes, English, and drawing, both mechanical and decorative.[23]

At times development societies urged inhabitants to buy from local merchants. This helped create a sense of belonging to a barrio but also aided some members of the organization and the advertisers in its publication. The development society Belgrano R. in an article entitled "You Ought to Buy from the Businesses of the Barrio" said: "Commerce . . . brings with it as an immediate consequence, progress. . . . Commercial exchange plays the most important role in the life of a community or a people. The more momentum that it acquires, the more benefits that are obtained are translated into . . . economic, social, building infrastructure, and social betterment, thus cementing the base for . . . collective prosperity."[24]

Development societies also tried to create an identity for their barrio. The Sociedad de Fomento José Enrique Rodó fought for the use of the name Nueva Chicago for its barrio, displaying pride in that name and rejecting the alternative, Mataderos.[25] In other words, the societies played a major role in creating the social world of the barrios and helped barrios establish an identity.

BETTERING THE BARRIO

The key function of the sociedades de fomento was to improve living conditions. A vast gap existed between inhabitants' hopes and actual conditions due to the subdivision of land in sectors that lacked infrastructure. In the more outlying barrios, parks and plazas frequently did not exist, streets remained unpaved and without lighting, and flooding was frequent. The city's response was initially slowed by the difficulty porteños faced in placing political pressure on decision makers. With the establishment of a popularly elected city council, voters had a government branch that depended on them. Some intendentes tried to use sociedades de fomento to mobilize support and circumvent hostile city councils. The sociedades de fomento also pressured the national government.

Even when authorities attempted to deal with the lack of urban infrastructure, which areas received attention first frequently depended on the generation of political pressure. Many barrios lacked water and sewer pipes. The provision of water and sewer services was the responsibility of the national government, and it responded. In 1915, 146,630 locations had running water, and that number climbed to 386,192 by 1925. After the mid-1920s most inhabitants had running water, though the provision of sewer connections lagged. The government claimed that all areas of the city had water. In the summer months in certain barrios, however, problems existed with the supply of water due to low pressure. The city government also made improvements. Between 1915 and 1923 the average number of blocks paved yearly was 198. However, when a community received services was not foreordained, and pressure created by sociedades de fomento on either the national or the city government often proved critical in determining who obtained what and when.[26] The authorities did respond to bad publicity generated by the development societies and to the demands of politicians building ties to barrios, but not all needs could be met. Even a largely middle-class outlying barrio such as Villa Devoto, despite being founded at the end of the nineteenth century, still had serious infrastructural problems in 1930.[27]

Development societies handled many small problems themselves. For example, during one year in the late 1920s the Sociedad de Fomento de Versailles (today, the name is spelled Versalles) planted 1,250 trees, most of which it obtained from the national government. An employee of the sociedad cleaned vacant lots and pulled weeds.[28] The Sociedad de Fomento of Villa Lugano also had an employee who cleaned streets and ditches and a tractor with which to level streets.[29] In mid-1929, the development society Villa Luro Norte owned a tractor and a machine to level streets with which it improved more than seventy blocks. Enough development societies owned equipment that a Socialist city councilor proposed that the municipality provide fuel and up to two workers to help with their use.[30] Many societies could not afford employees, however, let alone a tractor.

Some development societies advocated for what one could call respectability, a concept that merged perceptions of what was proper with the livability of a neighborhood. They did this by complaining to the police or others with enforcement powers, or they used social pressure. The development society

Belgrano R. pushed hard on this issue. For example, in the first number of its publication it argued: "The road to follow is full of rough places because unfortunately there exist remiss proprietors and egotistical owners of large mansions and infected empty lands that laugh at the ordinances and rent their property in full contradiction [of the ordinances]. . . . From these pages we will energetically fight the attitude of these true landowners for whom it appears sanctions never reach." Belgrano R. promised to see that all ordinances were obeyed. For example, the society denounced the bad conditions of the large properties owned by Dr. Carlos Decasse, which were mostly vacant. It applied social pressure by hanging a thousand wall posters in the barrio protesting the properties' condition and by showing the land to the intendente. This was not its only such action.[31]

This attitude was not unique. One sociedad de fomento complained about the quantity of advertising on walls. Others wanted the police to control the playing of football in the streets or in vacant lots because of damage to vehicles or the windows of houses. In one case a society complained because players allegedly changed their clothes in the open, thereby offending morals; another complaint was that the players got into a fight. In 1930 the Asociación de Fomento de Villa Devoto protested what it called "transients" using a portion of San Nicolás street to urinate, bothering the neighbors and the many women who walked down it.[32] In 1934 the development society Manuel Belgrano requested that the city council publish a letter in its session papers complaining that the city did nothing about the daily parking at the same location of a truck containing dead animals, which leaked blood, and the killing of animals in a nearby lot, hoping to place pressure on the municipal authorities. The society had political support. Its letter was published at the request of city councilor José Penelón, representing the splinter left party Concentración Obrera, and Fernando Ghio, who sat on the council for the Socialists, claimed that he had already intervened with the city, and it was now a police question.[33]

LOBBYING

Large infrastructure problems could only be dealt with by the development society calling attention to issues and using whatever leverage it possessed to get government agencies to act. Sociedades de fomento also made appeals to private companies that provided urban services, such as the trolley companies and bus lines.[34] Success usually depended on connections to politicians or individuals with ties to decision makers. The most direct path was to approach the executive branch of the municipality. Since intendentes were appointed, they and their staff were partially protected from political pressure. Nevertheless, they could be embarrassed, and ultimately even the president cared about popularity in the capital since it possessed an oversized impact on politics.

A development society could also appeal to the political body most directly subject to the will of the city's populace, the city council. City councilors could vote money for improvements, including extremely specific projects, bring pressure on the intendente, or publicize the needs of certain sectors of the city. Like politicians everywhere, both branches of the city government were keenly aware of what the press published. The sociedades de fomento turned to Congress on certain issues, but its jurisdiction was limited, and many members had little interest since they represented distant provinces.

Here, I briefly examine the interaction with the government of a development society for a period covered by an annual report. The society's impact was what it claimed it was, but one cannot be sure that the authorities did not act for other reasons. In the year from April 1929 to May 1930, the Sociedad de Fomento General Benito Nazar claimed that it had dealt with the municipal executive departments, Congress, the city council, the police, and local businesses. It stated that it obtained the construction of the Plaza General Benito Nazar. It also achieved the installation of drainage on one street and the paving of three others, as well as work on sewerage and water issues. The sociedad stated that through its efforts the city supplied crews to respond to the needs of the inhabitants. Although the organization had internal conflicts, it arranged to have a banquet in honor of the intendente, José Luis Cantilo. The ties to Cantilo's Radical Party may have come through María Inés Nazar and Benito Nazar Anchorena, who had given the organization the land and money to build a headquarters. The land for the plaza also had come from the family. Benito Nazar Anchorena was close to the Radicals, and his brother was a personal friend of President Yrigoyen.[35]

On a few issues the national government had direct control, and development societies petitioned Congress. This was difficult because, as has been pointed out, most deputies came from other districts and were indifferent to most of the pressure that the societies could generate. For example, there was a drawn-out attempt to remove the tracks of the Ferrocarril Pacífico branch that went to the Villa Luro station, which was in a peripheral barrio of the city. The building of the ring road around Buenos Aires made the continued use of this stretch of railroad questionable because a bridge over the road would have to be built, and the branch saw limited traffic. The railroad company, the city council, and the executive branch all believed that not enough traffic existed to keep the line open. The sociedad de fomento that represented Villa Luro Norte argued that lifting the rails would encourage further development, especially permitting completion of several streets. For unclear reasons, the Congress failed to authorize the removal of the rails even after the trains stopped running. The development society resorted to futile complaints to Congress about shacks being built alongside the rails and the spread of rats, bringing what it charged was the threat of bubonic plague.[36]

The Asociación de Fomento 12 de Octubre solved a critical problem by pressing the city government. A factory that produced oil (presumably vegetable oil of some type) generated a smell—because of either the manufacturing process or the use of inferior materials—that bothered neighbors for six or seven blocks. The owners ignored the association's protests, and the initial complaints to municipal authorities and the National Department of Hygiene brought no results. The company then opened a warehouse from which also emanated a foul odor, bothering a school with hundreds of students. According to the association, the school had to leave windows and doors closed to minimize the smell. After a petition was sent to the intendente, he asked to speak to a delegation, and when he met them he promised to visit the site. He did not do so, but the company was closed despite, according to the association, its owners trying to bribe various inhabitants and the school director to retract their complaints.[37]

Given the sizeable needs, a significant percentage of requests for municipal action could not be met. If influential figures intervened, the organizations would more likely have their requests granted. In most cases such interventions left little written evidence. Still, it is possible to see the connections that helped win governmental action. After the Asociación de Fomento de Villa Devoto complained several times about a serious flooding problem, a delegation arranged to meet with Intendente Cantilo, who subsequently visited the development society and toured the barrio. Cantilo promised to act. It is unlikely that Cantilo would have made the trip without the intervention of some influential figure, most likely the organization's president, who by 1938 had been both a police comisario and a justice of the peace.[38]

To successfully lobby the city council, sociedades de fomento usually required intervention by politicians. For example, in 1939 councilman José Rouco Oliva, who had belonged to the Independent Socialist Party but had become a Conservative, presented a resolution calling on the executive branch to pave Calle Tafí leading up to the rail station in Villa Lugano. This longtime wish had been postponed by a jurisdictional dispute, but by 1939 it had been cleared up, and the resolution passed. Slightly over a year later, a Villa Lugano neighborhood publication praised Rouco Oliva for his labor on public works: "It has created among our neighbors a true halo of esteem and popularity and it would not be hyperbolic praise that he is considered as one of the paladins of our progress."[39]

Influential men frequently played an oversized role. The Asociación General Alvear de Fomento Edilicio was created in December 1922 in the northern portion of the largely middle-class barrio of Caballito, which was underdeveloped. The association's name was political: the general's grandson had just become Argentina's president. The Dagnino family, which had moved to the neighborhood in 1912, played a crucial role in the organization. The family's father, José, allowed the new society to operate from the family's home. According to his son Lorenzo, José also recruited more than a hundred members by going house to house. José, two of his sons, and a son-in-law all served as the group's president. Especially influential was the journalist, geography professor, and urbanist Lorenzo Dagnino Pastore. In 1938 he served as president of the organization, while a brother and a brother-in-law sat on the governing board.

Other men in the development society also had connections. Eduardo Robirosa, who served as president and as editor of the organization's periodical, owned the local paper *El Baluarte*. Jorge Robirosa, almost undoubtedly a relative, ran for political office as a Progressive Democrat and was close to the party's founder, Lisandro de la Torre. The society's periodical took the unusual step of lauding the appointment of Jorge Robirosa as economic minister of the province of Buenos Aires. Another president of the sociedad de fomento, David Beltrán Núñez, had been a successful politician in the province of Santiago del Estero.

Much of the organization's success in the late 1930s came through ties to city councilor Rouco Oliva, who was active in Los Amigos de la Ciudad, an organization interested in the design of the city, of which he was president in 1939. Lorenzo Dagnino Pastore had been on the board of directors of Los Amigos de la Ciudad from 1925 to 1930. In the 1930s Rouco Oliva presented close to thirty projects of the Asociación General Alvear to the city council. For example, he played a pivotal role in the city acquiring the land to accomplish a longtime goal of the organization, the completion of Acoyte Street, which had been stalled. The street developed into an important artery. What did Rouco Oliva gain politically? The organization's periodical gave him considerable favorable publicity. In addition, an important member of the society, who served several terms as president, praised Rouco Oliva as acting like he was "one of us." The sociedad de fomento honored Rouco Oliva with a reception and made him its first honorary member. This type of recognition and ties to locally influential people would have helped any politician. In addition, in 1942 Alejandro Rouco Oliva sat on the society's board of directors, undoubtedly a close relative.[40]

Politicians and Development Societies

Despite the importance of lobbying for sociedades de fomento, politicians' roles are less visible than in football clubs. After the mid-1920s, municipal regulations prohibited municipal officeholders from positions in the development societies.[41] In addition, sociedades de fomento—like bibliotecas populares—were numerous but had few members, so for a politician to dedicate a lot of time to one might yield little advantage. Aspiring politicians did play roles, however. A politician who helped a development society could be rewarded with loyalty and potentially campaign aid or at least with favorable publicity, as with Rouco Oliva. For historians, spotting aspiring politicians is difficult since we can only notice them if they become successful.

Frequently, politicians provided aid, especially in their home barrio. A good example is Rómulo Vinciguerra, who was active in the Radical Party and served on the city council in the 1930s and in Congress after the fall of Perón. He built and maintained a base in the barrio of Villa del Parque, partly by aiding local civic associations. For example, he persuaded the city council to exempt the local development society's building from taxes. In return the organization's periodical published a favorable interview with him, which included a large photograph. He also played a role in the universidad popular in the barrio (see chapter 6).[42]

Help came in many forms. In submitting a report to its members, the Sociedad de Fomento Asociación Belgrano R. thanked, among many others, four members of the city council, especially José Claisse, an Antipersonalist Radical, who was a "great friend and collaborator who is virtually our legal advisor and to whom we owe a great part of the work that we have done."[43] The same development society was not above referring to Radical councilor Abelardo Boullosa as "occupying himself intensely with Belgrano R."[44]

In the late 1920s the Sociedad de Fomento de Versailles wanted the city to pave several streets, and with the intercession of two powerful men, José Guerrico and Tomás R. Cullen, it felt that it would succeed. (It is unclear if it did.) Guerrico was an honorary member of the society and a Conservative politician who served on the city council off and on for two decades. In 1930 he was made intendente by the postcoup military government. He was also a developer, and he had named the barrio; a contemporary journalist referred to him as one of the magicians who had transformed the barrio after the first subdivision was made in 1912. Guerrico also helped the sociedad de fomento get a school placed in the barrio. Cullen was a member of the traditional elite, a Conservative and former cabinet member, and he had served in Congress for the province of Santa Fe.[45]

Some politicians held offices in development societies. An example is the historian and politician Emilio Ravignani, who built political support by dispensing patronage while holding a bureaucratic post and by participating in civic associations. In the 1920s he served in an important administrative position in the city government and became the center of an extensive web of patronage. In addition to an extremely active career in the academic world, he held posts in several civic associations. He sat on the board of the Automovil Club Argentino, and in 1936 he ran for the governing board of the elite sporting club Gimnasia y Esgrima de Buenos Aires on a list that failed in its challenge to the longtime president, Ricardo C. Aldao. In 1935–1936, Ravignani was president of the Sociedad de Fomento Teniente General Luis María Campos and was a member for much longer.[46] Ravignani won election to Congress on Radical Party lists in 1936, 1940, 1946, and 1952.

Individuals with influence in different spheres of the social-political world also served on boards of sociedades de fomento. For example, the D. Santiago Diz who sat on the board of El Progreso de Villa Lugano in 1931 was almost undoubtedly Domingo Santiago Diz, a railroad union activist of long standing, an anarcho-syndicalist, and a member of the governing board of the railroad workers union, the Unión Ferroviaria, in its early days. He won a seat on the national railroad workers pension board in an industry-wide election on the slate of the union and briefly held an important post in the Unión Ferroviaria directly after the 1943 military coup. He served the sociedad de fomento during a period of upheaval on the board in a relatively new community composed largely of the working class.[47] His experience in a much larger and more complex organization undoubtedly helped him play a role, as did the connections that he had developed in the political arena.

Perhaps the most conspicuous chaser of votes through efforts to aid development societies was José Penelón. He seems an unusual person to follow this strategy, since he first won election to the city council as a Communist. A printer by trade, he became a key figure in the Communist Party shortly after its founding, including becoming secretary-general, and he won election to the city council in 1920 and again in 1926. Penelón was expelled from the party in 1927 after charges that he had abandoned revolution for municipal policies, though the reasons were more complex. He established a dissident branch of the party, which after the 1930 coup became Concentración Obrera. He won election twice to the city council during the 1930s.

Penelón pursued a tactic of aiding barrios and their sociedades de fomento and worked extremely hard to benefit municipal workers. After his expulsion from the party, his electoral successes came almost entirely from his careful cultivation of municipal issues. He supported sociedades de fomento, through visits to barrios, which highlighted their problems, and through constant actions on the city council. While he was a member of the Communist Party, the party periodical emphasized the bad conditions in the outlying barrios, Penelón's visits to these areas, and his proposals to fix the deficiencies. Betterment of conditions in those neighborhoods was a key element of the Communist Party's 1926 plan for the municipality, which among other things called for draining excess water in working-class neighborhoods, building plazas and playgrounds, and making electric street lighting, piped drinking water, and electricity available everywhere in the city.[48]

In late 1928 at the request of an organization called Comité Vecinal de Simpatizantes de Nueva Pompeya, for example, Penelón made a tour of that barrio. In his excursion he was joined by delegates from the Sociedad de Fomento Emilio Mitre, with which he had previously visited the neighborhood. In Penelón's subsequent presentation to the city council, he made clear that visits to poorer barrios were part of his party's program to improve life in outlying districts. He underlined the poor conditions of the neighborhood and presented concrete proposals, including having the city fix road drainage and a bridge and fill a marshy area.[49] Penelón behaved similarly in the 1930s.[50]

Although Penelón seems to have been the most diligent pursuer of this tactic, politicians from all sectors of the city's political spectrum visited barrios accompanied by delegations from development societies, who pointed out bad conditions. The visits brought publicity in the press and usually proposals for legislation.[51] At times these strategies met with success. For example, in 1921 three Democratic Progressive councilmen toured the barrio of Flores Sud at the request of the local sociedad de fomento. They reported on a series of specific problems with drainage and paving and called on the city's executive branch to correct the conditions. The call for action was passed by the council.[52]

Sociedades de Fomento Acting Together

At times development societies addressed problems that stretched beyond their barrio. For example, as Lila Caimari has shown, many sociedades de fomento wanted the government to hire more police so that they could better patrol outlying barrios because a perception of insecurity existed. In 1934 development societies sent a wave of petitions to Congress asking that next year's budget include funding for a thousand more police. Several stressed that patrolling was inadequate and that the development society had gone to the local police station asking for more agents on the street but had been told that there were not enough officers available. A number of sociedades echoed the wish in 1940.[53]

To address such larger issues, sociedades de fomento joined together in congresses. These were frequently tied to the goals of politicians, which does not necessarily mean that they did not reflect the desires of barrio inhabitants. Some questions could not be handled on a barrio-by-barrio basis. For example, in 1920 during a period of inflation, thirteen institutions met to exchange ideas about ways to lower costs. They created a commission to draw up a plan, which would be presented to a subsequent meeting. They also resolved to send a note to Yrigoyen requesting that he limit the export of meat and wheat to make them more affordable.[54]

Drainage was a major issue in large sectors of the city, and groups of development societies tried addressing this together. For many years the Arroyo Maldonado, a ravine that traversed a goodly segment of the city, posed a major impediment to development because of the need to bridge it and because it flooded regularly. The arroyo drained 5,900 hectares in the city and almost as much in the province of Buenos Aires. The national government had the responsibility to deal with it. Pressure to enclose the arroyo had existed for some time, and in the mid-1930s a group of development societies lobbied the authorities to acquire the necessary land and begin the process. The societies formed a permanent committee to advocate for enclosure and met with officials at all levels. The arroyo was covered over—at least in the capital.[55]

Another example of collective action, which proved totally unsuccessful, occurred on the largely affluent northern side of town. The original plan for a subway line under construction in 1939 was for it to run from downtown practically to the northern edge of the city, essentially the path of the current D line. The plan was altered to make the last stop at Palermo, about halfway through the original trajectory. The development society Belgrano R., which represented a barrio through which the line would have gone, organized a meeting of similar organizations to lobby for the original plan. They met regularly and sent petitions to the national government, to the city, to the company that was building the subway, and to others; they received a good deal of attention from the press. They printed 6,000 posters to be placed in businesses. According to the major newspaper *La Prensa*, they won support from businesses and homeowners in the affected area. The development societies also gained backing from important political actors, including the city council and the influential civic association Los Amigos de la Ciudad. However, the pressure proved futile since the national government had the power to make the decision and did not alter it. Only in the last decades of the twentieth century were subway stops added farther to the north, reaching almost to where the line had been originally planned to go.[56]

The Socialist Party frequently called congresses of development societies, despite the organizations supposedly being nonpartisan. For example, responding to a call from a Socialist group and organized by Socialist city councilors, in January 1935 a congress of seventy development societies met at the party's headquarters. The Socialist Party dominated, since in a contested election the Socialist president of the city council had won the right to preside over the congress. When the congress created three committees to present motions on the situation of the electric company, a matter of sharp political debate, on the controversial monopoly of public transportation in the capital, and on the question of paying for paving, Socialist city councilors sat as "advisors" on each committee. Clearly the party did not want motions to stray too far from its positions. The role of high-profile Socialists was not limited to city councilors. Angel Borlenghi, the secretary-general of the retail clerks union—a Socialist though never trusted by the party establishment—sat on the congress's credentials committee. He represented an organization that at least in 1942 was not recognized by the city. Borlenghi had great political skills and later served as Perón's longtime interior minister. Not all the participants approved of the party's role.[57]

The Attempt to Channel Development Societies

As Luciano de Privitellio and Adrián Gorelik have shown, tensions between the executive branch of the municipality and the city council pushed the former to try to use sociedades de fomento to build political support, since intendentes needed their own popular base. This occurred in the 1920s and 1930s.[58] The nature of the municipal political system, with the intendente a presidential appointee and the council popularly elected, led to intense friction when the president's party was weak in the capital. In both cases strong intendentes faced extremely hostile councils. The intendentes' actions led to attempts to control the societies, but also resulted in greater attention being paid to the outlying regions of the city. The intendentes had the power to channel public works, and they used that to push for improvements in urban infrastructure.

In the mid-1920s under President Alvear, after the splintering of the Radical Party, the pro-Alvear Radicals lacked a powerful base in the capital. The strong intendente Carlos Noel attempted to build political support by encouraging the formation of a federation of sociedades de fomento and a political party based on development societies. The latter failed miserably at the ballot box. According to Privitellio, the Personalist Radicals (pro-Yrigoyenist) and the Socialists responded by limiting the development societies' ability to become directly involved in politics while Noel turned to more direct contact with the organizations.[59] In late 1927 the city council passed ordinance 2.329, which set rules for sociedades de fomento that wanted to be recognized by the city and therefore would be attended to by the government. The rules were amended several times but remained essentially unchanged. The organizations were empowered to approach both branches of city government. They were supposed to have at least a hundred members (in 1930 this was lowered to fifty) who were over eighteen years old; the members could be of either gender. Dues could be no higher than one peso per month. In the heart of the old city, the sociedades de fomento were to cover an entire electoral circuit but elsewhere just thirty square blocks. Elections for the governing board were to be by secret ballot, and no city councilors or municipal employees could hold these posts. The development societies could join similar organizations in local conferences or citywide congresses, but these could not be permanent.[60]

After the return to the ballot box following the 1930 coup, the abstention of the Radical Party led to an excellent showing by the Socialists with the administration's supporters not doing well. Hostility developed between the Socialists and the powerful intendente, Mariano de Vedia y Mitre, who served from late 1932 until 1938. To woo development societies de Vedia y Mitre used as his point man a lawyer, Amílcar Razori, who served as secretary of public works. In March 1934, a special office in Razori's department was created to handle requests from development societies, which became the focal point of the strategy. In 1935 Razori announced that he would receive delegations from development societies on Tuesday mornings and would use the information to address infrastructure problems.[61]

The government increased its efforts to improve conditions, using a multi-pronged strategy. For example, in 1932 and 1933 the city planted no more than 200 blocks with trees each year, although authorities fielded constant requests for more. In 1934 it planted 1,843 blocks with 40,184 trees.[62] A key element was to deal effectively with sociedades de fomento. In 1936, according to the municipality, eighty-three development organizations submitted 633 requests to the city of which 580 were decided favorably, a remarkably high percentage. Razori collected many of these petitions during tours of outlying barrios accompanied by representatives of development societies. In 1935 Razori went on at least seventeen tours that resulted in significant publicity.[63]

Earlier, in mid-May 1934, Razori had toured the territories of the development societies José Enrique Rodó and Roque Sáenz Peña. He promised the enclosure of a stream on Calle Albariños, which was done and earned Razori a celebration in his honor hosted by those two development societies plus that of Emilio Castro. The society José Enrique Rodó continued to be close to Razori. It participated in a large ceremony for Francisco Traba, who headed the bureau dealing with the sociedades de fomento, and its journal printed fulsome praise of Razori.[64]

This was not unusual. On October 23, 1935, Razori toured sections of northwestern Vélez Sarsfield accompanied by representatives of the development societies Manuel Belgrano, 25 de Mayo, and 12 de Octubre. They showed him various deficiencies, and Razori promised to investigate some of them while others he pledged would be taken care of. He received a detailed petition.

Contacts with Razori continued, and some of the issues facing the societies seemed to have been addressed. The results for the city administration proved promising. The Manuel Belgrano participated in a homage to Razori and made Traba its honorary president. This development society seemed to have leaned leftward. For example, in January 1936 its executive committee donated five pesos to the striking union of carpenters, which was dominated by Communists, and it seemed in general to have been sympathetic to the Socialists. The shift to open ties with the Conservative government coincided with an internal struggle whose causes are not clear from the official publication. It seems safe to hypothesize that stress over such a shift in position would have worsened existing fissures. This does not mean that the Manuel Belgrano became a creature of the government, since it continued to oppose the monopoly of transportation that the government had established.[65]

Razori used almost all occasions to further his ties with development societies. When the Asociación Fomento y Cultura Flores Sud inaugurated its new headquarters, Razori attended. Similarly, when the Asociación de Fomento y Cultura Los Olivos celebrated the inauguration of a playground on public property for which it had raised the funds for the equipment, Razori came. Los Olivos later honored Traba, and Razori was awarded a gold medal at a cinematic function (see above).[66]

Despite all of this, it does not appear that Razori had a major political impact, since Conservatives continued not to do well in elections in the capital. By the late 1930s ties to other political groups were too solid as were the personal ties that had been established. Probably more important is that frequently government policies went against what many porteños perceived as their interests. Government actions on public transportation, labor conditions, unions, and other issues limited the governing coalition's appeal.

For example, many sociedades de fomento actively opposed the government's creation of a public corporation that controlled trolleys, buses, subways, and similar vehicles. The government's action was perceived as worsening service and raising costs. An article in the publication of the development society Manuel Belgrano summed up the attitude of many: "The development societies should not limit their actions in the defense of the interests that they were entrusted with to the narrow limits of problems related to buildings as some believe. Such a thing would ... diminish them, make them smaller and restrict the great benefits that they are called on to bring to the progress of the city. ... In modern life the means of locomotion are a vital thing."[67] Sociedades de fomento protested, and letters poured into Congress in a failed effort to derail the measure. In June 1942 development societies created the Asociaciones Vecinales de Fomento de la Ciudad de Buenos Aires to fight an adjustment of fare structures perceived as increasing commuting costs. The petition that it drew up had signatures from 135 organizations from different parts of the city.[68] Larger issues outweighed the smaller ones. The government's infrastructural improvements were important, but the rewards were few since other factors outweighed them in the minds of the voters.[69]

Conclusions

The sociedades de fomento played a large role in the barrios of Buenos Aires in the first decades of the twentieth century. They had multiple impacts. Along with other civic associations, they helped create the sense of belonging to a particular neighborhood by becoming centers of sociability. They also benefited barrio inhabitants by providing social services. They advocated for fostering the commercial world of the barrio, since many members were local businesspeople, and given the nature of transportation, local businesses provided conveniences for the inhabitants.

The key difference between sociedades de fomento and other civic associations is that their primary purpose was to advocate for the material betterment of their barrio. They worked to improve the inhabitants' physical world and helped bring a sense of respectability. Through their own actions or through persuading the government to act, the sociedades de fomento brought changes to their barrio. They also entered the conversations on larger issues.

Although barrio elites frequently dominated the sociedades de fomento (but the barrio elites were usually not part of the citywide or national elites), on many issues the societies could speak for a considerable percentage of local inhabitants. Almost all would benefit from streetlights, better drainage, or better garbage collection. When they ventured into political questions, however, it is difficult to generalize about the support they generated in the barrio. Still, their lobbying pushed the authorities to improve the conditions for many.

More than other civic associations, sociedades de fomento needed close ties to the powerful to gain access to the government. Politicians needed to build local bases, and favors done for sociedades de fomento brought publicity and ties to influential figures in a barrio. Both sides got something. In forming these relationships, these sociedades partially shaped the nature of politics and the city itself.

CHAPTER SIX

The Search for More Education

Universidades Populares

IN THE FIRST HALF of the twentieth century many porteños hungered for further education, and they created universidades populares to fulfill that very real need. For those who had left formal education and already entered the workforce, further education was difficult to acquire. This proved especially true for people who desired practical training to allow them to advance in the work world. Universidades populares were established to help fill that gap.

Learning was considered a good in itself, but it also was a way of achieving social and economic advancement. The public primary schools provided basic literacy and numerical ability. However, as the urban economy grew more complex, this was not sufficient. The secondary education system tended to be academically focused and only available during traditional times. Many, both elites and average inhabitants, perceived a need for practical, skill-related education. Plus, many young porteños needed to work, so education had to be available in hours that did not coincide with work.

Early on, some perceived the benefits of an education that could be used in the workplace. For example, in 1909 in an article in *El Monitor de Educación Común*, a periodical of the Consejo Nacional de Educación (National Council of Education), Raúl B. Díaz praised adult public education in New York City with the clear implication that it would be an ideal model for Buenos Aires. For Díaz, what was happening in New York was education whose "essential purpose is not to teach science per se but to improve adults in their daily pursuits."[1]

Shortly thereafter in Buenos Aires, efforts were made to enlarge the opportunities for adult education, although frequently not on the model of New York. Many of the courses were offered by nonprofit private schools organized as civic associations, the universidades populares. Lack of funding, however, limited their ability to meet their goals, and not all parts of the city possessed them. Many universidades populares received aid from the government, but the financing was inconsistent, not systematically planned out, and inadequate. In several ways this resembled the situation of the bibliotecas populares. There seems to have been little correlation between the number of students served and the quantity of government assistance. Institutions with excellent political connections appear to have fared particularly well. Nevertheless, the universidades populares provided classes that were unavailable from other sources.

The relatively high costs of maintaining universidades populares forced them to seek help from the state. Teachers had to be paid, though frequently they received paltry sums, and if universidades populares offered technical courses, special equipment and classrooms were required. Almost all universidades populares did not charge their students, and since they were barrio-based, resources from membership dues and fundraising were limited, and state aid became critical. Politicians and important individuals played a crucial role in procuring that support. Alone among the civic associations I studied, members gained nothing from belonging except the feeling that they were participating in a greater good. More than the other civic associations I studied, the universidades populares were dominated by those with some means.

Universidades Populares and the Hunger for Education

As mentioned, a belief existed that upward mobility was possible for either porteños or their children through education and hard work. Traditional education was frequently not the answer. As Juan Brugnara, a founder of five universidades populares, argued, working-class families needed alternatives to high schools since they could not afford the fees nor the time required to attend. Families needed income from their children. Government statistics indicate that the average working-class family needed more than one wage earner to survive.²

Many porteños took advantage of opportunities to take classes outside of traditional times. These were offered by a wide variety of institutions, from the public school system to football clubs to sociedades de fomento and bibliotecas populares. However, the offerings were frequently ad hoc and insufficient to meet demand, failing to slake the inhabitants' thirst for knowledge. Residents partially filled the void by establishing universidades populares to provide instruction to those who wanted more education and lacked the time or the opportunity to go to traditional *colegios* (high schools). They wanted to provide practical training that would open paths to better economic opportunities and social mobility. A desire to create better citizens also existed.

Like the bibliotecas populares, the location of the universidades populares depended on private initiatives, and so some barrios lacked them. Also, many universidades populares did not have the resources to adequately carry out their missions. For example, the Universidad Popular de Villa del Parque in the mid-1930s had only nine typewriters, some of which had been donated by its board of directors, and it had to turn away more than a hundred students who sought typing courses. In numerous cases popular universities functioned at night in public primary schools, many of which only begrudgingly shared their space, lacked places to store materials, and were designed for smaller students.³ Teacher compensation was nowhere near sufficient to be a principal source of income. In 1936 in twelve universidades populares, which were part of a coalition, most instructors taught four to six hours a week and earned between twenty and forty pesos a month.⁴ One of the arguments given for the continued role of private organizations in this form of education was that their schools were significantly cheaper than state-run schools.⁵

Early Attempts at Popular Education

Despite claims that the Universidad Popular de La Boca, founded in 1917, was the first such institution, similar schools had existed previously. As early as 1904 a popular university was created under the auspices of various elites. Others followed, although they weren't always called universidades populares. A couple had some success.[6] Institutions run by anarchists or Socialists, which concentrated primarily on the enlightenment of the individual and not on professional training, existed as well and predated the widespread rise of universidades populares.[7] Until the twenty-first century, there was little attention in Argentina to the type of popular universities examined in this chapter.[8]

Institutions with the name universidad popular appeared throughout the continent from Mexico to Uruguay with examples in countries as different as Cuba, Guatemala, Peru, and Bolivia. The schools appear to have been led by people who were part of the university reform movement that swept Latin America after 1917, or they were interested in radically transforming the society. Several of the key figures in these institutions went on to play crucial roles in the political life of their countries by helping to forge revolutionary movements. For example, critical to starting the universidad popular in Lima was Victor Raúl Haya de la Torre, the founder and longtime leader of the Aprista Party. In Cuba Julio Antonio Mella played a similar role in the creation of a popular university, and he was among the founders of the country's Communist Party.[9]

The universidades populares examined in this book had a very different type of founder; they were not in general inspired by the university reform movement, nor were they interested in a radical transformation of the society. The university reform movement in Argentina did lead to the founding of some popular universities; one such institution, for example, was created in the city of La Plata in the mid-1930s, but it did not resemble those I focus on here.[10] Also, unlike in Argentina, in much of the rest of Latin America the experiment with popular universities tended to be truncated by political forces.

The Argentine state did establish schools for adults that offered courses beyond those of the traditional school system. These can be divided into two categories. One type provided basic literacy, but it became less necessary with time. The other offered classes that resembled those of the universidades populares. Attendance in adult education courses in the city of Buenos Aires stood at 13,605 in 1917, 9,554 in 1922, and 12,155 in 1929. In 1933 the literacy courses had 12,714 students, and the courses that resembled those of the universidades populares had 27,741 students. In the latter category, the classes with the most students in descending order were embroidery, dressmaking, typing, drawing, English, bookkeeping, and French. In 1936 there were 47,000 students in adult education classes, a major increase, and some 23,000 attended universidades populares operating in public schools.[11] Other universidades populares used private buildings. Also, the government operated industrial schools, which were relatively small, but efforts were made to enlarge them.[12] Clearly, government offerings remained inadequate, since the number of courses resulting from private initiatives was vast.

Purportedly nonsectarian and nonpolitical, civic associations designed to provide adult education of a practical bent underwent a rapid expansion in the late 1920s and the 1930s. By 1937 twenty-two universidades populares received subsidies from the municipal government of Buenos Aires.[13] The national budget for 1938 contained a slightly different twenty-two popular universities in the city of Buenos Aires.[14] More such institutions existed but did so without consistent outside assistance.

Nature of Popular Universities

The universidades populares usually stressed their nonpartisan and secular nature in a manner similar to the declaration of Universidad Popular de Villa Pueyrredón:

> The social and educational work that we have been doing has merited the open support of the neighborhood since we have always tried to create an educational atmosphere in which is observed the strictest political and religious neutrality, making our establishment a true place of peace and intended for the physical, moral, and intellectual formation of the students who attend our classes. We always seek that they understand and have learned the material, giving them in this way the technical specialization necessary to better their possibilities in the struggle for life.
>
> We want to underline that the political and religious neutrality that we impose on our labor does not signify indifference to the problems that

impact the very existence of the nation and the principles and the constitutional and legal underpinnings that we have adopted to organize our life in common.[15]

While claiming political neutrality, the institution expressed a clear ideological position.

Some universities went further; the Universidad Popular Bartolomé Mitre had as one of its goals "endeavoring to spread nationalistic culture." The national government appears to have pushed these institutions in the same direction, as the principal government inspector for adult education for several years in the 1930s, Clotilde Arrieta de Acuña, helped found a right-wing nationalist organization.[16]

Since universidades populares were civic associations, their governance structures resembled those of the other organizations discussed in this book. A good example is the Universidad Popular Florentino Ameghino. Its board of directors had nine members with three substitutes elected by an annual assembly of dues-paying members.[17] The popular universities differed from other civic associations, however, in that members only received the benefit of supporting the organization, making them mostly institutions created and controlled by the more comfortable classes. Membership dues sometimes represented a significant percentage of income. In 1937 the Universidad Popular de Villa del Parque had 299 members, and their dues were 41 percent of its yearly income, the largest category.[18]

Because of their role and the assistance they received from the state, three government agencies monitored the universidades populares' performance. Usually, the inspectors of schools for adults of the Consejo Nacional de Educación did the evaluations. The inspections appear to have been done regularly. For example, inspectors visited the Universidad Popular Bernardino Rivadavia four times between July 1939 and April 1940. The inspectors could take severe actions. They closed the two-year-old Universidad Popular Cervantes because of problems with its governing board despite it being the only such school in the barrio of Nueva Chicago.[19]

Like almost all the civic associations I discuss, most universidades populares were male-dominated. Most of the boards of directors were all male, though several exceptions existed. The people who led the schools on a day-to-day basis also tended to be male. However, the universidades populares José M. Estrada and Achával Rodríguez both had women directors. Female students comprised a significant percentage of many universities' attendees, and especially in the all-female schools, women comprised a high percentage of the teachers.[20] Teaching was one of the few professions in this period in which women played a critical role.

The universidades populares provided some of the same social functions as most other civic associations. For example, the popular university in Boedo during the years between its founding in 1928 and 1937 sponsored forty lectures on a wide variety of topics, including literature, science, history, and travel. It also organized celebrations of patriotic holidays and held four theatrical performances and twenty athletic tournaments.[21] In its annual report for 1934–1935, the Universidad Popular de Flores Sud insisted that it carried out the celebrations of the national holidays not only because it was required to do so, but it did so with real enthusiasm. In addition, it had acquired a field for sporting events and installed a tennis court, a place to play bocce, and playground equipment, and it was constructing a basketball court. During the summer, physical education classes for children were held at the field as was a sports festival. The Universidad Popular Florentino Ameghino had a free medical office for its students and established a sports club and a student orchestra.[22]

Like other civic associations, popular universities sponsored some events primarily to raise money, but these also helped build a sense of community. The Universidad Popular de Flores Intendente Torcuato de Alvear held several fundraisers that only stand out because of their potential to raise large sums. It sponsored a tea dance on board a ship of the Italian American Line to celebrate the end of classes in 1926. It also benefited from a special football match between River Plate and Platense for a cup donated by the intendente with the proceeds going to the university.[23]

Universidad Popular de La Boca

The surge in the creation of private educational institutions focused on practical subjects began in 1917 in La Boca, where much of the maritime-related industry of the city was concentrated. Although the school was supposedly nonpolitical, the idea for the Universidad Popular de La Boca was hatched in the local headquarters of the Radical Party, and its founders were an elite group of what would later become the Antipersonalist Radicals. La Boca had become a Socialist Party stronghold, and the Radicals wanted to break that dominance. The university's founders included Tomás Le Breton, Leonidas Anastasi, Arturo Goyeneche, Roberto M. Ortiz, and Angel Gallardo, all of whom played major roles in politics before 1943.

Le Breton was the driving force behind the Universidad Popular de La Boca during its early years. Le Breton was an important politician who had a deep interest in La Boca, although it was not his home barrio. A lawyer, he had participated in the Radical Party since its founding. He served in both houses of Congress. He also held a cabinet post under Alvear, a personal friend, and served as ambassador to the United States, France, and Great Britain. According to Anastasi, Le Breton's motivation for founding the school lay in the problems of the maritime industry, which had been severely damaged by World War I. He wanted the *maquinistas* (machinists) to be able to transfer their skills to the countryside. Not only was he the intellectual force behind the university, but he personally provided significant funds. When he went on leave from the lower house of Congress, he gave his salary to the university and contributed other sums. By mid-1919 he had donated more than 15,000 pesos, and he continued to make major gifts.[24]

Anastasi was a congressman and a lawyer who represented the Shipboard Workers Union (Federación Obrera Marítima) for a time. He was heavily politically invested in La Boca and had a deep interest in education, helping to found an earlier educational institute in La Boca and serving on the first board of the Universidad Popular del Oeste in the neighborhood of Caballito, which was reasonably distant from La Boca. Goyeneche, besides being the longtime president of the popular university in La Boca, sat in the lower house of Congress and served as president of that body between 1918 and 1921. When Roberto M. Ortiz was president of Argentina in the late 1930s and early 1940s, he made Goyeneche the intendente of Buenos Aires. Ortiz before his presidency had been both a congressman and minister of public works under Alvear and treasury minister under Justo.[25] Gallardo, a scientist, served as president of the Consejo Nacional de Educación during the founding of the popular university. He later was ambassador to Italy, and during the presidency of Alvear he served as minister of foreign affairs and culture.[26]

The largely working-class composition of La Boca made it a barrio in which vocational education could greatly enhance the opportunity for occupational mobility. Given the political clout of the school's founders, if they simply wanted to provide vocational education for the district, they could have done so by creating a state-run institution. Although they never revealed their thinking, the creation of a state institution would have yielded short-term political benefits but would have had almost no longer-term political impacts. Instead, the founders continued to be identified with the popular university and therefore continued to receive whatever goodwill it produced.

During its first year the Universidad Popular de La Boca had 1,500 students, and another 250 wished to attend but there was no space. The school offered thirty-two courses, including agricultural machinery, French, English, Spanish, bookkeeping, typing, maritime law, and bird raising. Several important companies, including the metallurgical firm Vasena and the railroad company Sud, made contributions. By 1919 the school had over 3,000 students, and the course offerings were even more diverse, including various agricultural courses and automobile mechanics. Some funding came from the national government, 6,000 pesos, while the Consejo Nacional de Educación, headed by Gallardo, provided the use of an existing school in the evenings and some teaching materials. The elite Jockey Club gave 23,000 pesos, and as already stated Le Breton contributed generously. In addition, a Dr. Pereira donated a thousand liters of milk a month for the classes on that industry. During the twenties, the university received some support from the municipality of Buenos Aires as well.[27] In 1923 there were three separate sections: farming, which was taught almost entirely by university professors as a public service; commerce; and industry.[28] In 1927 it had slightly fewer than 3,000 students taking twenty-eight courses. The percentage of students who were Argentinian-born was 84. Educating each student cost slightly over seven pesos annually, a ridiculously low figure.[29]

By 1941 the institution's political ties were less evident. Its honorary president was Le Breton, but its governing board lacked major political figures. It did contain men who held elected office in the football clubs Boca Juniors and

River Plate, and there were some Radicals of importance in La Boca. The person in charge on a daily basis was Emilio Leveratto, an important figure in the barrio: a lawyer, a teacher, and principal of the school where the university was housed. In 1940 he had sat on the city council for a minor party, Unión de Contribuyentes, which began as a representative of grocery store owners but evolved into a municipal party supporting conservative interests. In 1956 Leveratto was elected president of Boca Juniors.[30]

In 1941, the student body had reached almost 3,100, and they took a wide range of classes. Offerings had moved away from rural agricultural-related education to more relevant courses for an urban neighborhood, including bookkeeping, English, Italian, typing, shorthand, industrial and artistic drawing, electricity, radiotelegraphy, radiotelephony, combustion engines, naval construction, electricity for aviation, classification and commercialization of grain, and oil production. Most of the university's funds came from the national government in the form of a subvention, and various ministries supported specific courses. Donations also came from individuals and from General Motors, Ford, General Electric, and the textile and footwear company Alpargatas, among others.[31] The support from the large corporations indicates that they needed more skilled workers.

In 1942 the Universidad Popular de La Boca's preparation of ship crews earned the thanks of the Liga Naval Marítima, and approved students received twenty-day cruises on the vessels of the state oil company YPF. All those trained for the petroleum industry obtained jobs from YPF, as they had since 1937. The institution's income was 20,071 pesos; the national government's share was 78 percent.[32] Not included in the calculations are the savings from the use of a public school at no cost.

The Universidad Popular de La Boca differed from its peers in certain aspects. It received more national government support than most. The Antipersonalists were politically crucial both before and after the 1930 coup, and they procured for the university important sums, which were needed because the equipment was expensive. The money permitted the institution to become a vocational school offering training in industrial-related fields. Almost all other universidades populares could only offer clerical training, such as bookkeeping and typing, or classes that needed little expensive equipment, such as the needle trades. They lacked the funds. Given the growth of the industrial sector, more schools like that in La Boca would have proved useful.

Universidad Popular de Boedo

The Universidad Popular de Boedo was created in 1928 in a more socioeconomically mixed barrio than La Boca. At its founding, it had extraordinarily good political connections, but its ties were to the Personalist Radicals, which after Yrigoyen's overthrow in September 1930 appears to have hurt the university. Its political connections are revealed by its 1929 honorary commission, composed almost entirely of Personalist Radicals, including two senators, five deputies, and two city councilors.[33] One of the congressmen, Pedro Bidegain, and a city councilor, Pedro Villemur, were key figures in San Lorenzo de Almagro. As has been discussed, Bidegain was the dominant Radical in the district and pursued political capital by aiding civic associations.

The university met a need, since students filled its first set of courses within three days. It served both men and women, though they received instruction on different days in the public school that permitted the universidad popular to use its facilities. The institution also wanted to bring ideas to the barrio and planned to present weekly talks, though many fewer occurred. Its founders displayed neighborhood boosterism; they wanted to compete with other neighborhoods. In a newspaper interview José González Castillo, the president of the board of directors, after mentioning the economic and cultural progress of Boedo, said: "What Boedo lacked to complete its autonomy was the popular university that would make it equal to La Boca, one of the rival neighborhoods in football and in progress."[34]

In its second year the Universidad Popular de Boedo possessed a student body of 846 males and 500 females. Given the institution's connections, it is unsurprising that the city council voted it a sizeable subvention in just its second year, even before it formally received legal recognition (*personería jurídica*). Congress acted similarly. After the 1930 coup, however, the university's connections proved less useful than those of its peer in La Boca, since Boedo received over time much less government support than La Boca. For example, in 1936 Boedo's subsidy was only slightly higher than the income from the university's membership dues.[35]

In 1940 the popular university had expenses of 11,813.97 pesos and ran a deficit of 741.43. The national government subsidy comprised 32.6 percent of the income, with the remaining funds coming from private sources. In several earlier years when the national government subvention was larger (all subventions were lowered) and aid also came from the municipality, private contributions were less important but still vital. In 1937 municipal and national contributions were 59 percent of income. Not figured into these calculations was the university's free use of a public school.[36]

The university referred to itself as the "postescuela" (afterschool), a correct characterization. From its founding through 1940, of the 15,768 students who attended, 69 percent had a primary education, 30 percent had secondary education, and 1 percent had university education. The students were 70 percent male and 92 percent Argentinian-born. Most had ended their formal schooling; 24 percent were listed as students, 20 percent were workers, 30 percent were employees (*empleados*), 3 percent were categorized as various professions, and 1 percent were merchants. Twenty-two percent claimed no profession. Those from fourteen to sixteen years old comprised 40 percent of the attendees, while the seventeen-to-nineteen age group represented an additional 27 percent; the numbers declined from there. The age distribution partially explains the heavy percentage of Argentinian-born, since most of the young were locally born; this would also account for the large number of students and those without a listed profession.

In the university's first year (1928) it had 1,393 students; the figure increased the following year, but then the numbers began a steep descent, bottoming out at 758 students in 1932. Enrollment then started an upward trajectory, reaching 1,477 students in 1940. The post-1929 decline reflected the impact of the Depression plus the turmoil caused by the 1930 coup, especially the persecution of Radicals, which would have affected institutions identified with that party.

In 1932 students at the Universidad Popular de Boedo took fifteen courses; this had increased to thirty-one by 1935. In 1940 the university offered thirty-four courses, including English, French, bookkeeping, typing, shorthand, calligraphy, embroidery, dressmaking, combustion engines, and telegraphy. In earlier years, seemingly less practical courses had been taught, including music, guitar, declamation, and native songs and dances. The changed nature of the course selection may explain why the percentage of women students declined over the years. Most women did not stay long in the job market and faced limited job opportunities, so they might have been attracted to courses that seemed less career-oriented.[37]

Universidad Popular Bernardino Rivadavia

In May 1926 the Universidad Popular Bernardino Rivadavia was created under the auspices of the *cooperadora* (a parent-teacher organization) of school number 8 of the twelfth school district to serve the northern end of the barrio of Caballito, a largely middle-class neighborhood. The founders wanted to "contribute to the education and the intellectual betterment of the young . . . to whom we offer an excellent opportunity to obtain new knowledge or acquire a career." During its first year, all funds came from the 150 families who belonged to the cooperadora, and the instructors received no pay. The school was free, and the students had to have finished fourth grade or the equivalent. Courses were given in Spanish, French, English, typing, shorthand, bookkeeping, and business arithmetic, as well as electricity, geometry, and music. It managed to obtain in its first year a 10,000-peso national subsidy for the following year.[38]

The university evolved during the 1930s. In 1936 over a thousand students attended, and they were almost evenly divided between men and women. They could take twenty-five different classes. The subject matters had shifted; some had been dropped, and others intended for females had been added, such as embroidery and dressmaking. However, the only language offered was English, and while music courses were offered, the practical courses were not numerous. The early 1930s had been financially tight. The university continually informed Congress that it had financial troubles and requested that its subvention return to what it had been in 1929. Its 1937 annual report said that the city government had boosted its support from 416.50 pesos to 1,500 because of the personal intervention of Rómulo Magnani, a member of the university's governing council. Magnani, a police comisario, had earlier been president of the Biblioteca Popular Alberdi of Villa Crespo, a neighboring barrio. The following year the annual report was even more evocative of the need for personal connections. It mentioned the work of Magnani and Luis Boffi (who was vice president of the board of directors) "who thanks to their enthusiastic and selfless efforts succeeded in obtaining in one case the payment of late portions of the national subsidy and in the other . . . the Honorable City Council agreed to subsidies corresponding to the years 1939 and 1940, which given the state of municipal finances ran the risk of not being agreed to."[39] Boffi was a Radical city councilor who built support through civic associations (see chapter 2). Those with political connections made a tremendous difference in the lives of institutions.

Who Were the Students?

The Universidad Popular de Flores Intendente Torcuato de Alvear deserves a great deal of attention because it produced a unique registry of students, which allows researchers to develop some idea of the student body's composition.[40] Flores, like most barrios in Buenos Aires, was of mixed socioeconomic status, but the institution claimed that it served a working-class area. Founded in 1925, the universidad received the name of a transformative intendente of the city, who also was the father of the sitting Argentine president.

The university's initial governing council included Ricardo Hermelo, a controversial prefect of the port with political aspirations, and Juan Guereño, the Spanish-born soap manufacturer and Radical who, as already discussed, was a president and benefactor of the Sociedad de Fomento Democracia y Progreso. More illustrative of the universidad popular's connections was that its honorary council included the Argentine president's wife, Regina P. de Alvear; the country's vice president; the foreign minister, Gallardo; the minister of war and a future president, Justo; the intendente of the city; and several other key politicians. The nation's president and the minister of justice and public education attended the official inauguration of the university. This level of support allowed the school to receive subventions from 1926 onward from both the city of Buenos

Aires and the national government. Like most other such institutions, it operated in the evening in a public school. It differed from most other coed popular universities in that its student body was overwhelmingly female.

Students could study embroidery by hand and machine, dressmaking, hat making, weaving, artificial flowers, typing, shorthand, Spanish, English, and the playing of various musical instruments. In 1929 the Universidad Popular de Flores claimed that its focus was on useful instruction and blamed its lack of male students on its inability to offer courses that would train them for employment in careers such as carpentry, furniture making, or plumbing because it lacked shops.[41]

In 1928 as part of a request for funds, the university had sent Congress a roster of its students, divided by gender. It gave each student's age, nationality, home address, and the profession of their father or, if no father was listed, their mother's profession.[42] Many of the older women students for whom no parent was mentioned were married, which was determined by their names. The extremely varied nomenclatures of the occupations indicate that they were supplied by either the student or a parent. The school had 1,005 female students and just 176 males. The females were 94.9 percent Argentinian-born with the rest being foreign-born or listing no origin. The males were 97.7 percent Argentinian-born.

The age of the female students was more diverse than the males'. Although the university's minimum age was fourteen, 62 females (6.2 percent) were younger. Fifty percent were from fourteen to sixteen years old, 24.2 percent were between seventeen and nineteen, and 11.2 percent were from twenty to twenty-two. Older students represented 8.4 percent of the total. Male students were more concentrated with a higher percentage of students from fourteen through nineteen. Mothers were listed for 10 percent of the females and 10.2 of the males. Neither parent was given for 4.2 percent of the women and 8.5 percent of the men; these were usually older students. If a mother was listed instead of a father, we can assume that in most cases the father was not present in the household.[43]

The occupations of the parents varied greatly. For female students, 11.9 percent of their parents worked in one of the construction trades; 30.3 percent were empleados or empleadas (employees); and an additional 23.2 percent had what can be considered middle-class jobs, including 10.7 percent of the entire universe of parents who were listed as merchants (the term undoubtedly masked very different incomes). Nonconstruction blue-collar jobs represented some 17.7 percent. Others were difficult to classify, were potentially upper class, or were not listed. The occupations of the parents of the male students did not differ greatly from this breakdown.[44] In this universidad popular many parents belonged to what could be labeled the middle strata. Whether this is representative of the other universidades populares is difficult to say, but it probably represents the barrio from which the school pulled most of its students.

The overwhelming percentage of students lived within easy walking distance. Seventy-five percent of female students lived within a kilometer of the school, and only 6 percent lived more than two kilometers from the institution. The figures for male students varied little from this, though they tended to live slightly farther away. Sixty-five percent lived within a kilometer of the school while 14 percent lived more than two kilometers away. The Universidad de Flores served a relatively small area of the city and was very much a barrio institution.

Table 6.1. Distance Students Lived from Site of the Universidad Popular de Flores (in kilometers)

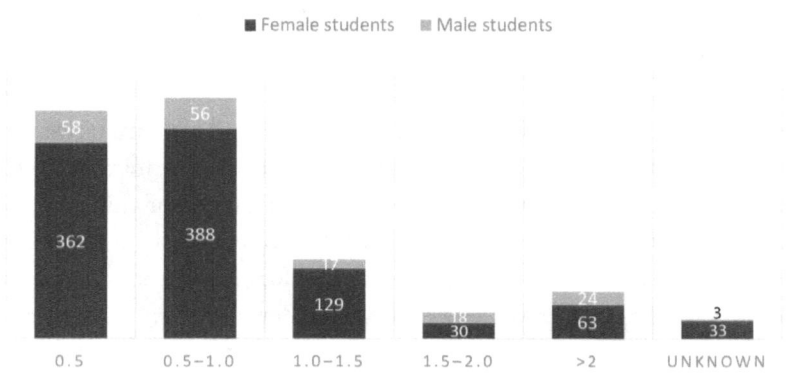

Methodology: The location of the school and the addresses of the students listed in the 1928 petition were mapped on Google Earth Pro. Many street names and numbers had not changed between 1928 and 2018. Although most addresses were located using this system, some streets were not found. I consulted a list of former street names prepared by Piñeiro, *Las calles de Buenos Aires*, which identified a significant number of streets with name changes. The 1976 *Guía de planos* was also consulted. However, ten streets, representing thirty-six students, remained unlocated. These are labeled in the table as "unknown." To measure distances, circles of 0.5 kilometers, 1.0 km, 1.5 km, and 2.0 km, centered on the address of the universidad popular, were placed on the map using the Google Earth ruler.

Trying to Exist without Government Support

Not all universidades populares followed the same path. An excellent example is the institution created in August 1930 in the barrio of Belgrano, which contained the homes of many wealthy people, the Universidad Popular de Belgrano. It was a precarious time to form a university since politics were in turmoil; it was the month before the coup that overthrew Yrigoyen, and the economy had already felt the first impacts of the Depression. The university, however, shunned outside support, saying in 1938: "Never has our institution enjoyed official help, in no moment has it required subventions from the nation, the municipality or from elsewhere. Its directors are resolved to maintain that orientation in order that the work be sustained by private efforts and break with the time-honored custom of expecting everything from the state."[45] It claimed that all its funds came from members and the small fees that were charged to students who could afford them. Such fees were highly unusual, since the classes of almost all universidades populares were free. The university in Belgrano also derived some money from fundraising activities. There is a certain irony in the comment about self-funding, since the Belgrano had received 9,000 pesos from the city to construct a building for the institution. That was insufficient, and it sought additional money from Congress, receiving a one-time subvention of 30,000 pesos. Previously, the universidad had been renting a building, which consumed 20 percent of its expenditures, although it could use the space for just two hours a night, five days a week. In 1937 it received a 900-peso subvention from the city.[46] It also began petitioning for funds from the national government to help pay for rent and equipment.

The institution had over a thousand students in 1938 and offered thirty-nine courses whose range did not differ from those of many similar organizations. It did offer more language courses: Spanish, French, German, and English. The school tried to create a sense of community. Besides celebrating patriotic holidays and conducting fundraisers, in 1940 it sponsored a chamber music performance and a discussion of Uruguayan poetry. The university also helped found an organization of students, alumni, and community members dedicated to putting on sporting activities.

Like many popular universities, the Belgrano cultivated ties with politicians.

At the end of 1938 it held a celebration at the Club Belgrano attended by members of its board, teachers, and the speakers at its cultural events. One special guest was a former member of the city council, Enrique Vago, whom the institution's president lauded for "the importance of the cooperation given by Mr. Vago in his role as a neighbor." In 1940 it made former president Justo a "patron member," and he toured the facilities. The institution's ability to raise large sums of money from membership dues indicates that many members were wealthy. Interestingly in 1938 three members of the governing board were women, which was unusual. One, Emma Day de Oliva, was a distinguished educator from Belgrano who was a feminist and Socialist.[47]

Even an organization supported by well-heeled individuals and that wanted to survive without government aid felt it necessary to turn to the state for assistance.

Problems with Depending on the Government

The largely working-class barrio of Barracas had a universidad popular named Bernardo de Irigoyen, which was founded in 1917, roughly simultaneously with the one in La Boca. Two existing organizations, which had been created to help barrio schools, played a critical role in its establishment. The initiative came from an important local figure, Pedro F. Arias, who was president of the local school board. Appointments to the local school boards were always political. A doctor and head of a local sanatorium, Arias was active in a sociedad de fomento, the Boy Scouts, and the Red Cross.

The Bernardo de Irigoyen's honorary president was vice president of the Consejo Nacional de Educación, and not surprisingly the university gained permission to operate in two local public schools, one for females and the other for males. It had two women on its inaugural board of directors. In its first year 1,500 students took a wide variety of classes, including such unusual courses as preparation for the colegio nacional (national high school) and for the school of midwives, as well as agricultural machinery.[48] As early as 1919, during a school year that ran from April to November, its library was well used, having some 3,000 readers.

The university grew rapidly; in 1920 it had 1,396 female students and 952 males. Both genders could take bookkeeping, stenography, typing, French, English, drawing, and painting. The women could study dressmaking, embroidery, repoussé, hat making, and music while men could study spelling and editing, mechanical drawing, and telegraphy, a much less ambitious curriculum than what was initially offered.[49]

The university quickly began receiving subventions, and by the mid-1920s it obtained annual subsidies of 10,000 pesos from the national government and 5,000 from the city. This allowed teachers to receive small stipends. During the post-1930 era things changed dramatically as a result of the political situation plus the Depression. Subsidies ended for a time. Even after the national subsidy was restored, the university received just 2,500 pesos annually from mid-1939 to 1945, and expenses had increased greatly, despite the piddling sums paid to those who worked for the organization. The director made 60 pesos a month while an instructor earned 20 pesos. Clearly the teachers did not depend on this job. At least in its early years, the teachers were also employed in the city's public schools.[50] This was not unusual.

A Dream of a Network of Popular Universities

The Universidad Popular Florentino Ameghino was founded in 1926 as an all-male institution in the barrio of Villa Crespo. The driving force was Juan Brugnara, who had a wide vision of what universidades populares should be and used the Florentino Ameghino as the cornerstone of a coalition of such organizations.[51]

From its beginnings, the Florentino Ameghino had excellent political connections that it used for its benefit. Its first head was Remigio Iriondo, a politician and barrio activist (see chapter 2). It first opened in a private school that was run and owned by Iriondo.[52] The Florentino Ameghino had just 126 students its first year. However, what it lacked in size it compensated with political pull. Its leaders desired to operate in a public school, and when authorities rejected its petition, the universidad turned to its honorary president, Alvear, who obtained the use of a school.[53] The early years were difficult as teachers worked for little or no pay. In 1929 the situation of the institution improved after the historian and sitting Radical Party senator Diego Luis Molinari helped obtain a national subvention of 20,000 pesos.[54]

It grew to be a medium-size popular university. By its second year it had 354 students, and by 1930 there were 722. It stayed near the latter figure until 1939 when its student body topped 1,000. The students tended to be older than those who attended the Universidad Popular de Flores Intendente Torcuato de Alvear. In 1937, 30 percent of the Florentino Ameghino students fell in the range of fourteen to seventeen years old, with an additional 50 percent from eighteen to twenty-five; the remaining students were even older. They were overwhelmingly Argentinian-born. In 1932 the attendees' professions were listed: 43 percent were students, and 30 percent were empleados with the remainder working a range of jobs. They studied bookkeeping, commercial law, calligraphy, English, mathematics, commercial arithmetic, and wireless telegraphy, among other subjects.[55]

The Florentino Ameghino regularly received support from both the national and municipal governments. Like other institutions, subsidies were drastically trimmed whenever the governments faced budgetary problems. Additionally, the universidad could not depend on what it had been promised. For example, according to its 1934 annual report, the national government owed it the third-quarter subvention for 1933, the second-quarter subvention for 1934, and a month's support for the third quarter of that year. The municipal government also was late with a quarter of its payment. This was not unique, but it was problematic because of a dependence on public funding. In 1938 almost three-quarters of its revenue came from government sources with the rest from membership dues.[56]

Like many other universidades populares, the Florentino Ameghino operated in a public primary school with no rent being charged. The situation was less than optimal because the school's principal function determined its furnishings. As the organization pointed out, a school designed for six- to fourteen-year-olds was inadequate for older students because desks and chairs were too small, and there was no place to store equipment. In 1938 Congress voted to give the Florentino Ameghino 80,000 pesos for a building, but that proved insufficient to buy land and construct a building. In 1942 Congress approved an additional 150,000 pesos.[57]

The institution became the center of a citywide network of universidades populares. The schools that comprised the consortium shared a governing council. It had the visionary leadership of Brugnara, but it also had good political connections. The Florentino Ameghino's honorary council in 1936 continued to have Alvear as its president. The honorary council also contained several other important Radicals, especially intellectuals, but there were also Democratic Progressives and Socialists. The university was not above appealing to the Conservative vice president and acting president, Ramón Castillo. On July 9, 1939, Independence Day, the Florentino Ameghino arranged for some 5,000 popular university students to parade past Castillo.[58]

Plans to establish a universidad popular for women was presented to the administrative structure of the Florentino Ameghino in 1933. Difficulty obtaining the use of a public school created a delay, but the Universidad Popular Femenina de Palermo opened in 1935. Students took classes in embossing, hand weaving, dressmaking, embroidery, shorthand, bookkeeping, arithmetic, English, French, piano, and painting. There were annual variations in the offerings. The number of attendees grew rapidly from 205 in 1935 to 594 in 1939.[59] Like all the institutions connected with the Florentino Ameghino, the Palermo received generous subsidies from the national government. In 1938, for example, it gave the Palermo 10,000 pesos and the Florentino Ameghino 15,000 (only the university in La Boca received as much). The affiliated Universidad Popular de Villa Pueyrredón got 6,000 pesos. The first two universities obtained smaller but significant subsidies from the city.[60]

Two coed institutions were part of the network. The Universidad Popular de Villa Pueyrredón was founded in 1937 with the idea that "by taking care of the teaching of people, without distinction of age, inasmuch as there are students of 14 and others who are 35, without distinction of nationality since in our universidad popular are accepted equally Argentines as well as foreigners, without prejudices about religion or political beliefs, will be created men and women useful in the home and to the nation." The university had separate courses for men and women; the offerings were similar except for those stereotypically identified with one gender, such as dressmaking or telegraphy. Shorthand, typing, English, and bookkeeping could be taken by any student. The students were predominantly male, and the male student body grew quickly, while the number of females remained relatively unchanged. In 1939, out of 627 attendees, 74 percent were male, and over 90 percent were Argentinian-born. Its connections to the Florentino Ameghino ensured that it received a subvention just a year after its founding. It, like all institutions that received subsidies, had them slashed when the government had budget shortfalls. For example, in 1940 instead of obtaining the 6,000 pesos included in the original budget, it received 4,435.[61]

A similar organization, the Universidad Popular de Villa del Parque, was started in 1934 at the suggestion of Brugnara. It maintained some independence from the Florentino Ameghino but had Brugnara overseeing its day-to-day operations. By 1940 it had become part of the larger group, and as such was included in the free medical services mentioned earlier. In 1940 it had 508 students, and 89 percent were Argentine. The courses resembled those available in its sister institution, Villa Pueyrredón.[62]

Before it began to receive subsidies, Villa Parque's funds primarily came from membership dues. In mid-1935 it had 160 members who paid 2.50 pesos per month. In 1937 it obtained 3,000 pesos from the municipality and 4,000 from the nation. The support from the municipality came through the efforts of Enrique Vago, a city councilor sitting for the Antipersonalist Radicals, who regularly supported universidades populares. The national subvention had the support of Radical congressman Mario Sáenz, the chair of the appropriate committee in the lower house, who served on the university's honorary committee. The honorary committee contained a very impressive combination of Radical and Socialist politicians plus distinguished intellectuals. In addition, according to an article in the 1960s in the newsmagazine *Primera Plana*, Radical barrio boss Rómulo Vinciguerra helped found the popular university and used it to aid his operations. His headquarters was just down the street. Vinciguerra sat on the city council in the late 1930s and won election twice to Congress after the fall of Perón. In 1939 the university had a national subsidy that was supposed to be 10,000 pesos, but it suffered a 15 percent reduction like all similar institutions, and the following year the amount was reduced by another 15 percent. In 1940 its municipal subsidy had been lowered to 400 pesos. Not surprisingly it had severe financial problems.[63]

The most ambitious school in the consortium, the Universidad Popular Industrial de Buenos Aires, was founded in January 1938. It provided what many universidades populares had promised but could not do: training for the changing economy of the city. This made it like the university in La Boca. Its courses included motors, commercial art, electricity, bookbinding, carpentry, and industrial chemistry. The need for equipment made training for blue-collar jobs expensive plus the school rented a building for 600 pesos a month. It quickly received government support, despite starting with only 157 students. It reached 452 students in 1940.[64] It did not have much time before the 1943 coup to fulfill its promise.

The ability of the popular universities in the consortium to receive sizeable aid from the government, despite not having very large student bodies, indicates the importance of connections. However, it is impossible to judge the quality of the instruction offered compared to other institutions.

Conclusions

The universidades populares came about because individuals perceived a need for education beyond that provided by the public schools for those over fourteen. The universidades populares differed from other civic associations in that dues-payers received little or no benefit. Undoubtedly almost all members were economically comfortable. Still, universidades populares became an important part of barrio identity: centers of sociability for barrio inhabitants and sources of important services for their children. The universities became dependent on ties to politicians since they needed state aid. Unfortunately, the aid was inadequate, unreliable, and not distributed based strictly on need. The number of students had little to do with the size of government subventions, but it is impossible to know the quality of the courses.

The efforts by private citizens, even with the help of important politicians and other people of standing in the society, could not provide adequate education in technical skills. The institutions lacked the funding. Teacher salaries remained exceedingly small; the institutions were a supplemental source of income for most of them. Almost all the buildings housing the universidades populares were inadequate. Most popular universities operated in public elementary schools that were designed for the younger students. The rest rented buildings, which consumed a significant portion of their budgets, and those edifices were not necessarily suitable either. It was difficult to erect shops, and the universities could not afford expensive machines. Most of the training for males was for white-collar jobs and not for industrial employment nor for skilled manual labor. Women's classes taught clerical skills or the needle trades, which could also be transferred to the home.

The universidades populares did fill a void for those who had left school but wanted more education. The state's provision of vocational education remained inadequate, either in its own institutions or through aiding universidades populares. The institutions created by individuals, while critical, were insufficient. The popular universities did furnish an important opportunity for politicians to build ties to crucial local actors. The universidades populares comprised an important part of the web of barrio institutions that created a sense of neighborhood, while simultaneously becoming part of a clientelistic political system.

Conclusion

PORTEÑOS IN THE FIRST decades of the twentieth century built thousands of civic associations. In doing so, they created a crucial galaxy of institutions that bettered their lives, displaying great ingenuity, persistence, and dedication. Most of these associations were run democratically, and many fulfilled at least some of their founders' goals, providing recreational opportunities, maintaining libraries, offering educational opportunities, and improving neighborhoods. They gave porteños institutions that they could identify with and helped create and solidify a sense of barrio identity. What they achieved was limited by a lack of resources, however. The search for resources led civic associations to turn to politicians and other important individuals. Civic associations became key components of the political system as men searched for influence and votes. The need for political assistance shaped many civic associations, and they did not become schools for democracy.

At the beginning of the twentieth century, Argentina and the city of Buenos Aires were growing and relatively wealthy places. The rapid expansion of the city presented serious challenges for the inhabitants, but the increasing wealth of the society and the resourcefulness of its inhabitants gave hope that many problems could be overcome. However, the nature of the political system dimmed that prospect. The clientelistic relationship that politicians created with civic associations limited the organizations' ability to become fully independent and limited politicians' desires to create larger, more efficient government institutions or private ones with reliable sources of income. Politicians preferred systems in which their roles were visible. Civic associations were shaped by the society in which they were located.

The civic associations, besides attempting to carry out the primary reasons for which they were founded, became places of sociability. Many porteños' worlds revolved around the barrio-based organizations. People mingled in those facilities and shared activities. Those who ran the institutions spent a high percentage of their "leisure" time working for their civic associations. Members developed webs of acquaintances and friends from their relationship with the associations. Activities such as dances and celebrations were particularly important since these offered young men and women opportunities to intermingle in the respectable world of the civic associations, supposedly under the watchful eyes of their elders. Although the role of women in the civic associations was relatively limited, it grew over time, and women did play a vital role in organizing many of the social events. Their importance in holding the organizations together and in creating the sense of barrio should not be underestimated. For many porteños, civic associations became the center of their social life and were important to a barrio's identity. The institutions became "our" football team, "our" library, and so on.

But the civic associations did not act as schools for democracy in the sense meant by Robert Putnam. This should not be at all surprising. Civic associations are products of the society in which they are created, and the Buenos Aires of the first decades of the twentieth century was a society in which both politicians and civic associations needed things. The exchange was not equal, however, and in many senses, the clientelism that still exists in Argentina has been shaped by this period.

The ties that some politicians established to voters in the years prior to 1943, in part through civic associations, were often long-lasting. Some politicians who built their political career in such a fashion survived the political changes and the enlarged state that emerged under Perón. Politicians such as Elena, Vinciguerra, and Boffi won elections after the overthrow of Perón in 1955. They benefited from the banning of the Peronist party, but the connections that they had created still resonated with voters.[1] Clientelism remains critical in the politics of greater Buenos Aires, though it has altered with the passage of time.

The clientelism in greater Buenos Aires in the late twentieth century and early twenty-first has operated in a very different environment than in the 1920s and 1930s. Leaving aside the many technological changes, in the more recent period much larger structural impediments have existed to gaining meaningful employment, social mobility, and a relatively decent living environment. There has been for the poor a smaller sense of hope. Therefore, dependence on material aid from governments directed through politicians has become much larger. For the poor there have been fewer alternatives. However, the manner of mobilizing popular support bears some resemblance to earlier periods.

Civic associations have continued to play a crucial role in politics and in clientelist exchanges. For example, Steven Levitsky in his examination of the political machinery of the Peronist party in greater Buenos Aires in the 1990s says: "The Peronist organization consists of a vast collection of informal neighborhood-based networks that operate out of a range of different entities, including local clubs, cooperatives, soup kitchens." He also mentions that sociedades de fomento and football clubs play key roles. Similarly, Mariela Szwarcberg argues that local leaders often begin by helping people, frequently through civic associations, before moving into politics.[2]

Some authors argue that local political figures (brokers) do favors for communities or individuals without exerting pressure for votes or other quid pro quos, depending on goodwill and a sense of reciprocity. Other authors claim that politicians do pressure the beneficiaries of largess to vote correctly and to do political work. Some say that those "correct" votes are even monitored, although it is not totally clear how this would be done.[3] The development of these kinds of ties seems similar to what occurred in earlier eras. Politicians helped an organization achieve a goal or get a street paved, and a sense of reciprocity developed. Undoubtedly if the politicians believed that they did not receive their "due," they would not continue to provide services. Alternatively, the politicians could lose their positions and be unable to continue providing aid.

In the first decades of the twentieth century, porteños created a myriad of civic associations that functioned with at least the formal rules of democracy. The internal problems that they faced were not that different than those in other societies, though some reflected the tensions and antagonistic nature of Argentine politics. The country has not had an easy time achieving a functioning democratic system. The period from 1930 to 1983 was marked by military coups, which often came with a great deal of popular approval but then produced increasing levels of repression. Even the periods when the military did not govern were scarred by fundamental denials of a free political culture, since the dominant parties were frequently banned. Intervals of truly fair elections were rare. Even after the reemergence of democracy in 1983, the politics of Argentine democracy have been extremely difficult. The economy has suffered from periods of hyperinflation and deep economic turndowns that have matched or surpassed the Great Depression of the 1930s. Politics has been made more complex not only by a deep-seated clientelism but also by a political style that has left sharply etched divisions between parties, even when ideological differences have been relatively small.

Porteños have maintained many older civic associations and created new types of organizations in order to survive in an increasingly complex country. The older civic associations still play a sizeable role in the culture, especially the football clubs. They have in some cases become extremely large institutions. At the end of 2018, Boca Juniors claimed 206,078 members while River Plate had 151,435, Independiente had 83,428, Racing had 70,006, and San Lorenzo de Almagro had 61,108.[4] The scope of their social activities is at least as large as it was in the 1930s.[5] And politics is ever-present in their internal affairs.

The politicization of football clubs intensified in the Perón years. They received many benefits (stadiums, for example), but at the same time, like labor unions, they lost some of their autonomy. Like much else that changed during these years, the break with the past was not as sharp as many thought. The politicization also continued in subsequent years but not in a linear fashion.[6]

Influential figures have remained important. In 2012 Hugo Moyano, then head of one of the national labor confederations, indirectly controlled five football clubs, which played at different levels. Moyano's son-in-law Claudio Fabián Tapia became president of the football federation in 2017, and as of mid-2023 he still held the post. Macri's influence in Boca Juniors lingered even after the club had catapulted him into politics to first run the city of Buenos Aires and then the nation. His hegemony only ended after his failure to be reelected president of Argentina and the defeat of his candidate in the Boca elections. The Peronists who defeated Macri in the national election are also deeply involved with football: the president of San Lorenzo was appointed to a cabinet position.[7]

Politicians of almost all stripes attempted to use the popularity of the great football star Diego Maradona to enhance their own reputation, almost from the moment that he first demonstrated his great skills to the public. Upon his death in 2020, the national government attempted to use his popularity by scheduling a viewing of his body in the Casa Rosada (the seat of the government). The attempt backfired, and the event ended in great chaos.[8]

The economic position of football clubs is not good. In part this is due to the deteriorated economic situation of the country, but the problems are more complex. The clubs cannot compete with those in Europe and elsewhere for good players. The best Argentine footballers usually only play with local clubs when they are very young and just before they retire. Fans see the heroes of the national team only on television broadcasts of European games. The level of club football is not as good as it is at the best European clubs, which weakens local teams' appeal. An additional problem is that too many teams are based in greater Buenos Aires, making the competition for attendance and members fierce. Also, the opportunities for other types of diversion have increased, providing more competition for people's attention.

The emergence in the late 1950s of the so-called *barras bravas*, the violent organized bands of fans attached to football clubs, who are frequently involved in criminal activities of many sorts, has made the problems of the clubs even more complicated. These groups have ties to club factions, which makes it difficult to control them, and politicians use them for their own purposes. They have corrupted the internal workings of many clubs and have made attending games dangerous, forcing limitations on fan attendance.[9]

Despite the problems that the football clubs have had in recent decades, they command the love of many. Television has extended their bases nationwide, but some barrio loyalties remain quite strong, as with Boedo and San Lorenzo de Almagro. The football clubs remain centers of sociability, nodes of entertainment, and anchors of community just as they have been since early in their histories. Their roles may have shifted somewhat, but they have continued to help give people a sense of identity. Public figures are often identified by their support for a particular club. Even Pope Francis is identified with a team, San Lorenzo de Almagro.

The bibliotecas populares continue to exist, although their numbers are fewer than previously, and they still play a vital role, offering books and other forms of learning, since public libraries are in short supply. Anyone using a major research library in Buenos Aires has ample proof of that; for example, every afternoon the Biblioteca Nacional is full of students of high school age. There are more public libraries than before but clearly not enough. Nationwide in mid-2019, there were 1,270 CONABIP-recognized bibliotecas populares; there were 36 as of mid-2020 in the city of Buenos Aires.[10] This is despite the periodic waves of economic distress and the problems created by the military during the last dictatorship, which ran from 1976 to 1983.[11] A number of the libraries mentioned in this book have survived, among them Ciencia y Labor, Cornelio Saavedra, and the Alberdi in Villa Crespo.

Popular libraries still display what they did a century ago: the ability of the average Argentine to fill a need in their society through organizing and hard work. They still have the aid of the CONABIP, but like everything else that depends on government financing, its ability to help varies tremendously. Porteños continue to possess a tremendous desire to read. As of 2019 there were some 450 bookstores in the city; according to the Spanish newspaper *El País*, this gives Buenos Aires the distinction of having the most bookstores per capita in the world.[12] However, not everyone can buy books, and the hunger for them persists.

The role of sociedades de fomento, as both social institutions and organizations aimed at improving living conditions in neighborhoods, has been altered by changing societal and government structures. Although they have continued to be recognized by the city in a similar fashion to previously, they appear to have a much diminished role in the pushing for barrio improvements. These organizations have become increasingly barrio clubs with largely social functions, including sports. However, the fact that the government has continued to regulate them indicates that they do perform some of the basic lobbying activities that they did before.[13] They have been joined by political and informal organizations of many types that push for improvements in conditions.

The universidades populares became increasingly obsolete. The Peronist government rapidly expanded the school system with particular attention to vocational education, which made the universidades populares less necessary. The elite nature of the founders and of the mainstays of many universidades populares probably contributed to their weakening since many would have been anti-Peronist. Porteños' educational level continued to rise after the fall of Perón. Of the universidades populares that existed in the 1930s, only the Universidad Popular de La Boca appears to have continued to exist with its original mission intact, offering vocational classes. The Universidad Popular de Belgrano has survived as well, but it is focused on cultural activities.[14]

Other types of civic associations also continue in Buenos Aires, but like in many other parts of the world the joining of such organizations is less common than formerly. Still, porteños have created organizations and survival tactics to get them through the vicious economic crises of recent years. This is the same pattern as in the first years of the twentieth century. Inhabitants created civic associations that attempted to fulfill some of their desires for recreation, education, books to read, and basic urban amenities. In doing so they displayed skill and determination. Like any such organizations, they faced continual problems, and many survived only for a short time; others proved long-lasting and grew into crucial institutions. They provided barrios with a sense of identity by being points of pride but, more important, centers of sociability. People developed ties to their neighbors through them.

These institutions also became the focus of politicians, who could establish relationships with influential figures in the barrio and become one of "us" even when they were really not. The politicians aided the civic associations and in return received favorable publicity, and they hoped to get campaign aid or votes. These were symbiotic, if uneven, relationships since the civic associations needed the politicians to help fulfill their goals. Money was always short, and the state was frequently the only place to turn. Government aid was needed for other reasons as well, and politicians were crucial in obtaining it. The civic associations, while retaining a great deal of autonomy, became part of the political system. This should not be surprising since the system of clientelism was entrenched before 1912, and it continued. Civic associations are shaped by the society where they are created.

Notes

Introduction

1. Weitz-Shapiro, Curbing Clientelism in Argentina, 5n13.
2. Horowitz, *Argentina's Radical Party*; Horowitz, "Patrones y clientes."
3. Zarazaga, "Brokers beyond Clientelism," 29.
4. Tocqueville, *Democracy in America*; Putnam, *Bowling Alone*, esp. 19, 338–39, 345–46; Sabato, *The Many and the Few*, esp. 12.
5. Putnam, *Making Democracy Work*, esp. 10–11, 90–91, 183; Almond and Verba, *Civic Culture*, esp. 245. For the importance of civic culture in the democratic traditions of Latin America, see Sabato, *Republics of the New World*; Forment, *Democracy in Latin America*, vol. 1.
6. "¿Dónde anida la democracia?"; Sabato, *The Many and the Few*; Gutiérrez and Romero, *Sectores populares, cultura política*; Privitellio, *Vecinos y ciudadanos*.
7. See, for example, Riley, *Civic Foundations of Fascism in Europe*; Romero, "La política en los barrios"; Privitellio and Romero, "Organizaciones de la sociedad civil"; Di Stefano et al., *De las cofradías*.
8. Bermeo and Nord, *Civil Society before Democracy*.
9. Their success was partially due to Peronists being blocked from politics.
10. Given the nature of secondary sources and the difficulty of defining which organizations are civic associations, it is impossible to make a valid estimate about whether the density of such institutions in Argentina was greater than in other countries.
11. Torre, *Los años peronistas*; Ballent, *Las huellas de la política*.
12. Gravano, *Antropología de lo barrial*, 70.

Chapter One

1. Clemenceau, *South America Today*, 35.
2. Gorelik, *La grilla y el parque*; Gorelik, "El color del barrio," esp. 38–40; Prignano, *Barriología*, 51–52. For a different vision, see Landau, *Gobernar Buenos Aires*, 125–34.
3. See Horowitz, *Argentina's Radical Party*.
4. The literature is vast. For an excellent summary of the twentieth century, see Bellini and Korol, *Historia económica*, esp. 17. See also Hora, *Historia económica*; Cortés Conde, *Political Economy of Argentina*; Rocchi, *Chimneys in the Desert*.

5. Political parties in the 1930s frequently had to deal with internal scandals. For the impact on one type of civic association, see Horowitz, *Argentine Unions*, 151–79.
6. See Forment, *Democracy in Latin America*, for the idea of colonizing. For other cities, see *El Gráfico*, Aug. 17, 1935, 14–15; "Historia de C. A. Estudiantes," www.taringa.net/posts/deportes/6868259/Historia-deC_A_-Estudiantes.html; Ramírez, "Política y fútbol," 39–42; García, *El caso Vigil*, 25.
7. Bunge, *Una nueva Argentina*, 417–70, esp. 418.
8. Gutman and Hardoy, *Buenos Aires*, 124; Gorelik, *La grilla y el parque*, 279.
9. Korn, *Buenos Aires*, 153–86. Once is not a recognized barrio and lies within Balvanera.
10. Ferreres, *Dos siglos de economía argentina*, 136; Comisión Nacional del Censo, *Tercer censo nacional*, 3:3–12.
11. Halperín Donghi, "Una ciudad entra en el siglo XX," 64–65.
12. Scobie, *Buenos Aires*; Sargent, *Spatial Evolution*, 78; Torres, "Evolución de los procesos," 285–89.
13. *Revista Municipal*, Dec. 12, 1910, 14, as quoted in Rocchi, "Industria y metrópolis," 279. Barrio Norte is not a legally recognized barrio and lies within the current boundaries of Recoleta and Retiro.
14. Gutman and Hardoy, *Buenos Aires*, 341, 345; Bourdé, *Buenos Aires*, 109.
15. Francos Rodríguez, *Huellas españolas*, 257.
16. Armus, "La idea del verde," esp. 16–19; Armus, *Ailing City*, esp. 333.
17. Comisión Nacional del Censo, *Tercer censo nacional*, 2:109.
18. Ferreres, *Dos siglos de economía Argentina*, 133–34. For a good overview of immigration, see Devoto, *Historia de la inmigración*.
19. Germani, *Estructura social*, 75; Mora y Araujo and Llorente, *El voto peronista*.
20. Recchini de Lattes, "La populación," 232; Armus, *Ailing City*.
21. García Heras, *Transportes, negocios y política*, 80; *Revista de Estadística Municipal*, July–Sept. 1939, 252–53, 301; Sargent, *Spatial Evolution*, 69–71.
22. The nature of class in interwar Buenos Aires is highly controversial and is not addressed here. For different views, see Gutiérrez and Romero, *Sectores populares, cultura política*, esp. 9–20; Iñigo Carrera, *La estrategia*, esp. 13–40; Adamovsky, *Historia de la clase media argentina*.
23. Gerchunoff, *El eslabón perdido*; Hora, "Izquierda y clases populares"; Pastoriza and Torre, *Mar del Plata*.
24. Bard, *Estampas de una vida*.
25. Silvestre, *Como se llega*.
26. Gorelik, *La grilla y el parque*, esp. 273–306. For a discussion of the social science literature on barrios, see Gravano, *El barrio en la teoría social*. Jablonsky, *Pride in the Jungle*, esp. xv, argues that in Chicago a civic association helped establish a sense of neighborhood identity.
27. The official nomenclature leaves out several barrios that everybody knows. Other barrios that did not receive legal recognition are largely forgotten.
28. Horowitz, "Football Clubs and Neighbourhoods," 566–67; Scobie, *Buenos Aires*, esp. 160–207.

29. Aiscurri, *La tribu de mi calle*, 31; Prignano, *Barriología*, 54; Vargas Llosa, *Fish in the Water*, 60–64.
30. Privitellio, "Inventar el barrio"; *La Nación*, June 30, 2019.
31. Agulhon, *Le cercle dans la France bourgeoise*; Agulhon, "La sociabilidad como categoría histórica"; Gayol, *Sociabilidad en Buenos Aires*; Bruno, *Sociabilidades y vida cultural*; Calhoun, *Habermas and the Public Sphere*.
32. Gayol, *Sociabilidad en Buenos Aires*, esp. 13. For an overview of cafés in Buenos Aires, see Bossio, *Los cafés de Buenos Aires*; Banchik, *Buenos Aires, los cafés*; Armus, "'Milonguitas' en Buenos Aires."
33. Ferrera, "Vivir en Soldati," 126.
34. Hora, *Landowners of the Argentine Pampas*; Sabato, *The Many and the Few*; Botana, *El orden conservador*; Alonso, *Between Revolution and the Ballot Box*; Alonso, *Jardines secretos, legitimaciones públicas*; Bonaudo, *Liberalismo*; Lobato, *El progreso*.
35. See Horowitz, *Argentina's Radical Party*.
36. Falcón, *Democracia*; Horowitz, *Argentina's Radical Party*; Halperín Donghi, *Vida y muerte*.
37. Cattaruzza, *Crisis económica*; Halperín Donghi, *La república imposible*; Halperín Donghi, *La Argentina*.
38. Walter, *Politics and Urban Growth*, 60.
39. In the 1930 congressional elections in the city of Buenos Aires, for example, Yrigoyen's branch of the Radical Party did badly. In the rest of the country it performed respectably, but the results were pictured as a defeat for the Radicals.
40. Horowitz, "Patrones y clientes."
41. Gorelik, *La grilla y el parque*, 127. See also Gorelik, "Ensayo introductorio," 30.
42. Walter, *Province of Buenos Aires*.
43. Avellaneda, *Boletín Municipal*, Jan. 1920, 11.
44. Raga, "Workers, Neighbors and Citizens," esp. 249–50. See also Cisneros, *Historia*; Fernández Hirsuta, "Alberto Barceló"; Vicente, *La Avellaneda de Barceló*; Folino, *Barceló*; Pignatelli, *Ruggierito*; *El Gráfico*, July 6, 1935, 10–11, 28.

Chapter Two

1. Horowitz, *Argentina's Radical Party*; Privitellio, *Vecinos y ciudadanos*; Sabato, *The Many and the Few*; Alonso, *Between Revolution and the Ballot Box*. In "¿Qué reforma la reforma?" Privitellio questions the use of 1912 as a major breaking point.
2. Lever, *Soccer Madness*, 57; Brennan and Rougier, *Politics of National Capitalism*, 112.
3. Caimari, *While the City Sleeps*, esp. 10–19, 161–90; photographs of parts of issues of *Magazine Policial* between 1925 and 1937 provided by Caimari plus conversations with her in the fall of 2018. See also Salvatore, *Wandering Paysanos*; Caimari, *Apenas un delincuente*; Horowitz, *Argentina's Radical Party*; Rodríguez, *Historia de la policía*.
4. Walter, *Socialist Party of Argentina*, esp. 59–60; Rock, "Machine Politics"; Horowitz, *Argentina's Radical Party*.

5. See, for example, Valdez, "Algunas hipótesis," 47–50.
6. Horowitz, *Argentina's Radical Party*, esp. 70–71; Viguera, "Participación electoral"; Valdez, "Algunas hipótesis"; Valdez, "Prácticas electorales." For a Radical campaign, see *La Época*, March 12–22, 1919. See *La Prensa* during any electoral season for other parties.
7. Small, *Unanticipated Gains*, 6. Political scientists use the term somewhat differently.
8. Horowitz, *Argentina's Radical Party*, 65–94; Sabato, *The Many and the Few*; Alonso, *Between Revolution and the Ballot Box*; Yablon, "Patronage and Party System."
9. Municipalidad de la Ciudad de Buenos Aires, *Censo de personal administrativo*, 21.
10. Horowitz, *Argentina's Radical Party*, 77.
11. Ibid., 65–94; Horowitz, "Patrones y clientes."
12. See, for example, Sikkink, "Las capacidades y la autonomía," esp. 549–50.
13. *Acción Comunal*, Apr. 1937, Aug. 1939; "Su historia," Aquí Mataderos: Revista Social, Cultural y Deportiva de Mataderos, http://r-aquimataderos.com.ar/nueva_chicago_1911.htm, 8/8/14.
14. Horowitz, "Patrones y clientes."
15. *Crítica*, Oct. 19, 1922. For other examples, see Oct. 10 and Nov. 1, 1922.
16. *La Vanguardia*, May 23, 1914, May 4, 1938; Vecchio, *Mataderos*, esp. 58, 149, 177, 190–201; Biblioteca y Asociación Vecinal de Nueva Chicago, *Memoria, 1933–1934*; *Magazine Avellaneda*, Aug. 1934, July 1935; "Su historia," Aquí Mataderos; Cecchi, *Sinopsis histórica*, 1:158, 160, 256–57, 271, 277, 2:197, 199, 330, 338, 350–51; "Sitios de interés cultural: Bar 'Oviedo,'" www.bibleduc.gov.ar/areas/cultura/cpphc/sitios/detalle.php?id=102, 2/16/07, "Don Fernando Ghio," Foro de la Memoria de Mataderos, Feb. 4, 2008, www.forommataderos.blogspot.com/2008/02/don-fernando-ghio.html; Cutolo, *Historia de los barrios*, 1:522; Privitellio, *Vecinos y ciudadanos*, 235.
17. Bucich, *La Boca*, 342; "Dirigentes radicales de La Boca: Reinaldo Elena (1899–1987)," www.laboca.radicales.org.ar/reinaldoelena.htm, 12/23/11; Horowitz, *Argentina's Radical Party*, 76–77; Archivo General de la Nación, Fondo Agustín P. Justo, caja 141bis, sala 7, 3324, n.d., documento 159 E, Reinaldo Elena to General Justo, and documento 160, Reinaldo Elena to Sr. Presidente; "Intereses del magisterio," 1927, http://repositorio.educacion.gov.ar/dspace/handle/123456789/108182.
18. *La República*, Apr. 3–4, 1938; *La Razón*, Apr. 2, 1938.
19. *La República*, Feb. 10, 1938; *La Libertad* (Avellaneda), Mar. 8, 1936; Privitellio, *Vecinos y ciudadanos*, 137; *Última Hora*, Dec. 16, 1925, Dec. 28, 1927; Asociación Amateurs de Football, *Memoria, 1925*, 71; Asociación Amateurs de Football, *Memoria, 1926*; "Club Atlético Boca Alumni," https://it.wikipedia.org/wiki/Club_Atl%C3%A9tico_Boca_Alumni; "Algo más que fútbol... Desde el barrio (Boca Alumni 1922)," http://carolsaira.blogspot.com/2011/04/desde-el-barrio-boca-alumni-1922.html, 12/23/11; Concejo Deliberante de la Municipalidad de Buenos Aires, *Actas*, Dec. 5, 1933, 2085–86, Dec. 24, 1933, 4263–65, July 11, 1939, 186–93, Dec. 27, 1939, 3998–99; *La Vanguardia*, Dec. 12, 1934, Dec. 16, 1937; *Primera Plana*, Mar. 16, 1965, 11; *La Prensa*, Jan. 12, 1936.
20. Francavilla, *Historia de Villa Crespo*, 52, 64, 69–70, 102–3, 111–12; Del Pino, *El barrio de Villa Crespo*, 76–77; Del Pino, "Un buen caudillo"; Universidad Popular

Florentino Ameghino, *La Universidad Popular Florentino Ameghino en su XV aniversario*, 6, 9, 15; Library of the Instituto Ravignani, Colección Emilio Ravignani, ARV 37, no. 38, 54; Patrimonio Legislativo, Asociación de Fomento Defensa Vecinal a la Cámara de Diputados, Sept. 4, 1938, 1760-p-1938; *Fomento y Cultura*, Feb. 1, 1926; Concejo Deliberante de la Municipalidad de Buenos Aires, *Actas*, Apr. 15, 1921, 278–79, Nov. 17, 1921, 2403; "Remigio Iriondo," es.wikipedia.org/wiki/Remegio_Iriondo; "Barrio Villa Crespo: Habitantes notables," http://www.geocities.ws/rodr-305/historia/Prestigiosos/PRESTIGIOSOS.html.

21. Boffi, *1259 días*, 11–26; Archivo General de la Nación, Fondo Agustín P. Justo, caja 73, Municipalidad de la Ciudad de Buenos Aires, 1930–1938, sala 7, 3255, nos. 75–79.

22. Concejo Deliberante de la Municipalidad de Buenos Aires, *Actas*, Dec. 5, 1939, 3325; "El ciclón se sigue ampliando," Oct. 16, 2008, http://debatecuervo.blogspot.com/2008_10_01_archive.html, 10/13/12.

23. Boffi, *1259 días*, 29; Patrimonio Legislativo, Universidad Popular Bernardino Rivadavia a la Cámara de Diputados, June 19, 1940, 348-p-1940.

24. Unlike the records of most football clubs, the official list of Almagro's presidents is incorrect. Ortiz de Zárate is listed as president between 1919 and 1927. Contemporary sources had others as president in some years and had him as president again in the 1930s and 1940s. Club Almagro, "6 de enero de 1911: Historia en tres colores," http://www.elsitiodealmagro.com.ar/6deenero1911/, 7/22/20; *Crítica*, July 26, 1919, Dec. 23, 1920, Apr. 19, 1922; *La Opinión* (Avellaneda), Feb. 4, 1939; *La Vanguardia*, Feb. 23, 1942.

25. Club Almagro, "Historia en tres colores," www.calmagro.com.ar/historia.htm, 7/22/20; *Crítica*, Nov. 14, 1919.

26. Club Almagro," http://es.wikipedia.org/wiki/Club_Almagro; "Cuando Almagro estuvo en Parque Chas," www.parquechasweb.com.ar/parquechas/notas/Nota_almagroch.htm; *La Época*, Aug. 30, 1920; *La Opinión*, Jan. 25, 1936; *La Prensa*, Nov. 3, 1924; *La Hora*, May 9, 1940; *Crítica*, Nov. 21, 1920; Iwanczuk, *Historia de fútbol amateur*, 243; Scher and Palomino, "Fútbol," 106, 224; *Noticias*, Aug. 27, 1974, 15.

27. Concejo Deliberante de la Municipalidad de Buenos Aires, *Actas*, Dec. 29, 1920, 1287, Apr. 12, 1921, 267, May 10, 1921, 585, May 13, 1921, 644–48, Nov. 17, 1921, 2438–39; Cámara de Diputados, *Diario de sesiones*, Sept. 13, 1929, 3:445–46.

28. Club Almagro, "Historia en tres colores," www.calmagro.com.ar/historia.htm, 7/22/20.

Chapter Three

1. See, for example, *Clarín*, Nov. 16, 2012, Nov. 15, 2013, June 30 and Dec. 13, 2019; *Perfil*, June 28, 2019; *El País* (Madrid), July 2, 2019.

2. In the twenty-first century, Buenos Aires still has seventy-nine stadiums where professional football is played. Gaffney, *Temples of the Earthbound Gods*, 131.

3. *Caras y Caretas*, Mar. 9, 1935, 90.

4. See, for example, Frydenberg, *Historia social del fútbol*; Frydenberg, "Espacio urbano y práctica"; Iwanczuk, *Historia de fútbol amateur*; Lorenzo, *Historia del fútbol argentino*.
5. Hora, *Historia del turf argentino*, esp. 10–14, 201–5, 225–29.
6. Scher and Palomino, *Fútbol*, 237–39.
7. Armus, "Contextualizando la enfermedad"; Armus and Scharagrodsky, "El fútbol en las escuelas y colegios argentinos"; Archetti, *Masculinities*.
8. River Plate, *Revista Gráfica e Informativa*, Sept. 1930, 18–26, Jan. 1931, 27–31; Club Atlético River Plate, *Memoria, 1930–1931*, 55.
9. More than 350 barrio clubs were forced to close at least temporarily by the coronavirus disaster of 2020. *Clarín*, Apr. 8, 2020. For a historical overview, see, for example, Prignano, "Seis clubes de fútbol," 26–36; Frydenberg, *Historia social del fútbol*, 154–59.
10. Frydenberg, "Espacio urbana y práctica"; Frydenberg, "Redefinición del fútbol," 51.
11. "El último patriarca bohemio," *Sentimiento Bohemio* 4:10 (July 8, 2003), https://sentimientobohemio.wordpress.com/2018/05/26/el-ultimo-patriarca-bohemio. See also Club Atlético Atlanta, "Historia del club," www.atlantapasion.com.ar/historia.php, 1/12/07.
12. For the founding of clubs, see Fabbri, *El nacimiento de una pasión*. See also Rosatti, *Cien años de multitud*, 1:41–47; *El Gráfico*, Jan. 19, 1935, 21.
13. *Última Hora*, Dec. 17, 1935; Ventieri, *Historia del Club Atlético Temperley*, 28, 39, 43.
14. Scher and Palomino, *Fútbol*, 46, 49.
15. Camarero, *A la conquista obrera*, 241–53; Mateu, "Política e ideología," 67; Barrancos, *Educación, cultura y trabajadores*, 115–17; *La Internacional*, Nov. 7, 1924, June 21, 1925, July 9, 1926; *La Vanguardia*, Aug. 24, 1930.
16. Elsey, *Citizens and Sportsmen*; Archetti, *Masculinities*, 121–22.
17. Morales, *Fútbol, identidad y poder*.
18. Frydenberg, "Los nombres de los clubes"; Gaffney, *Temples of the Earthbound Gods*, esp. 62–64; Bocketti, "Italian Immigrants, Brazilian Football"; Panfichi and Theroldt, "Identity and Rivalry," 143–49; Elsey, *Citizens and Sportsmen*; Reyna, *Cuando éramos footballers*.
19. Frydenberg, "Redefinición del fútbol," 52; Iwanczuk, *Historia de fútbol amateur*, esp. 206, 224–26; *La Vanguardia*, Feb. 22, 1929; Asociación del Fútbol Argentino, *Memoria, 1942*, 116.
20. Elsey, *Citizens and Sportsmen*; Stein, "Case of Soccer."
21. Rein, *Los bohemios de Villa Crespo*, 12. For identification between barrio and football clubs, see Archetti, *Masculinities*, esp. 6, 121; Frydenberg, *Historia social del fútbol*, esp. 126–29, 255–58.
22. Frydenberg, "Espacio urbano y práctica."
23. Gálvez, "El tango en su época de gloria"; Saítta, *Recuerdos de tinta*, 151.
24. "Reinauguración de la sede social," *Sentimiento Bohemio* 7:193 (May 21, 2007), http://guia-collado.com.ar/pages-39106.html, 12/1/07; "15 años después,"

Sentimiento Bohemio 7.175 (Jan. 6, 2007), https://sentimientobohemio.wordpress.com/2017/02/22/15-anos-despues/; Club Atlético Atlanta, "Historia del club"; Rein, *Los bohemios de Villa Crespo*, 116.
25. Club Atlético Chacarita Juniors, *Memoria, 1930*, 10; Club Atlético Chacarita Juniors, *Memoria, 1936*, 15; Club Atlético Chacarita Juniors, *Memoria, 1940; C. A. Chacarita Juniors: Órgano Oficial de la Institución* 2:5–9, Apr. 1943, 21–22.
26. *La Nación*, Dec. 16, 1934; Club Atlético Chacarita Juniors, *Memoria, 1930*; Club Atlético Estudiantes de La Plata, *Memoria, 1928–1930*, 15.
27. Boca Juniors Social y Deportivo, Aug. 1935, 7, 32; *Boca . . . !*, Dec. 12–26, 1942.
28. Elsey and Nadel, *Futbolera*, esp. 17–60; Club Atlético River Plate, *Memoria, 1932*.
29. Club Atlético Chacarita Juniors, *Memoria, 1941*, 14; Club Atlético Lanús, *Memoria, 1931*; *La Libertad*, Mar. 25–28, 1936; *La Hora*, Nov. 13, Dec. 23 and 30, 1941.
30. River Plate, *Revista Gráfica e Informativa*, Sept. 1930, 18–26; Jan. 1931, 27–31; Club Atlético River Plate, *Memoria, 1922*; Club Atlético River Plate, *Memoria, 1925*, 3; Club Atlético River Plate, *Memoria, 1927*, 12; Club Atlético River Plate, *Memoria, 1930*, 42–43; Club Atlético River Plate, *Memoria, 1931*, 51–55; *La Vanguardia*, Nov. 11, 1936, Feb. 19, 1939; *La Libertad*, Jan. 4, 1936.
31. Club Atlético Lanús, *Memoria, 1931*, 23; Club Atlético Lanús, *Memoria, 1937*, 12; Club Atlético Lanús, *Memoria, 1942*.
32. *La Opinión*, Dec. 12, 1935; Club Atlético Estudiantes de La Plata, *Memoria, 1928–1930*, 8; Club Atlético Estudiantes de La Plata, *Memoria, 1937–1938*, 16; Club Atlético Estudiantes de La Plata, *Memoria, 1940–1942*.
33. "El fútbol," www.eldiariodeltango.com/especiales/El%20Futbol.htm, 1/24/07; "San Lorenzo," https://sanlorenzoyeltangoayerhoyysiempre.bandcamp.com/track/san-lorenzo-2; Ziperstein, *Tango y fútbol*, esp. 81–88.
34. *El Gráfico*, Jan. 8, 1927, 16, Mar. 6, 1937, 18–20; *Última Hora*, Dec. 4 and 6, 1935; *El Mundo*, Dec. 28, 1935; Rosatti, *Cien años de multitud*, 2:22.
35. Panzeri, *Burguesía y gangsterismo*, 187.
36. Verbitsky, "Grandeza y decadencia," esp. 77, 80.
37. "Historia de Defensores de Belgrano-Taringa!" www.taringa.net/posts/deportes/10076959/Historia-de-Defensores-de-Belgrano.html; *Crítica*, Aug. 28, 1923; Cutolo, *Historia de los barrios*, 1:185.
38. Frydenberg, *Historia social del fútbol*, 120; *La Vanguardia*, Apr. 5, 1916; *Crítica*, May 6, 1922; *El Gráfico*, Nov. 17, 1928, 12, Jan. 4, 1930, 19, June 6, 1931, 40, Sept. 22, 1934, 22, 38; Scher and Palomino, *Fútbol*, 215. For where players worked, see *El Gráfico*, Nov. 3, 1928, 8.
39. *Crítica*, Jan. 24, May 11–June 12, Nov. 26, 1922; *Fomento y Cultura*, Dec. 1926, 2; *El Gráfico*, July 19, 1924, 28, Jan. 8, 1927, 16, 32, Jan. 27, 1927, 42; "Historia de Boca Juniors," www.informexeneize.com.ar/historia_1.htm, 1/29/07; Barovero, *Caudillos y protagonistas*, 34. Another important figure in the club, Francisco Galli, was the lieutenant of the dominant Radical Party member in the barrio, Nicolás Selén.
40. Scher, *La patria deportista*, 127–34; Fraga, *El general Justo*, 157; Archivo General

de la Nación, Fondo Agustín P. Justo, caja 34, file B, no. 211, Ruperto Molfino to Justo, June 27, 1932; *La República*, Feb. 6, 1938; *El Gráfico*, Feb. 2, 1938, 38–39; "Historia de Boca Juniors," www.informexeneize.com.ar/historia_1.htm, 1/29/07; *Boca . . . !*, Dec. 5, 1942, 10.

41. Asociación del Fútbol Argentino, "Registro de instituciones afiliados," 21; Club Atlético Vélez Sarsfield, *Memoria, 1940*, 10–17; *Clarín*, Mar. 3, 1998; Cutolo, *Historia de los barrios*, 1:508; Comisión de Asuntos Históricos, Club Atlético Vélez Sarsfield, *La historia*, 16–143; Rao, "José Amalfitani," esp. 20–23; "Autoridades de Vélez Sarsfield," https://velez.com.ar/club/autoridades; Departamento Nacional del Trabajo, División de Estadística, *Investigaciones sociales 1938*, 19.
42. Asociación Atlética Argentinos Juniors, "Historia," http://www.argentinosjuniors.com.ar/club/historia/historia/1920-1940, 8/8/14.
43. "Presidentes de Talleres: Francisco Agnelli," http://talleresdeescalada.blogspot.com/2015/08presidentes-de talleres-francisco.html; Gruschetsky, "Fútbol y clubes"; Chiti and Agnelli, *Cincuentenario*.
44. Frydenberg, "Espacio urbano y práctica"; *El Gráfico*, Dec. 15, 1937, 3–6, 50–51; "Historia de Boca Juniors," www.informexeneize.com.ar/historia_1.htm.
45. Scher and Palomino, *Fútbol*, 20.
46. *El Gráfico*, Feb. 2, 1935, 22; Semanario Quemero, "Historia 1 and 2," www.semanarioquemero.com.ar/historia, 8/29/08; Newton, *Historia del Club Atlético Huracán*, 28.
47. Concejo Deliberante de la Municipalidad de Buenos Aires, *Actas*, Nov. 30, 1934, 3157; Sirvent, *Cultura popular*, esp. 19–49, 89, 289–90; Vecchio, *Mataderos*, esp. 74, 282–83, 299–300, 334–35; Vecchio, *Aquí entre nosotros*, 64–65, 202–5; Lentini, *Crónica de un milagro*, 8; "Historia del Club Atlético Nueva Chicago," www.chicagopassion.com.ar/historia.htm, 2/17/09; "Su historia," Aquí Mataderos: Revista Social, Cultural y Deportiva de Mataderos, http://r-aquimataderos.com.ar/nueva_chicago_1911.htm, 8/8/14; Cutolo, *Historia de los barrios*, 1:541; "Pueblo de Nueva Chicago: Presentación," www.pueblodechicago.com.ar/presentacion.htm, 2/13/10.
48. "Historia del Club Atlético Nueva Chicago"; "Historia barrial," Aquí Mataderos, www.r-aquimataderos.com.ar/historia_barrial1911.htm, 1/9/07; Romero, "La política en los barrios," 38–39; Concejo Deliberante de la Municipalidad de Buenos Aires, *Actas*, Nov. 30, 1934, 3156–57.
49. Vecchio, *Mataderos*, 203, 303, 335.
50. Ibid., 104, 207; the dates of these events have not been recorded. Advertisements for the pharmacy were frequent; see, for example, *Acción Comunal*, June 1937, 1–3, Apr. 1938, 10, June 1938, inside cover; *Liniers*, Apr.–June 1941, 8–9.
51. "Historia barrial," Aquí Mataderos, www.r-aquimataderos.com.ar/historia_barrial_1931.htm, 1/25/11; "Historia del Club Atlético Nueva Chicago," www.chicagopassion.com.ar/historia.htm, 2/17/09; Vecchio, *Mataderos*, 303; Concejo Deliberante de la Municipalidad de Buenos Aires, *Actas*, Oct. 15, 1940, 1842; "Mercado de hacienda de Liniers," http://www.mercadodeliniers.com.ar/dll/institucional1.dll/insthist00001.

52. "La conquista de avenida La Plata," http://gloriosociclon.ar.tripod.com/metro. htm, 2/7/07; Lorenzo, *Historia del fútbol argentino*, 1:245–47; Deán, *San Lorenzo querido*, 11–30; Ana di Cesare and Gerónimo Rombolá, "Para futuras memorias— Lorenzo Massa," May 7, 2009, www.parafuturasmemorias.blogspot.com/2009/05/lorenzo.massa.html.
53. Bernal, "Pedro Bidegain"; Bidegain, *Mi radicalismo*; "Pedro Bidegain: 'El propulsor de la grandeza azulgrana,'" http://simplementesanlorenzoweb.blogspot.com/2012/11/pedro-bidegain-el-propulsor-de-la.html; *Crítica*, Aug. 28, 1923; *El Gráfico*, Jan. 12, 1935, 21–22.
54. *Almagro*, Apr. 20, 1935; Rodríguez, "Club Social Mariano Boedo"; Llanes, *El barrio de Almagro*, 79–86; Anexo: Presidentes del Club Atlético San Lorenzo de Almagro," https://sanlorenzo.fandom.com/es/wiki/Anexo:Presidentes_del_Club_Atl%C3%A9tico_San_Lorenzo_de_Almagro.
55. Aníbal Lomba, "Los cafés de Boedo," in Banchik, *Buenos Aires, los cafés*, 1:226–30; *La Nación*, Aug. 7, 1933; *Caras y Caretas*, June 19, 1937, 130–32; Daskal, *Los clubes*, 100; "Restitución histórica para el Club Atlético San Lorenzo de Almagro," www.somoscuervos.com.ar/wiki/ley_de_restitucion_historica_-_volver_a_boedo, 6/6/14.
56. *Última Hora*, Dec. 22, 1928–Feb. 4, 1929, esp. Jan. 24, 1929; *La Internacional*, Nov. 22, 1924; *La Vanguardia*, Apr. 27, 1926, Jan. 23–Feb. 4, 1929; *Crítica*, Jan. 24 and Feb. 3–4, 1929; *La Nación*, Jan. 27 and Feb. 4, 1929; *La Prensa*, Jan. 28–Feb. 4, 1929 ; *La Razón*, Jan. 15–Feb. 5, 1929; *El Gráfico*, Aug. 11–18, 1928, Jan. 12–19, 1929.
57. Concejo Deliberante de la Municipalidad de Buenos Aires, *Actas*, Jan. 1, 1929, 7; *El Gráfico*, Mar. 2, 1929, 14, Nov. 7, 1929, 9; *La Prensa*, Feb. 1, 1926; *La Vanguardia*, Jan. 20, 1930; *Crítica*, Jan. 24, 1922; Club Atlético San Lorenzo de Almagro, *Memoria*, 1924–1930; Bernal, "Pedro Bidegain," 94–99; Iwanczuk, *Historia de fútbol amateur*, 243.
58. *El Gráfico*, Feb. 7, 1931, 42, Mar. 7–21, 1931; *La Vanguardia*, Dec. 30, 1930, Jan. 23–27, 1931, Jan. 29 and Feb. 3, 1932.
59. "El ciclón se sigue ampliado," Oct. 16, 2008, http://debatecuervo.blogspot.com/2008_10_01_archive.html.
60. Fabbri, *El nacimiento de una pasión*, 88–90; Folino, *Barceló*, 96–97; Luís Paso Viola, "Como era la ciudad de Buenos Aires y su entorno en los albores del siglo XX," Jan. 2, 2004, www.culteducaavellaneda.com.ar/noticias/wmview.php?ArtID=66, 2/15/10; "Racing Club," www.rsssf.com/tablesr/racingclub.html.
61. Racing Club, "Historia," www.racingclub.com/historia.php, 6/6/09; Fabbri, *El nacimiento de una pasión*, 98–99.
62. Cascante, *Barracas al sud*, 154; Frydenberg, *Historia social del fútbol*, 191; Cisneros, *Historia*, 137; Walter, *Province of Buenos Aires*, 42–48.
63. Archetti, *Masculinities*, 54–61; Racing Club, "Historia," www.racingclub.com/historia.php; Asociación Amateurs de Football, *Memoria, 1926*; Asociación de Football Argentino, *Memoria, 1934*, 130; Asociación del Fútbol Argentino, "Registro de instituciones afiliados," 3, 11; *El Gráfico*, Apr. 11, 1931, 31; *La Opinión*, Dec. 1 and 20, 1935.

64. *La Opinión*, May 23, 1931, Jan. 12, 20, and 25, Feb. 3, Apr. 11 and 29, Nov. 19 and 22, and Dec. 15, 1933, Jan. 25, 1934, Nov. 23, 1935, Sept. 3 and Oct. 29, 1938; *La Hora*, Aug. 2, 1940, Nov. 14 and Dec. 19, 1941; *La Libertad*, Mar. 15, 1936; *Magazine Avellaneda*, Dec. 1934, Feb. 1935, Feb. 1936; Cascante, *Barracas al sud*, 128–32.
65. Folino, *Barceló*, 73–74, 193n3; Juan Corradi, pers. comm., 4/21/07.
66. Folino, *Barceló*, 98. How this information was gathered is unclear.
67. Cisneros, *Historia*, 133, 177–78; Folino, *Barceló*, 57; *Quién es quién en la Argentina*, 2nd ed., 312; Abad de Santillán, *Gran enciclopedia Argentina*, 3:629; *La Opinión*, Jan. 4, 1934.
68. Cisneros, *Historia*, 189.
69. *La Opinión*, July 29, Aug, 16–17 and 21, and Dec. 30, 1932, Jan. 1 and Mar. 24, 1933, Sept. 3 and 25, 1937; *La Vanguardia*, Jan. 12 and 18, and Dec. 24, 1932, Nov. 26, 1933, Dec. 5, 1934; Scher and Palomino, *Fútbol*, 216.
70. *La Opinión*, Jan. 1, 1934; *La Vanguardia*, May 30 and Dec. 16 and 31, 1934.
71. *Última Hora*, Nov. 20–Dec. 29, 1935; *La Opinión*, Nov. 25–Dec. 29, 1935; *El Mundo*, Dec. 28–29, 1935; *La Vanguardia*, Nov. 30–Dec. 30, 1935; *La Libertad*, Jan. 4, 1936. For Della Latta, see La Ciudad de Avellaneda, "Anuarios, año 1964, política," http://anuarioslaciudadavellaneda.blogspot.com/2009/08/ano-1964.html.
72. *La Opinión*, Jan. 11 and 16, 1936, Sept. 29, Oct. 7 and 8, Nov. 4 and 5, Dec. 2–31, 1937; *Última Hora*, Dec. 15–27, 1936; *La Libertad*, Oct. 30–Dec. 27, 1936; *La Prensa*, Dec. 28, 1936; *Caras y Caretas*, Oct. 10, 1937, 10; *La Razón*, Dec. 4–31, 1937; *La República*, Dec. 3, 1938.
73. *La Opinión*, Sept. 3, 1937.
74. *La Razón*, Jan. 12 and May 7–8, 1938; *La Opinión*, May 7–19, Sept. 21 and 25, Oct. 27, Nov. 2–6 and 24, Dec. 3–31, 1938; *La Vanguardia*, Dec. 9, 1938–Jan. 3, 1939; *La República*, Jan. 26, Apr. 2, and May 5–31, 1938; *La Prensa*, Dec. 25, 1938.
75. *El Gráfico*, Mar. 3, 1928, 38, Mar. 10, 1928, 16–17.
76. *La Opinión*, Sept. 7, 1932, Sept. 22, 1933, Nov. 26 and 29, 1935, Sept. 15 and Dec. 10, 1937; *La Libertad*, Nov. 8 and Dec. 7, 1929, Dec. 30, 1930, Jan. 30 and Mar. 18, 1931, Jan. 31, Feb. 3–5, and 21, Nov., and Dec. 25 and 27, 1936; *La Vanguardia*, Jan. 31, 1936; *La Prensa*, Dec. 23–24, 1936; *Magazine Avellaneda*, Feb. 1936; Cascante, *Barracas al sud*, 128–32; Daskal, *Los clubes*, 102–3.
77. "Listado de presidentes de Independiente hasta hoy," https://www.taringa.net/+deportes/listado-de-presidentes-de-independiente-hasta-hoy_11nlf6; Cisneros, *Historia*, 127, 134, 138, 257; Rudi Varela, "¿Qué periódicos leía la gente de Avellaneda y Lanús? 1822–1994," *La Ciudad*, June 7, 2006, www.laciudadavellaneda.com.ar, 4/8/09; Scher and Palomino, *Fútbol*, 220; *La Libertad*, Dec. 13, 1929, Mar. 9, 1931; *Última Hora*, Dec. 16, 1927; *El Gráfico*, Jan. 12, 1935, 30; Asociación del Football Argentino, *Memoria, 1934*, 63.
78. *La Libertad*, Nov. and Dec. 1930, Sept. 24, 25, and Nov. 26–Dec. 7, 1936; *La Prensa*, Dec. 17, 1931, Dec. 20, 1932, Dec. 23, 1938; *La Opinión*, Apr. 6, Nov., and Dec. 1933, Jan. 1, 1934, Dec. 1935, Oct. 31–Dec. 27, 1937, Dec. 8–27, 1938; *La Vanguardia*, Dec. 1934, Dec. 31, 1939, Jan. 1, 3, 5, 19, and 23, and Dec. 29, 1940, Dec. 6–29, 1941, Feb. 23, 1942; *Magazine Avellaneda*, Dec. 1934; *La Nación*, Dec. 27, 1934, Dec. 6–29, 1941, Feb. 23, 1942;

Última Hora, Dec. 3–7, 1936; *La Hora*, Oct. 7 and Nov. 13–Dec. 30, 1941; Cascante, *Barracas al sud*, 199; Asociación del Fútbol Argentino, *Memoria, 1940*, 173–76; Asociación del Fútbol Argentino, *Memoria, 1941*, 117–18; *Perfil*, June 6, 2013.
79. Juan Corradi, pers. comm., 4/21/07.
80. Centro para la Investigación de la Historia del Fútbol, "Fundación del Club Atlético River Plate"; *Clarín*, May 25, 2001; Bertolotto, *River*, 25–29.
81. Bucich, *La Boca*, 357.
82. *La Hora*, Nov. 20, 1941.
83. "Los estadios," www.sitioriverplatense.com.ar/estadios-ant.htm, 1/19/07; "Todos los presidentes de la historia de River," https://www.dobleamarilla.com.ar/rosca/todos-los-presidentes-de-la-historia-de-river-_a5a3708aab654133663a5c4e8.
84. "Todos los presidentes de la historia de River"; Cámara de Diputados, *Diario de sesiones*, Oct. 14, 1959, 4045, https://www4.hcdn.gob.ar/intervenciones/Intervencion%20Blanco%20Ruben%20V%20M/D%201959/06%20DSD%2014-10-1959%20pto%204.pdf; Centro para la Investigación de la Historia del Fútbol, "Fundación del Club Atlético River Plate"; Abad de Santillán, *Gran enciclopedia Argentina*, 8:532–33; *La República*, Apr. 3, 1938.
85. Club Atlético River Plate, *Memoria, 1922*; Club Atlético River Plate, *Memoria, 1923*; Tarcus, *Diccionario biográfico*, 717–18; Sanguinetti, *Los socialistas independientes*, 35–36.
86. Lorenzo, *Historia del fútbol argentino*, 1:212–14; "Los estadios"; "José Bacigaluppi en la historia riverplatense," www.agbacigaluppi.com.ar/bacigia.htm, 1/29/07. For the Bacigaluppi family business, see real estate advertisements in *La Prensa* in the 1920s.
87. *Revista River Plate*, Nov. 1931, 1; *La Vanguardia*, Nov. 28 and June 26, 1935, Mar. 12, 1936, Nov. 28, 1941.
88. "Estadio Monumental," www.cariverplate.com.ar/estadio-monumental/, 6/6/14; "Historia del Estadio Antonio Vespucio Liberti," www.geocities.com/Colosseum/Ring/3814/Estadio.htm, 6/6/14; Club Atlético River Plate, *Memoria, 1933*, 8–10; River Plate, *Revista Gráfica e Informativa*, Feb. 1930, 18; *El Gráfico*, Jan. 30, 1926, 16; *La Prensa*, Jan. 23, 1926; *La Opinión*, Aug. 5, 1932, Nov. 25, 1933; Concejo Deliberante de la Municipalidad de Buenos Aires, *Actas*, May 16, 1941, 89, Oct. 3, 1941, 1759–60; Scher, *La patria deportista*, 129; *La Vanguardia*, Feb. 19, 1939.
89. *Boletín Oficial del Club Atlético River Plate*, Jan. 1929, 13; *La República*, Mar. 23, 1938; *La Razón*, Apr. 11, 1938.

Chapter Four

1. See Gutiérrez and Romero, *Sectores populares, cultura política*, and for a much less optimistic vision, see Romero, "La política en los barrios."
2. Biblioteca Popular del Centro de Cultura Juventud Israelita de Boca y Barracas, *Almanaque 1911–enero 1931*, 47–48. For Jewish libraries in Argentina, see Dujovne, *Una historia del libro judío*, esp. 242–47.

3. Archive of CONABIP (hereafter CONABIP), Asociación de Fomento y Biblioteca Popular Cornelio Saavedra to CONABIP, Jan. 27, 1919, 077, 26-b-19.
4. *Federación*, Feb. 1931, Oct. 1930.
5. *Boletín de la Asociación de Fomento de Villa Devoto*, Aug. 1932.
6. Lidia González, "Horacio González, el abuelo Ulderico y la casa de Villa Pueyrredón," *Página 12*, Feb. 1, 2022; "Testimonio de Horacio Luis González: Primera parte, 21 octubre 2015," https://www.bn.gov.ar/micrositios/multimedia/ddhh/private-video-1.
7. *Acción Comunal*, Nov. 1932, 1.
8. American Society of Editors, *International Yearbook*, 290; Cane, *The Fourth Enemy*, 33–47; Diego, *La otra cara de Jano*, 113–36; García, "Historia de la empresa editorial," esp. 34, 97; Sarlo, *Una modernidad periférica*, 19–20; Cedro, "El negocio de la edición"; Abraham, *La Editorial Tor*.
9. Biblioteca Popular del Municipio B. Rivadavia, "Presupuesto para la compra de libros, elaborado por la Librería Perlado," Jan. 1, 1930, http://v.conabip.gob.ar/archivo_historico/results.The libraries covered on this website are in the capital unless otherwise indicated.
10. Departamento Nacional del Trabajo, División de Estadística, *Condiciones de vida*, 28.
11. Miranda, *Las bibliotecas públicas*, esp. 31.
12. Biblioteca Popular Democracia y Progreso, "Estatutos de la biblioteca," 1915, http://v.conabip.gob.ar/archivo_historico/results.
13. CONABIP, Biblioteca Popular General Pueyrredón de la Sociedad de Fomento Flores Sud, 1840, 17-b-19, "Estatuto," 1918 or 1919; CONABIP, Liga de Fomento de Villa General Mitre, 0046, 525-b-17, "Reglamento," 1917.
14. Asociación Liga de Fomento de Villa General Mitre, *Memoria, ejercicio, 1932–1933*, 10.
15. *Acción Comunal*, Oct. 1938, 4.
16. Archivo Intermedio de la Nación, Fondo Inspección General de Justicia, Registro de Asociaciones Civiles, caja 95, 360485, Biblioteca Popular Iberoamericana; Rovere y Oddino and Cocchi, *Aspiración*; "La biblioteca que llegó a Don Bosco," *Pueblo Kilmes*, Aug. 6, 2021, https://pueblokilmes.com.ar/escritos/don-bosco/biblioteca-don-bosco/.
17. Biblioteca Popular Juana Manso, "Informe de inspección de biblioteca realizado por la Comisión Protectora," Aug. 26, 1933, and "Conformación de la comisión de la biblioteca," June 7, 1945, http://v.conabip.gob.ar/archivo_historico/results.
18. Patrimonio Legislativo, Asociación y Biblioteca Popular Hijas de María de Guadalupe a la Cámara de Diputados de la Nación, Sept. 27, 1928, 1415-p-1928.
19. CONABIP, Biblioteca Popular Florencio Sánchez, 137-5, 243-b-23, Luis M. Moretti to CONABIP, May 2, 1938; reply, May 11, 1938.
20. Fiorucci, "La cultura, el libro y la lectura," 544–45; CONABIP, *Memoria, 1915–1916*, esp. 3–16, 28–33, 40; CONABIP, *Memoria, 1935*, 6; CONABIP, *Nómina de las bibliotecas*, 1938, 3–8; Patrimonio Legislativo, Juan Nigro y otros, "Subvenciones a bibliotecas populares," Cámara de Diputados, Sept. 22, 1932, 600-d-1932.
21. CONABIP, *Ley, decreto, reglamento e instrucciones*, 5–9; *Libros y Bibliotecas: Acción*

Interna (revista de Comisión Nacional de Bibliotecas Populares) 1:1 (Oct. 1926), 98–103, esp. 102–3.
22. CONABIP, *Memoria, 1915 y 1916*, 5–6, 14–15; CONABIP, *Memoria, 1936*, 20; CONABIP, memo to the president of CONABIP, Aug. 8, 1935, in response to an earlier inquiry from Liga de Fomento de Villa General Mitre, in file of that organization, 0046, 525-13-17.
23. See, for example, Concejo Deliberante de la Municipalidad de Buenos Aires, *Actas*, May 23, 1930, 657–58, June 20, 1930, 1014, May 31, 1932, 636–37; Cámara de Diputados, *Diario de sesiones*, June 20, 1934, 2:619–24, 652–53; Sept. 26 and 27, 1934, 6:311–16; 1937, 2:2 Anexo L, 225–27; July 30, 1941, 2:698; Patrimonio Legislativo, Biblioteca Popular Ciencia y Labor de Villa General Mitre a la Cámara de Diputados, Oct. 30, 1933, 1432-p-1933.
24. For the Ghio family, see chapter 2. The library's inability to grow may have been partially due to the sociedad de fomento not having placed emphasis on it. Biblioteca y Asociación Vecinal de Nueva Chicago, *Memoria, 1931–1932*; Biblioteca y Asociación Vecinal de Nueva Chicago, *Memoria, 1933–1934*; CONABIP, Asociación Vecinal de Fomento Nueva Chicago, 1760, 40-b-33, inspection, Apr. 16, 1933, July 26, 1933, Sept. 10, 1937, June 2, 1939, Sept. 30, 1942; Reglamento de la Biblioteca Nueva Chicago, 1933; inspection, Sept. 16, 1962, http://v.conabip.gob.ar/archivo_historico/results; Cámara de Diputados, *Diario de sesiones*, 1937, 2:2, 226.
25. Harris, *History of Libraries*, 150–57, 184–85; Altick, *English Common Reader*, 190–96.
26. Boston Public Library, "BPL History," https://www.bpl.org/bpl-history/; Boston History and Architecture, "Population Trends in Boston, 1640–1990," http://www.iboston.org/mcp.php?pid=popFig.8/30/2019; *Annual Report of the Trustees of the Public Library of the City of Boston*, 78.
27. Pan-American Union, *Cuban Books and Libraries*, esp. 8–9; Miguel Viciedo Valdé, "Breve reseña sobre la biblioteca pública en Cuba antes de 1959," *Revista Cubana de Información en Ciencias de la Salud* 14:1 (2006), http://scielo.sld.cu/scielo.php?script=sci_arttext&pid=S1024-94352006000100010; García Puertas and Botana Rodríguez, "Las bibliotecas públicas cubanas"; Abellá and Larrique, *Sistema nacional de bibliotecas públicas*, esp. 31.
28. See, for example, Cámara de Diputados, *Diario de sesiones*, Sept. 21, 1926, 6:59–65; Sept. 26, 1932, 6:390–96; Jan. 17, 1938, 2:1 (1937), 142–51.
29. Contarelli, *Acción de las entidades*, 65–66; Bolan, *Biblioteca Popular Alberdi*, esp. 60.
30. *Función social de la escuela*, 44.
31. Horowitz, "Patrones y clientes," 592, 594–95.
32. *Vélez Sarsfield Social*, Nov. 30, 1933; *La Libertad*, Jan. 31, 1936.
33. For example, see Biblioteca Popular General Benito Nazar, "Invitación a cine y baile a realizar en la sede de la biblioteca," Oct. 10, 1943, http://v.conabip.gob.ar/archivo_historico/results; *La Libertad*, Nov. 2, 1930, Feb. 7 and 21, Sept. 4, Oct. 24, 1936.
34. *Pueyrredón*, Oct. 1934, 6–7, Jan. 1936, 6.

35. Klineberg, *Palaces for the People*, esp. 26–39, 111–16.
36. Barrancos, *Educación, cultura y trabajadores*, 96; Graciano, *Entre la torre de marfil y el compromiso político*, 217.
37. Camarero, *A la conquista obrera*, 218–33; Vicente Francomano and Antonio López, "Biblioteca Popular José Ingenieros: Apuntes para su historia," https://flornegra.wordpress.com/2007/06/25/biblioteca-popular-jose-ingenierosapuntes-para-su-historia/; Domínguez Rubio, *El anarquismo argentino*.
38. Library of the Instituto Ravignani, Colección Emilio Ravignani, ARV 32, nos. 22 and 114; *Pueyrredón*, Aug. 1935, 3; *La Prensa*, May 22, 1917, Aug. 12, 1919, July 20, 1922.
39. See, for example, *La Acción*, Jan. 19 and 20, 1927; *La Bandera Proletaria*, Jan. 22, 1927; Horowitz, *Argentina's Radical Party*, 167–69.
40. *La Vanguardia*, Nov. 21, 1931; CONABIP, *Nómina de las bibliotecas*, 1933; Horowitz, "Occupational Community," 74–75; *Anuario Socialista*, 147–48; Unión Ferroviaria, *Memoria*, 89–91.
41. González, "Lo propio y lo ajeno," 118–25.
42. Lyons, "New Readers," 332; Giménez, "Que hacer de las horas libres."
43. Biblioteca Popular Juan Bautista Alberdi (Avellaneda), "Nota del secretario general de la biblioteca al ministro de instrucción pública," Dec. 21, 1919, "Informe de la inspección de la biblioteca," April 8, 1920, Province of Buenos Aires, http://v.conabip.gob.ar/archivo_historico/results.
44. Biblioteca Popular Juan Bautista Alberdi (Avellaneda), "Las autoridades de la biblioteca comunican el reinició de la actividad de la institución," June 13, 1933, "Informe de inspección de la biblioteca a cargo de la Comisión Protectora," Oct. 27, 1933, Province of Buenos Aires, http://v.conabip.gob.ar/archivo_historico/results; *Anuario La Libertad*; *Libros y Bibliotecas* 1:1 (Oct. 1926), 168; Di Tella, *Perón y los sindicatos*, 278–87; CONABIP, *Nómina de las bibliotecas*, 1933 and 1938, 12; Patrimonio Legislativo, Biblioteca Popular Juan Bautista Alberdi de Gerli a la Cámara de Diputados de la Nación, June 25, 1937, 414-p-1937; Cámara de Diputados, *Diario de sesiones*, 1937, 2:2, 50, 232.
45. Biblioteca Popular Alberdi, *Bodas de oro, 1910–8 de julio 1960*, http://biblio-alberdi.blogspot.com/2009/03/nuestra-historia.html; *El Progreso*, June 19, 1943, http://biblio-alberdi.blogspot.com/2009/03/hablan-de-nosotros-2.html; Bolan, *Biblioteca Popular Alberdi*; Francavilla, *Historia de Villa Crespo*, 42–45, 52–59, 69; Marcelo J. Bourdeu, "Notas sobre un vecino de Villa Crespo y de Buenos Aires, Julián Bourdeu," *Barriada*, June 1, 2009, http://www.barriada.com.ar/MarceloBourdeu/NotasSobreUnVecino.aspx; "Julián Bourdeu," https://es.wikipedia.org/wiki/Juli%C3%A1n_Bourdeu; CONABIP, *Memoria, 1915 y 1916*, 45; Lupano, *La gran familia industrial*, 139–84; "Barrio Villa Crespo: Habitantes notables," http://www.geocities.ws/rodr-305/historia/Prestigiosos/PRESTIGIOSOS.html; Patrimonio Legislativo, Biblioteca Popular de la Parroquia de San Bernardo a la Cámara de Diputados de la Nación, Aug. 26, 1916, 525-p-1916.
46. "Bio-cronología Leopoldo Marechal," http://biblioteca.unlam.edu.ar/

descargas/18_BiocronolgadeMarechal.pdf, 11/29/17; "Leopoldo Marechal," http://www.vorticelibros.com.ar/autor.php?id=36; Brock, *Boots and Shoes*, 83; *La Libertad*, Feb. 12, 1936; Biblioteca Popular Alberdi a la Cámara de Diputados de la Nación, Sept. 1, 1936, 487-p-1936; Magnani, *El agitador comunista*; Petra, "Hacia una historia," 110.

47. "La biblioteca popular de Belgrano," *Fray Mocho*, Feb. 13, 1914, 114–27; Córdoba, *El barrio de Belgrano*, 114–27; *El Monitor de Educación Común*, Mar. 31, 1910, 922–23; Concejo Deliberante de la Municipalidad de Buenos Aires, *Actas*, June 22, 1922, 1368–69; Landenburger and Conte, *La Unión Cívica*, 50; Saítta, "El periodismo popular," 439; Patrimonio Legislativo, Comisión Administrativa de la Biblioteca Popular de Belgrano a la Cámara de Diputados de la Nación, Sept. 17, 1924, 658-p-1924; Miranda, *Las bibliotecas públicas*, 40.

48. Asociación Biblioteca Popular Domingo Faustino Sarmiento, *Memoria, 1929–1930*, *Memoria, 1935–1936*, *Memoria, 1936–1937*, and *Memoria, 1940–1941*; *Sarmiento* (*Boletín de la Asociación Biblioteca Popular Domingo Faustino Sarmiento*), Aug.–Sept. 1934, 3–10, and Aug.–Sept. 1942, 3–10; Arata, *Villa Urquiza*, 193–98; Patrimonio Legislativo, Biblioteca Popular Domingo Faustino Sarmiento a la Cámara de Diputados de la Nación, Aug. 25, 1927, 529-p-1927.

49. *Sarmiento*, Aug.–Sept. 1934, 11; *Acción Comunal*, June 1937, 7; *Ateneo Popular de Villa Devoto*, Feb. 1941, 2–3; Asociación Biblioteca Popular Domingo Faustino Sarmiento, *Memoria, 1936–1937*, 8–9; *Quién es quién en la Argentina*, 346–47; Arata, *Villa Urquiza*, 195–96; Pablo Forcinito, "Las callecitas de Buenos Aires tienen ese no sé qué . . . ," http://www.elaleph.com/boletin.cfm?edicion=200210&seccion=4; Busich Escobar, "D. José Luis Cantilo."

50. In its first years this organization's nomenclature was confusing, going by both Sociedad de Fomento de Villa Leandro Alem and Sociedad de Fomento Democracia y Progreso de Villa Leandro Alem.

51. *Liniers*, Oct. 1940, 2–8; Biblioteca Popular Democracia y Progreso, "Solicitud de reconocimiento por parte de la biblioteca," Aug. 10, 1915, "Inspección de la biblioteca," Aug. 17, 1915, "Estatutos de la biblioteca," 1915, http://v.conabip.gob.ar/archivo_historico/results; Boragno, "Los talleres ferroviarios."

52. *Liniers*, Oct. 1940, 9–15; "Juan Guereño," http://cremenes.wordpress.com/hijos-ilustres/juan-guereno/; Navarro, *Evita*, 48; Rao, "José Amalfitani," 20; Gutiérrez and Romero, *Sectores populares*, 17.

53. *Liniers*, Oct. 1940, 9.

54. Ibid.

55. Ministerio de Gobierno de la Provincia de Buenos Aires, *Fomento y protección*, 25, 132–33, 138; Biblioteca Popular Juan N. Madero, "Informe de inspección de biblioteca," May 22, 1934, "Informe de inspección de biblioteca," May 18, 1946, Province of Buenos Aires, http://v.conabip.gob.ar/archivo_historico/results; "Biblioteca y Museo Popular Juan Nepomuceno Madero," http://sanfdomiciudad.blogspot.com/, 10/7/09.

56. CONABIP, Biblioteca Popular General Pueyrredón de la Sociedad Fomento Flores Sud, 1840, 17-b-19, inspection, Feb. 24, 1919, Feb.23, 1923, Mar. 13, 1923, Apr. 2, 1923, Biblioteca to CONABIP, Jan. 31, 1919, Mar. 20, 1919; Sociedad de Fomento Flores Sud, *Memoria*.
57. CONABIP, Biblioteca Popular General Pueyrredón de la Sociedad Fomento Flores Sud, 1840, 17-b-19, inspection, Mar. 13, 1935, Apr. 11, 1938, July 16, 1938, Oct. 17, 1938, Jan. 17, 1939, Dec. 15, 1939, Jan. 12, 1940, May 30, 1941, July 14, 1941, Apr. 14, 1943, Biblioteca to CONABIP, Jan. 9, 1935, Jan. 3, 1940; Patrimonio Legislativo, Asociación de Fomento y Cultural de Flores Sud a la Cámara de Diputados de la Nación, 1042-p-1941; *El Fomento de Flores Sud*, esp. Apr. 1935, 8, May 1935, 5–6, Apr. 1936, 2–4, 12, Sept. 1938, 11–13, 20; Cámara de Diputados, *Diario de sesiones*, 1937, 2:2, 227.
58. CONABIP, Biblioteca Popular de la Asociación Cultural Florencio Sánchez, 1375, 243-b-23, esp. inspection, June 25, 1929, Oct. 4, 1929, Mar. 25, 1930, Nov. 7, 1932, Jan. 10, 1934, June 17, 1935, Jan. 14, 1938, July 17, 1940, July 3, 1941, Mar. 26, 1942; Asociación Cultural Florencio Sánchez, *Memoria*; Cámara de Diputados, *Diario de sesiones*, 1937, 2:2, 226.
59. CONABIP, Asociación de Fomento y Biblioteca Popular Cornelio Saavedra, 0077, 26-b-19, esp. letter from biblioteca to CONABIP, Jan. 27, 1919; undated list of Comisión Directiva (probably from 1919); inspections, Oct. 14, 1919, June 15, 1923, Jan. 21, 1929, Aug. 29, 1932, Aug. 21, 1933, May 30, 1936, Dec. 27, 1937, Aug. 7, 1939, Oct. 1, 1940, Apr. 29, 1943.
60. See, for example, Stearns, *Lives of Labor*, 9; Roth, *Social Democrats in Imperial Germany*, 241; Felsenstein and Connolly, *What Middletown Read*, esp. 7.
61. Patrimonio Legislativo, Asociación Biblioteca Popular José E. Rodó a la Cámara de Diputados de la Nación, Sept. 12, 1938, 1842 1/2-p-1938; Biblioteca Popular Domingo Faustino Sarmiento a la Cámara de Diputados de la Nación, Aug. 25, 1927, 529-p-1927. In the 1970s and 1980s every afternoon the library of the Unión Ferroviaria was filled with students doing homework with books that they could not buy.
62. See, for example, CONABIP, Biblioteca Popular de la Liga de Fomento de Villa General Mitre, 0046, 525-b-17, inspections, May 30, 1934, Sept. 30, 1935, Aug. 5, 1937, Oct 7, 1943; Biblioteca Popular Carlos Vega Belgrano, 1115, 406-b-25, inspections, July 25, 1933, May 12, 1936; Asociación de Fomento y Biblioteca Popular Cornelio Saavedra, 0077, 26-b-19, inspection, May 30, 1936; Biblioteca Popular Florencio Sánchez, 1375, 243-b-23, inspections, June 17, 1935, May 20, 1936.
63. In research in a small city in the United States, it has been hypothesized that the proper atmosphere in the public library made working-class men uncomfortable, and they formed their own library. Felsenstein and Connolly, *What Middletown Read*, esp. 7.
64. CONABIP, *Memoria*, 1935, 17–19.
65. *Pueyrredón*, Sept. 1934–Jan. 1935, Jan. 1936, 6.
66. The figure for literature was somewhat lower than it was for other periods from 1915 to the middle of 1919. Biblioteca Obrera, "Informe de inspección de la Biblioteca

Obrera," Jan. 1, 1911, "Estadística correspondiente al primer trimestre de 1915," "Estadística correspondiente al cuarto trimestre de 1915," "Estadística correspondiente al segundo trimestre de 1916," "Estadística correspondiente al tercer trimestre de 1916," "Estadística correspondiente al primer trimestre de 1917," "Estadística correspondiente al segundo trimestre de 1917," "Estadística correspondiente al cuarto trimestre de 1917," "Estadística correspondiente al año 1918," "Estadística correspondiente al primer trimestre de 1919," "Estadística correspondiente al segundo trimestre de 1919," all at http://v.conabip.gob.ar/archivo_historico/results. For the early history of the library, see Tripaldi, "Origen e inserción."

67. *Boletín de la Biblioteca Obrera Juan B. Justo*, Mar.–May 1930, 14, Oct.–Dec. 1930, 3; Biblioteca Obrera Juan B. Justo, *Memoria, 1943*, 5. See also Biblioteca Obrera Juan B. Justo, *Memoria, 1938*, 8; Biblioteca Obrera Juan B. Justo, *Memoria, 1940*, 8; Biblioteca Obrera Juan B. Justo, *Memoria, 1941*, 8.
68. See Horowitz, *Argentina's Radical Party*, esp. 65–94.

Chapter Five

1. Some of these ideas were taken from a book about a case that is quite different: Seligman, *Chicago's Block Clubs*, esp. 4–11.
2. Sierra, *La Paz's Colonial Specters*, esp. 80–92, 116–17; Confederación Nacional de Juntas Vecinales, *El movimiento vecinal en Bolivia*, esp. 57–58; Duffau Soto, *De urgencias y necesidades*.
3. For example, see Archivo Intermedio de la Nación, Fondo Inspección General de Justicia, Registro de Asociaciones Civiles, caja 59, 924.150, Fomento Edilicio y Beneficia y Biblioteca Popular Emilio Mitre, "Estatutos."
4. *Boletín de la Asociación de Fomento de Villa Devoto*, Feb. 1931; *Los Olivos*, Feb.–Mar. 1936, 17–18; Library of the Instituto Ravignani, Colección Emilio Ravignani, ARV 31, 1936, ser. 2, caja 26, 257, Sociedad de Fomento Teniente General Luis María Campos, "Nomina de socios"; *Acción Comunal*, Apr. 1938, 10–11; *Boletín de Fomento Caballito*, Jan. 1940; *Censor Edilicio*, Mar. 1944, 9. A few lists occasionally contain initials instead of names but never enough to change the analysis.
5. Cubilla, "Sociabilidad y cultura," 81.
6. *Manuel Belgrano*, Aug. 1935, 5, July 1939, 3; *Verdades*, July 1940; *Fomento y Cultura*, May 1928, 1, Aug. 1928, 1–4.
7. Municipalidad de la Ciudad de Buenos Aires, *Memoria del Departamento Ejecutivo, 1933 y 1934*, 305–7; *La Prensa*, May 16, 1939.
8. *Censor Edilicio*, Feb.–Mar. 1942, 12–13.
9. *Clarín*, Mar. 24, 2014; Marcelo J. Bourdeu, "Villa Tallar: Un aporte sobre los orígenes y primeros años de un barrio casi desaparecido de Buenos Aires," *Barriada*, Nov. 14, 2008, https://www.barriada.com.ar/villa-talar-introduccion-y-origen-por-marcelo-j-bourdeu/. It was located in what are now the legal barrios of Villa Pueyrredón and Agronomía.

10. Archivo Intermedio de la Nación, Fondo Inspección General de Justicia, Registro de Asociaciones Civiles, caja 59, 924.150, Fomento Edilicio y Beneficia y Biblioteca Popular Emilio Mitre.
11. Ibid.; *El Sud*, July–Nov. 1944, 14–16, June 1946, 2–4; Patrimonio Legislativo, Asociación de Fomento y Biblioteca Popular Emilio Mitre a la Cámara de Diputados, Apr. 25, 1925, 10-p-1925.
12. Patrimonio Legislativo, "Extracto Sancerni Giménez: Prestamos a las sociedades de fomento que actúa en la Capital Federal," Cámara de Diputados, Sept. 19, 1939, 966-d-1939.
13. *Acción Comunal*, June 1933, 3, Apr. 1937, 11, May 1938, 37, Mar.–Apr. 1939, 6, May 1940, 5.
14. *El Sud*, Nov. 1943–Feb. 1944, 15.
15. *Verdades*, Aug. 1939–Nov. 1940, esp. Aug. and Oct. 1939.
16. *Boletín Mensual de la Liga de Fomento Federico Lacroze*, Jan. 1939–Dec. 1940, esp. Jan. 1939; *Anuario Kraft*.
17. "La Asociación Benito Nazar cumple 90 años," *AVC Amo Villa Crespo*, Jan.–Feb. 2017, https://issuu.com/amovillacrespo/docs/avc16web.
18. *Colón*, Mar. 1941, 4–5, Jan. 1942, 12.
19. *Acción Comunal*, Apr. 1932, 2, Nov. 1933, 2, Dec. 1933, 2, Feb. 1937, 2, Apr. 1938, 6; *Manuel Belgrano*, Feb.–Mar. 1940, 2.
20. *Los Olivos*, Feb.–Mar. 1936, flyer inside Apr.–June 1937, in Biblioteca Nacional.
21. Asociación Liga de Fomento de Villa General Mitre, *Memoria, ejercicio, 1918–1919*, 10, *Memoria, ejercicio, 1932–1933*, 13–14, and *Memoria, ejercicio, 1934–1935*, 10–12; *El Fomento de Flores Sud*, Sept. 1938, 5–6; *Censor Edilicio*, June 1941, 3; *Liniers*, July–Sept. 1941, 3–4; Sociedad de Fomento General Benito Nazar, *Memoria*, 10–14; *Boletín de la Corporación Mitre*, July 1940, 6–7.
22. *Liniers*, Oct. 1940, 19–20.
23. *Manuel Belgrano*, Aug. 1935, 5, July 1939, 3. For other examples, see *Verdades*, July 1940; *Los Olivos*, Apr.–June 1937.
24. *Verdades*, Aug. 1939. See also *Acción Comunal*, Feb. 1937; Cubilla, "Sociabilidad y cultura," 76.
25. For example, see *Acción Comunal*, July 1937, 7–8, Jan. 1939, 8–9.
26. *Anuario estadístico de la ciudad de Buenos Aires*, 145, 257; *Revista de Estadística Municipal*, Oct.–Dec. 1941, 161; Aguas Argentinas, *Buenos Aires y el agua*, 30–34; Obras Sanitarias de la Nación, *Memoria, 1923*, 7, 38; Obras Sanitarias de la Nación, *Memoria, 1941*, 173; *Fomento Edilicio y Cultura*, Aug. 1932–Feb. 1935; Concejo Deliberante de la Municipalidad de Buenos Aires, *Actas*, Apr. 19, 1927, 221–23, May 10, 1927, 435–36.
27. Cubilla, "Sociabilidad y cultura," 75.
28. Sociedad de Fomento de Versailles, *Memoria*, 5–8.
29. *El Progreso*, July 1931, 5.
30. Concejo Deliberante de la Municipalidad de Buenos Aires, *Actas*, June 25, 1929, 932.
31. *Verdades*, Aug.–Dec. 1939.

32. *Liniers*, Dec. 1940, 4; *Censor Edilicio*, Jan.–Feb. 1943, 11, Mar.–Apr. 1943, 4; *Boletín Mensual de la Liga de Fomento Federico Lacroze*, Dec. 1939, 3; *Boletín de la Asociación de Fomento de Villa Devoto*, Mar. 1930.
33. Concejo Deliberante de la Municipalidad de Buenos Aires, *Actas*, Sept. 21, 1934, 2198–99.
34. *Los Olivos*, Apr.–June 1937, 10; *Fomento Edilicio y Cultura*, Jan. 1933, 2–3, Feb. 1933, 2; *Pueyrredón*, Apr. 1935, 3.
35. Sociedad de Fomento General Benito Nazar, *Memoria*; "Benito Alberto Nazar Anchorena," https://es.wikipedia.org/wiki/Benito_Alberto_Nazar_Anchorena; "La Asociación Benito Nazar cumple 90 años."
36. Patrimonio Legislativo, Mensaje del Poder Ejecutivo a la Cámara de Diputados, "Levantamiento de las vías del ramal de Sáenz Peña a Villa Luro," Feb. 14, 1938, 241-pe-1937; Asociación de Fomento Edilicio, Cultural y Biblioteca Popular Villa Luro Norte a la Cámara de Diputados, Aug. 16, 1938, 1514-p-1938; Honorable Concejo Deliberante de la Ciudad de Buenos Aires a la Cámara de Diputados, "Se aboque al estudio de proyecto de ley sobre el levantamiento de las vías de ramal Villa Luro," Sept. 25, 1939, 93-ov-1939; Ferrocarril de Buenos Aires al Pacífico a la Cámara de Diputados, "Solicita que radicada en la Honorable Cámara una nota presentado al Senado . . . sobre levantamiento de ramal de Sáenz Peña a Villa Luro," July 11, 1939, 434-p-1939; Honorable Concejo Deliberante de la Ciudad de Buenos Aires a la Cámara de Diputados, "Se expresa que vería con agrado se trata con preferencia . . . levantamiento de las vías ferroviarias de ramal Villa Luro–Sáenz Peña," Aug. 27, 1940, 102-ov-1940; Asociación de Fomento Edilicio, Cultural y Biblioteca Popular Villa Luro Norte a la Cámara de Diputados, June 14, 1940, 311-p-1940; Manuel Palacín y otros, "Levantamiento de las vías . . . entre las estaciones de Villa Luro y Sáenz Peña," June 24, 1942, 476-d-1942.
37. Asociación de Fomento 12 de Octubre Caballito Noroeste, *Memoria, ejercicio*, 4–7.
38. *Boletín de la Asociación de Fomento de Villa Devoto*, Feb., Mar., and Apr. 1930; *Caras y Caretas*, Dec. 3, 1938, 86.
39. Concejo Deliberante de la Municipalidad de Buenos Aires, *Actas*, Dec. 27, 1939, 3999; *Lugano Social: Revista Ilustrada*, Jan.–Feb. 1941, 13–14; Sanguinetti, *Los socialistas independientes*; Tarcus, *Diccionario biográfico*, 590.
40. Dagnino Pastore, *Casi un siglo*, esp. 276–78, 305–6; *Caballito: Informativo de la Asociación General Alvear de Fomento Edilicio*, July 1938, inside front cover, Aug. 1938, 2–5, Oct. 1938, 4–5, Sept.–Oct. 1939, 1, 4–7, 12–13, Nov.–Dec. 1939, 11, Mar.–Apr. 1940, 3–4, 14–15, July–Aug. 1940, 4–6, Dec. 1940, 11; *El Centinela*, June–July 1939; *Censor Edilicio*, Jan. 1942, 17; Concejo Deliberante de la Municipalidad de Buenos Aires, *Actas*, Sept. 19, 1919, 1420, Apr. 22, 1927, 264, May 18, 1934, 152–53, Oct. 20, 1936, 1888–89; *Nueva Era*, Mar. 28, 1922, 1; *Boletín de Los Amigos de la Ciudad*, Jan. 1939, 51; Rogelio Alaniz, "Los duelistas," *El Litoral*, Aug. 14, 2013, https://www.ellitoral.com/index.php/diarios/2013/08/14/opinion/OPIN-02.html.

41. Ordenanza 2329, Nov. 30, 1927, Concejo Deliberante de la Ciudad de Buenos Aires, *Ordenanzas, resoluciones y minutas, 1927*, 426–29.
42. *Boletín de la Corporación Mitre*, Aug. 1940, 9.
43. *Verdades*, Nov.–Dec. 1939, n.p.
44. Ibid., Oct. 1939, n.p.
45. Sociedad de Fomento de Versailles, *Memoria*, 7, 11; Walter, *Politics and Urban Growth*; "Plazas de Versailles," http://plazas.faggella.com.ar/versalles.htm, 2/20/15; "Tomás Cullen," http://es.wikipedia.org/wiki/Tomás_Cullen; Parker, *Argentines of To-Day*, 1:471–72; *Caras y Caretas*, Dec. 6, 1930, 169–71.
46. Horowitz, *Argentina's Radical Party*, 76–77; Library of the Instituto Ravignani, Colección Emilio Ravignani, esp. ARV 9, nos. 7, 8; ARV 29, nos. 231, 232 234, ARV 32, nos. 59–75, ARV 39bis, nos. 312–14; Gimnasia y Esgrima de Buenos Aires, "Historia," https://hmong.es/wiki/Gimnasia_y_Esgrima_de_Buenos_Aires.
47. *El Progreso*, July 1931, 2–7, Jan. 1932; and, for example, *El Obrero Ferroviario*, Aug. 1, 1938; *CGT* (publication of the Confederación General del Trabajo), Nov. 1, 1943; Manuel F. Fernández, *La Unión Ferroviaria*, 153.
48. *La Internacional*, Oct. 23, 1926–Dec. 10, 1927; Horowitz, *Argentine Unions*, 110; "José F. Penelón," http://josefernandopenelon.blogspot.com; Campione, López Cantera, and Maier, "La cuestión Penelón"; Tarcus, *Diccionario biográfico*, 498–500; Camarero, *A la conquista obrera*, xxiii–xxxii.
49. Concejo Deliberante de la Municipalidad de Buenos Aires, *Actas*, Oct. 23, 1928, 2110–14; *La Internacional*, May 14, 1927. For another example, see Concejo Deliberante de la Municipalidad de Buenos Aires, *Actas*, May 29, 1928, 477–78.
50. *El Fomento de Flores Sud*, Dec. 1934, 6–8, Jan. 1935, 2–7, 10–11.
51. For example, see *Manuel Belgrano*, May–June 1938; *Acción Comunal*, Sept. 1932, 3.
52. Concejo Deliberante de la Municipalidad de Buenos Aires, *Actas*, June 7, 1921, 986–87, Nov. 8, 1921, 2182–83.
53. Caimari, *While the City Sleeps*, 88–90; *Fomento Edilicio y Cultura*, Oct. 1932, 7, July 1933, 1–2; Patrimonio Legislativo, Asociación de Fomento y Cultura Flores Sud a la Cámara de Diputados, June 21, 1934, 247-p-1934, and Aug. 24, 1934, 733-p-1934; Asociación Vecinal de Fomento Los Amigos de Villa Luro a la Cámara de Diputados, Aug. 17, 1934, 640-p-1934; Asociación Biblioteca Popular José E. Rodó y Fomento de Villa General La Madrid a la Cámara de Diputados, Sept. 14, 1934, 982-p-1934; Sociedad de Fomento de Villa Ortúzar a la Cámara de Diputados, Nov. 5, 1934, 1310-p-1934; Asociación Vecinal de Villa del Parque a la Cámara de Diputados, June 14, 1940, 319-p-1940; Asociación de Fomento de Villa Devoto a la Cámara de Diputados, July 15, 1940, 543-p-1940.
54. *La Vanguardia*, May 8, 1920.
55. Razori, *La obra de la intendencia municipal*, esp. 11; *Manuel Belgrano*, Dec. 1935, 4, Feb. 1936, 3, Apr. 1936, 5–6; Concejo Deliberante de la Municipalidad de Buenos Aires, *Actas*, Oct. 4, 1935, 2052–53. Also see Patrimonio Legislativo, Asociación de Fomento y Cultura Popular 25 de Mayo a la Cámara de Diputados, Aug. 23, 1929, 445-p-1929; *La Vanguardia*, June 2, 1930.

56. *Verdades*, Aug., Sept., Nov.–Dec. 1939; *Nuestra Lucha: Órgano Oficial de la Agrupación Progresista de Belgrano*, Aug. 1939, 12; Resolución 120.42, Concejo Deliberante de la Ciudad de Buenos Aires, *Ordenanzas, resoluciones y minutas, 1939*, 19; *La Prensa*, Mar.–June 1939. Development societies also pressed for subway lines in other areas. See *Acción Comunal*, Mar. 1934, 3; *La Prensa*, June 5, 1939.
57. *Acción Comunal*, Feb. 1935, 1–3, Mar. 1935, 2; *Fomento Edilicio y Cultura*, Feb. 1935, 1–5; *Manuel Belgrano*, Feb. 1935, 1–4; *La Vanguardia*, Nov. 18, 1934, Jan. 16 and 19–21, 1935; *Censor Edilicio*, Feb.–Mar. 1942, 12–13; Horowitz, *Argentine Unions*.
58. See Privitellio, *Vecinos y ciudadanos*, 105–47; Gorelik, *La grilla y el parque*, 392–451.
59. Privitellio, *Vecinos y ciudadanos*, esp. 70; *Pueyrredón*, Aug. 1935, 3.
60. Concejo Deliberante de la Ciudad de Buenos Aires, *Ordenanzas, resoluciones y minutas, 1927*, 426–29; Concejo Deliberante de la Municipalidad de Buenos Aires, *Actas*, Apr. 5, 1927, 122–24, May 10, 1927, 428–29, May 13, 1927, 482–84, Nov. 30, 1927, 2429–35, May 23, 1930, 707; Landau, *Gobernar Buenos Aires*, 130.
61. *Quién es quién, 1943*, 656; Razori, La obra de la intendencia municipal, esp. 59, 87; *Manuel Belgrano*, Dec. 1935, 4.
62. Razori, *La obra de la intendencia municipal*, esp. 44–45.
63. Municipalidad de la Ciudad de Buenos Aires, *Memoria del Departamento Ejecutivo, 1935*, 443–48; Municipalidad de la Ciudad de Buenos Aires, *Memoria del Departamento Ejecutivo, 1936*, 2:51–52.
64. *Acción Comunal*, Sept. 1936, 1–2, July 1937, 8–9, Aug. 1937, 1–4.
65. Municipalidad de la Ciudad de Buenos Aires, *Memoria del Departamento Ejecutivo, 1935*, 447–48; *Manuel Belgrano*, Jan. 1935–Sept. 1942, esp. Oct. 1935, Mar. and June 1936, Oct. 1937.
66. *El Fomento de Flores Sud*, Apr. 1936, 2–7; *Los Olivos*, June–July 1936, 8–10, Aug.–Sept. 1936, 8, Jan.–Mar. 1937, flyer inside Apr.–June 1937 in Biblioteca Nacional.
67. *Manuel Belgrano*, Mar. 1936, 2-4.
68. Patrimonio Legislativo, Centro de Fomento y Cultura Villa Mitre a la Cámara de Diputados, Sept. 6, 1940, 1125-p-1940; Asociación Belgrano R. a la Cámara de Diputados, Sept. 19, 1940, 1374-p-1940; Asociación Vecinal de Fomento Edilicio, Cultural y Social de Los Amigos de Villa Luro a la Cámara de Diputados, July 25, 1941, 765-p-1941; Sociedad de Fomento Vecinal Villa Miraflores a la Cámara de Diputados, July 6, 1942, 579-p-1942; *Manuel Belgrano*, May 1936, 7, May–June 1939, 3, Aug. 1942, 7, Sept. 1942, 3, insert inside Sept. 1942 of Las Asociaciones Vecinales de Fomento de la Ciudad de Buenos Aires, "Repudian todo aumento de tarifas en los transportes pasajeros," in Biblioteca Nacional. For an overview of the situation, see García Heras, *Transportes, negocios y política*, esp. 120–51.
69. The later government of President Macri (2015–2019) tried a similar strategy of building popularity through infrastructure improvements. Its crushing defeat in its reelection attempt demonstrates that other issues massively outweighed whatever goodwill had been developed.

Chapter Six

1. *El Monitor de Educación Común*, Feb. 28, 1909, 209–15, esp. 209.
2. Brugnara, *Universidades populares*, 5–6, 8–10; Departamento Nacional del Trabajo, División de Estadística, *Condiciones de vida*, 28.
3. Brugnara, *Universidades populares*, 32–34; Universidad Popular de Villa del Parque, *Memoria, 1937*.
4. Patrimonio Legislativo, Universidades Populares a la Cámara de Diputados, July 2, 1936, 202-p-1936.
5. Brugnara, *Universidades populares*.
6. See, for example, *La Universidad Popular: Revista Mensual Órgano de la Universidad Popular*, Apr. 1905; Brugnara, *Universidades populares*, 20–23.
7. Suriano, *Anarquistas*; Suriano, *Auge y caída*, 45–58; Barrancos, *La escena iluminada*.
8. For example, see Martín Yaverovski, "Tres repúblicas barriales"; Martín Yaverovski, "Francia, Brasil, México y Argentina"; Artienda, "Historia de la Universidad Popular Juan Ramón Lestani."
9. *Historia Caribe* (Barranquilla) 16:38 (Jan.–June 2021); Klaiber, "Popular University"; Torres Aguilar, *Cultura y revolución*; Medina Espada, *De la universidad popular*; Graciano, "Entre cultura y política."
10. See, for example, Graciano, "Entre cultura y política."
11. Barrancos, *Anarquismo, educación y costumbres*, 315; *El Monitor de Educación Común*, Nov.–Dec. 1933, 162–65; Patrimonio Legislativo, Universidades Populares a la Cámara de Diputados, July 2, 1936, 202-p-1936.
12. See, for example, Cámara de Diputados, *Diario de sesiones*, Sept. 27, 1935, 4:698–701, Sept. 14, 1938, 4:856–62.
13. Concejo Deliberante de la Municipalidad de Buenos Aires, *Actas*, Aug. 31, 1937, 1867–69.
14. Cámara de Diputados, *Diario de sesiones*, 1937, 2:2, 121.
15. Patrimonio Legislativo, Universidad Popular de Villa Pueyrredón a la Cámara de Diputados, Aug. 20, 1940, 933-p-1940.
16. *Las Universidades Populares*, Sept. 1933, 10; *Revista de las Universidades Populares*, Oct. 1936, 90.
17. Universidad Popular Florentino Ameghino, *Estatutos*.
18. Universidad Popular de Villa del Parque, *Memoria, 1937*.
19. Universidad Popular de Boedo, *Memoria, 1937*, 8; Universidad Popular de Flores Sud, *Memoria*; Brugnara, *Universidades populares*, 65; Canop, *Obra y acción*, 111; Patrimonio Legislativo, Universidades Populares a la Cámara de Diputados, July 2, 1936, 202-p-1936; Universidad Popular Bernardino Rivadavia a la Cámara de Diputados, June 22, 1936, 175-p-1936, and June 19, 1940, 348-p-1940; *Acción Comunal*, July 1936, 2.
20. *Las Universidades Populares*, Sept. 1933, esp. 23, 28; Universidad Popular de Villa del Parque, *Memoria, 1937*; Universidades Populares Florentino Ameghino, *Memoria, 1938*.

21. Universidad Popular de Boedo, *Memoria, 1937*, 15.
22. Universidad Popular de Flores Sud, *Memoria*; Universidad Popular Florentino Ameghino, *Informe*; Universidades Populares Florentino Ameghino, *Memoria, 1938*.
23. Patrimonio Legislativo, Universidad Popular de Flores Intendente Torcuato de Alvear a la Cámara de Diputados, Aug. 23, 1927, 512-p-1927.
24. Ricardo J. Siri, "Tomás A. Le Breton, 1868–1959," *Los Diplomáticos* 17 (1999), https://www.cari.org.ar/pdf/diplomaticos17.pdf; Bucich, "Ubicación boquense"; *Caras y Caretas*, July 21, 1917, 45–46, Feb. 2, 1919, 66–67; *La Vanguardia*, Dec. 22, 1917; Universidad Popular de La Boca, *Memoria, 1941*, 7; Universidad Popular de La Boca, *XL año lectivo*, 2; Cámara de Diputados, *Diario de sesiones*, Sept. 28, 1921, 5:427; *Las Universidades Populares*, Sept. 1933, 42–44.
25. Horowitz, *Argentina's Radical Party*, esp. 31; *Las Universidades Populares*, Sept. 1933, 60; Patrimonio Legislativo, Universidad Popular del Oeste a la Cámara de Diputados, Dec. 15, 1922, 877-p-1922; Walter, *Politics and Urban Growth*, 211; Patrimonio Legislativo, "Presidentes de la Cámara, 1854–2014"; Luna, *Ortiz*.
26. Gallardo, *Memorias de Angel Gallardo*.
27. *El Monitor de Educación Común*, Sept. 31, 1917, 203–4, Oct. 31, 1917, 43; *Caras y Caretas*, July 21, 1917, 45–46, Feb. 2, 1919, 66–67; *La Vanguardia*, Feb. 7, 1918; Concejo Deliberante de la Municipalidad de Buenos Aires, *Actas*, June 5, 1923, 790–91, Oct. 22, 1929, 1783–84.
28. Concejo Deliberante de la Municipalidad de Buenos Aires, *Actas*, June 5, 1923, 791–92.
29. Ministerio de Justicia e Instrucción Pública, *Estadística*, table 186.
30. Universidad Popular de La Boca, *Memoria, 1941*, 3; "Los comicios en los que se eligieron sólo vice y cargos menores," *Imborrable Boca*, Nov. 13, 2011, http://imborrableboca.blogspot.com/2011/11/; Club Atlético River Plate, "Nace el más grande," www.cariverplate.com.ar/tlp.php?cat=es&url=acta.php, 1/22/07; Barovero, *Caudillos y protagonistas*, 25–26, 45; Privitellio, *Vecinos y ciudadanos*, 71–79.
31. Universidad Popular de La Boca, *Memoria, 1941*.
32. Universidad Popular de La Boca, *Memoria, 1942*, 4–8.
33. Patrimonio Legislativo, Universidad Popular de Boedo a la Cámara de Diputados, Dec. 6, 1929, 840-p-1929.
34. Ibid., especially enclosures (the clipping that is the source of the quote does not include the newspaper's name or date); Horowitz, "Football Clubs and Neighbourhoods," 574–76; Busich Escobar, "D. José Luis Cantilo," 218–19.
35. Cámara de Diputados, *Diario de sesiones*, Sept. 24 and 25, 1928, 5:497, 1937, 2:2, 121; Concejo Deliberante de la Municipalidad de Buenos Aires, *Actas*, June 28, 1929, 1135; Universidad Popular de Boedo, *Memoria, 1937*, 35.
36. Universidad Popular de Boedo, *Memoria, 1940*, 17, and *Memoria, 1937*, 22.
37. Universidad Popular de Boedo, *Memoria, 1936*, 9–22, *Memoria, 1937*, 8–17, and *Memoria, 1940*, 8–13.

38. Universidad Popular Bernardino Rivadavia, *Memoria*, esp. 3; Cámara de Diputados, *Diario de sesiones*, Dec. 16, 1926–Feb. 1927, 8:735.
39. Patrimonio Legislativo, Universidad Popular Bernardino Rivadavia a la Cámara de Diputados, June 22, 1936, 175-p-1936, June 27, 1938, 721-p-1938, July 26, 1939, 328-p-1939, June 19, 1940, 348-p-1940, Aug. 12, 1941, 953-p-1941.
40. In its early years, the shortened references were to Intendente Torcuato de Alvear, but in later years, the name was more commonly shortened to Flores.
41. Patrimonio Legislativo, Universidad Popular de Flores Intendente Torcuato de Alvear a la Cámara de Diputados, Aug. 23, 1927, 512-p-1927, July 25, 1928, 456-p-1928, Sept. 24, 1929, 697-p-1929.
42. Ibid., July 25, 1928, 456-p-1928.
43. The figures for parents take no account for siblings, and many families sent more than one child.
44. Patrimonio Legislativo, Universidad Popular de Flores Intendente Torcuato de Alvear a la Cámara de Diputados, July 25, 1928, 456-p-1928.
45. Patrimonio Legislativo, Universidad Popular de Belgrano a la Cámara de Diputados, Sept. 15, 1938, 1894-p-1938.
46. Ibid., Sept. 15, 1939, 1198-p-1939.
47. Patrimonio Legislativo, Universidad Popular de Belgrano a la Cámara de Diputados, Sept. 15, 1939, 1198-p-1939, Sept. 20, 1940, 1360-p-1940, Aug. 21, 1941, 1047-p-1941, Sept. 1, 1941, 1175-p-1941; "Emma Day," es.wikipedia.org/wiki/Emma_Day. For another example of surviving without national government support for some time, see Patrimonio Legislativo, Universidad Popular Dalmacio Vélez Sarsfield a la Cámara de Diputados, Sept. 28, 1938, 2043-p-1938.
48. *Caras y Caretas*, Sept. 9, 1917, 48–49; "Genealogía de la familia Servén-Pedro Arias," http://rrsrgeneo.blogspot.com/2014/11/dr-pedro-f-arias.html; Consejo Nacional de Educación, *Escuelas primarias*; *El Monitor de Educación Común*, Nov. 30, 1917, 69, Dec. 31, 1918, 183–84.
49. Patrimonio Legislativo, Universidad Popular Bernardo Irigoyen a la Cámara de Diputados, Sept. 27, 1920, 969-p-1920.
50. Patrimonio Legislativo, Universidad Popular Bernardo Irigoyen a la Cámara de Diputados, Sept. 17, 1948, 2240-p-1948; Concejo Deliberantes de la Municipalidad de Buenos Aires, *Actas*, Dec. 28, 1923, 3320; Cámara de Diputados, *Diario de sesiones*, June 30, 1920, 2:802; Sept. 27, 1922, 4:753; June 12, 1923, 3:461; Dec. 16–Feb. 9, 1927, 8:735.
51. Brugnara, *Universidades populares*, 27.
52. Ibid.; Universidad Popular Florentino Ameghino, *La Universidad Popular Florentino Ameghino en su XV aniversario*, 5–9.
53. Brugnara, *Universidades populares*, 30–31; Universidad Popular Florentino Ameghino, *La Universidad Popular Florentino Ameghino en su XV aniversario*, 9, 13.
54. Universidad Popular Florentino Ameghino, *La Universidad Popular Florentino Ameghino en su XV aniversario*, 52–53; Cámara de Diputados, *Diario de sesiones*, Sept. 24 and 25, 1928, 5:407.

55. Universidad Popular Florentino Ameghino, *La Universidad Popular Florentino Ameghino en su XV aniversario*, 33; Universidades Populares Florentino Ameghino y Femenina de Palermo, *Memoria, 1935*; Universidad Popular Florentino Ameghino, *Informe*; Patrimonio Legislativo, Universidad Popular Florentino Ameghino a la Cámara de Diputados, Oct. 2, 1937, 1071-p-1937.
56. Universidad Popular Florentino Ameghino, *Memoria, 1934*; Universidades Populares Florentino Ameghino y Femenina de Palermo, *Memoria, 1935*; Universidades Populares Florentino Ameghino, *Memoria, 1938*.
57. Patrimonio Legislativo, Universidad Popular Florentino Ameghino a la Cámara de Diputados, Oct. 2, 1937, 1071-p-1937; Universidades Populares Florentino Ameghino, *Memoria, 1938*; Cámara de Diputados, *Diario de sesiones*, Sept. 3, 1942, 4:418–19, Sept. 25–26, 1942, 5:868.
58. Patrimonio Legislativo, Universidad Popular Florentino Ameghino a la Cámara de Diputados, Sept. 24, 1936, 580-p-1936; Universidad Popular Florentino Ameghino, *La Universidad Popular Florentino Ameghino en su XV aniversario*, 5, 28–29.
59. Universidad Popular Florentino Ameghino, *Memoria, 1934*; Universidades Populares Florentino Ameghino y Femenina de Palermo, *Memoria, 1935*; Universidades Populares Florentino Ameghino, *Memoria, 1938*, and *Memoria, 1939*; Patrimonio Legislativo, Universidad Popular Femenina de Palermo a la Cámara de Diputados, Sept. 24, 1936, 579-p-1936, July 24, 1940, 646-p-1940.
60. Cámara de Diputados, *Diario de sesiones*, 1937, 2:2, 121; Concejo Deliberante de la Municipalidad de Buenos Aires, *Actas*, Aug. 31, 1937, 1868.
61. Universidades Populares Florentino Ameghino, *Memoria, 1938*, and *Memoria, 1939*; Patrimonio Legislativo, Universidad Popular de Villa Pueyrredón a la Cámara de Diputados, Oct. 2, 1937, 1070-p-1937, Aug. 20, 1940, 933-p-1940.
62. Archivo Intermedio de la Nación, Fondo Inspección General de Justicia, Registro de Asociaciones Civiles, caja 74, 359221, Universidad Popular de Villa del Parque; Patrimonio Legislativo, Universidad Popular de Villa del Parque a la Cámara de Diputados, June 27, 1940, 398-1/2-p-1940.
63. Archivo Intermedio de la Nación, Fondo Inspección General de Justicia, Registro de Asociaciones Civiles, caja 74, 359221, Universidad Popular de Villa del Parque; Universidad Popular de Villa del Parque, *Memoria, 1937*, and *Memoria, 1940*; Patrimonio Legislativo, Universidad Popular de Villa del Parque a la Cámara de Diputados, Sept. 24, 1936, 578-p-1936, Oct. 2, 1937, 1072-p-1937, Aug. 24, 1938, 1619-p-1938, June 27, 1940, 398-1/2-p-1940; Universidades Populares Florentino Ameghino, *Memoria, 1939*; *Primera Plana*, Mar. 16, 1965, 11. I found no contemporary record of Vinciguerra's involvement with the institution.
64. Brugnara, *Universidades populares*, 77–83; Patrimonio Legislativo, Universidad Popular Industrial de Buenos Aires a la Cámara de Diputados, Sept. 30, 1938, 2075-p-1938, Sept. 17, 1940, 1296-p-1940, and Extracto Angel Beiró: Subvención a la Universidad Popular Industrial de Buenos Aires y otras instituciones, July 10, 1941, 560-d-1941; Universidades Populares Florentino Ameghino, *Memoria, 1938*, and *Memoria, 1939*.

Conclusion

1. *Primera Plana*, Jan. 26, 1965, 12–13, Mar. 16, 1965, 10–11.
2. Levitsky, *Transforming Labor-Based Parties*, esp. 30, 63; Szwarcberg, "Building a Following," esp. 6; Szwarcberg, "Micro Foundations," 33.
3. Auyero, *Poor People's Politics*, esp. 156–59; Stokes et al., *Brokers, Voters, and Clientelism*, esp. 19, 76; Zarazaga, "Brokers beyond Clientelism."
4. *Olé*, Oct. 10, 2019.
5. See the official websites of the clubs.
6. Rein, *La cancha peronista*. There is a vast literature on politicization after 1955. For an overview, see Scher and Palomino, *Fútbol*.
7. *La Nación*, Feb. 29 and Aug. 14, 2012; *El País*, Dec. 9, 2019; *Perfil*, Dec. 6, 2019.
8. *La Nación*, Nov. 25 and 28, 2020; *El País*, Nov. 27, 2020; *Perfil*, Nov. 29, 2020.
9. Duke and Crolley, "Fútbol, Politicians and People"; *Clarín*, Apr. 21 and Nov. 17, 2009, Dec. 23, 2012, Mar. 4, 2015; *Perfil*, Oct. 22, 2016; *La Nación*, Nov. 28, 2020; Gustavo Grabia, "Cómo las barras bravas mancharon la despedida de Diego Armando Maradona," TyC Sports, Nov. 28, 2020, https://www.tycsports.com/interes-general/barras-bravas-despedida-maradona-id305693.html.
10. *La Nación*, Apr. 9, 2017; *El País*, May 13, 2019; "Buscador BEPÉ," https://www.conabip.gob.ar/buscador_bp?province=Ciudad+Aut%C3%B3noma+de+Buenos+Aires&city=&field_nombre_de_la_biblioteca_value=&field_n_mero_de_registro_value=, 5/24/20.
11. For example, see García, *El caso Vigil*.
12. *El País*, May 13, 2019.
13. "Ordenanza J.-N. 8.522, Jan.13, 2016," *Separata del Boletín Oficial de la Ciudad de Buenos Aires*, https://boletinoficial.buenosaires.gob.ar/files/digesto/2016_I-J-AccionSocialComunitariaDeportesyActividadesRecreativas.pdf; Sociedad de Fomento Belgrano R., https://es-la.facebook.com/SociedadFomentoBelgranoR/; "Belgrano, R.," https://es.wikipedia.org/wiki/Belgrano_R; "Un club con tradiciones en el corazón de Chacarita," *Diario Z*, https://historico.diarioz.com.ar/#!/nota/un-club-con-tradiciones-en-el-corazon-de-chacarita-44998/; "Fomento, Edilicio, Cultural y Deportivo José Hernández," https://es.wikipedia.org/wiki/Asociaci%C3%B3n_de_Fomento_Edilicio,_Cultural_y_Deportivo_Jos%C3%A9_Hern%C3%A1ndez; "La Asociación Benito Nazar cumple 90 años," *AVC Amo Villa Crespo*, Jan.–Feb. 2017, https://issuu.com/amovillacrespo/docs/avc16web.
14. Plotkin, *Mañana es San Perón*, esp. 154–55; Rein, *Politics and Education in Argentina*, 34–42; Torre and Pastoriza, "La democratización del bienestar," 298–99; Silvia Vepstas, "Un siglo enseñando oficios," *Sur Capitalino*, Aug. 31, 2017, https://www.surcapitalino.com.ar/detalle_noticias.php?Id=4091; Universidad Popular de La Boca, https://www.facebook.com/uplaboca/; Universidad Popular de Belgrano, http://www.upebe.com.ar/.

Bibliography

Unless noted otherwise, all websites were available as of September 14, 2022. If a date is listed, the site may no longer be available.

Archival Sources

Archive of Comisión Nacional de Bibliotecas Populares (CONABIP), Buenos Aires
Archive of CONABIP online. http://v.conabip.gob.ar/archivo_historico/results
Archivo General de la Nación, Buenos Aires
Archivo Intermedio de la Nación, Buenos Aires
Cámara de Diputados, *Diario de sesiones*
Cámara de Diputados online
    Diputados, https://apym.hcdn.gob.ar/diputados
    Expedientes, https://apym.hcdn.gob.ar/expedientes
    Patrimonio Legislativo, https://apym.hcdn.gob.ar/
    Presidentes de la cámara, https://apym.hcdn.gob.ar/autoridades
Concejo Deliberante de la Municipalidad de Buenos Aires, *Actas*
Library of the Instituto Ravignani, Buenos Aires

Published Sources

Abad de Santillán, Diego. *Gran enciclopedia Argentina*. 8 vols. Buenos Aires: Ediar, 1956.
Abellá, Mario, and Laura Larrique. *Sistema nacional de bibliotecas públicas*. Montevideo, Uruguay: Instituto Nacional del Libro, 1990.
Abraham, Carlos. *La Editorial Tor: Medio siglo de libros populares*. Temperley, Buenos Aires: Tren en Movimiento, 2012.
Adamovsky, Ezequiel. *Historia de la clase media argentina: Apogeo y decadencia de una ilusión, 1919–2003*. Buenos Aires: Planeta, 2009.
Aguas Argentinas. *Buenos Aires y el agua: Memoria, higiene urbana y vida cotidiana*. Buenos Aires: Aguas Argentina, 2001.
Agulhon, Maurice. *Le cercle dans la France bourgeoise, 1810–1848: Etude d'une mutation de sociabilité*. Paris: Librairie Armand Colin, 1977.

———. "La sociabilidad como categoría histórica." In *Formas de sociabilidad en Chile, 1840–1940*, ed. Maurice Algulhon et al., 1–10. Santiago, Chile: Fundación Mario Góngora, 1992.

Aiscurri, Mario. *La tribu de mi calle*. Buenos Aires: Catálogos, 2007.

Almond, Gabriel A., and Sidney Verba. *Civic Culture: Political Attitudes and Democracy in Five Nations*. Boston, MA: Little, Brown, 1965.

Alonso, Paula. *Between Revolution and the Ballot Box: The Origins of the Argentine Radical Party in the 1890s*. Cambridge: Cambridge University Press, 2000.

———. *Jardines secretos, legitimaciones públicas: El Partido Autonomista y la política argentina de fines del siglo XIX*. Buenos Aires: Edhasa, 2010.

Altick, Richard D. *The English Common Reader: A Social History of the Mass Reading Public 1800–1900*. Chicago, IL: University of Chicago Press, 1957.

American Society of Editors. *International Yearbook, 1929*. New York: Editor and Publisher, 1929.

Annual Report of the Trustees of the Public Library of the City of Boston, 1900–1901. Boston, MA: Municipal Printing Office, 1901.

Anuario estadístico de la ciudad de Buenos Aires, 1915–1923. Buenos Aires: Briozzo Hnos., 1925.

Anuario Kraft. Buenos Aires: Guillermo Kraft, 1918.

Anuario La Libertad, 1931. Avellaneda, Buenos Aires: La Libertad, 1931.

Anuario Socialista, 1930. Buenos Aires: La Vanguardia, 1929.

Arata, Héctor F. *Villa Urquiza: Sus primeros cien años*. Buenos Aires: Editorial La Constancia, 1987.

Archetti, Eduardo P. *Masculinities: Football, Polo and the Tango in Argentina*. Oxford: Berg, 1999.

Artienda, Teresa Laura. "Historia de la Universidad Popular Juan Ramón Lestani (Chaco, Argentina, circa 1929–1960)." *Historia Caribe* 16:38 (Jan.–June 2021): 167–208.

Armus, Diego. *The Ailing City: Health, Tuberculosis, and Culture in Buenos Aires, 1870–1950*. Durham, NC: Duke University Press, 2011.

———. "Contextualizando la enfermedad: Educación física, fútbol y tuberculosis en el Buenos Aires moderno." *Estudios del ISHiR* 3:5 (2013): 7–13.

———. "La idea del verde en la ciudad moderna: Buenos Aires 1870–1940." *Entrepasados* 10 (1996): 9–22.

———. "'Milonguitas' en Buenos Aires (1910–1940): Tango, ascenso social y tuberculosis." *História, Ciências, Saúde-Manguinhos* 9, suppl. (2002): 187–207, http://www.scielo.br/scielo.php?script=sci_arttext&pid=S0104-59702002000400009&lng=en&nrm=iso.

Armus, Diego, and Pablo Ariel Scharagrodsky. "El fútbol en las escuelas y colegios argentinos: Notas sobre un desencuentro en el siglo XX." In *Del football al fútbol: Historias argentinas, brasileras y uruguayos en el siglo XX*, ed. Diego Armus and Stefan Rinke, 85–99. Madrid: Iberoamericana/Editorial Vervuert, 2014.

Asociación Amateurs de Football. *Memoria y balance general: Correspondiente al ejercicio.* Buenos Aires, 1925, 1926, 1927.
Asociación Biblioteca Popular Domingo Faustino Sarmiento. *Memoria y balance.* Buenos Aires, 1930–1941.
Asociación Cultural Florencio Sánchez. *Memoria y balance, 1932–1933.* Buenos Aires, 1933.
Asociación de Fomento 12 de Octubre Caballito Noroeste. *Memoria, ejercicio, 1919–1920.* Buenos Aires: C. A. Dionigi, 1920.
Asociación de Football Argentino. *Memoria y balance general.* Buenos Aires, 1935–1939.
Asociación del Fútbol Argentino. *Memoria y balance.* Buenos Aires, 1940–1943.
———. "Registro de instituciones afiliados, 1940–1944." biblioteca.afa.org.ar/libros/libro_31/.
Asociación Liga de Fomento de Villa General Mitre. *Memoria, ejercicio.* Buenos Aires, 1920–1935.
Auyero, Javier. *Poor People's Politics: Peronist Survival Networks and the Legacy of Evita.* Durham, NC: Duke University Press, 2001.
Ballent, Anahí. *Las huellas de la política: Vivienda, ciudad: Peronismo en Buenos Aires, 1943–1955.* Bernal, Buenos Aires: Universidad Nacional de Quilmes/Prometeo 3010, 2005.
Banchik, Mario, ed. *Buenos Aires, los cafés.* 3 vols. Buenos Aires: Ediciones Turísticas, 1999–2003.
Bard, Leopoldo. *Estampas de una vida: La fe puesta en un ideal "llegar a ser algo."* Buenos Aires: Talleres Gráficos J. Perrotti, 1957.
Barovero, Diego Alberto. *Caudillos y protagonistas en la Boca del Riachuelo.* Buenos Aires: Editorial Dunken, 2013.
Barrancos, Dora. *Anarquismo, educación y costumbres en la Argentina de principios de siglo.* Buenos Aires: Contrapunto, 1990.
———. *Educación, cultura y trabajadores (1890–1930).* Buenos Aires: Centro Editor de América Latina, 1991.
———. *La escena iluminada: Ciencias para trabajadores, 1890–1930.* Buenos Aires: Plus Ultra, 1996.
Bellini, Claudio, and Juan Carlos Korol. *Historia económica de la Argentina en el siglo XX.* Buenos Aires: Siglo Veintiuno, 2012.
Bermeo, Nancy, and Philip Nord, eds. *Civil Society before Democracy: Lessons from Nineteenth-Century Europe.* Lanham, MD: Rowman and Littlefield, 2000.
Bernal, Eduardo. "Pedro Bidegain, un hombre de Boedo." *Desmemoria* 4:13–14 (1997): 82–101.
Bertolotto, Miguel Angel. *River: El campeón del siglo.* Buenos Aires: Oceano/Temas, 2000.
Biblioteca y Asociación Vecinal de Nueva Chicago. *Memoria y balance periodo.* Buenos Aires, 1932, 1934.
Biblioteca Obrera Juan B. Justo. *Memoria.* Buenos Aires: La Vanguardia, 1938–1943.

Biblioteca Popular del Centro de Cultura Juventud Israelita de Boca y Barracas. *Almanaque 1911–enero 1931*. Buenos Aires: Talleres Gráficos Cultura, 1931.
Bidegain, Pedro. *Mi radicalismo*. Buenos Aires, 1929.
Bocketti, Gregg P. "Italian Immigrants, Brazilian Football, and the Dilemma of National Identity." *Journal of Latin American Studies* 40:2 (May 2008): 275–302.
Boffi, Luis L. *1259 días concejal de la ciudad de Buenos Aires*. Buenos Aires: Lotito Hnos., 1943.
Bolan, Eduardo Horacio. *Biblioteca Popular Alberdi: Recorridos por su historia*. Buenos Aires: Biblioteca Popular Alberdi, 2014.
Bonaudo, Marta, ed. *Liberalismo: Estado y orden burgués (1852–1880)*. Volume 4 of *Nueva historia argentina*. Buenos Aires: Editorial Sudamericana, 1999.
Boragno, Susana. "Los talleres ferroviarios en la geografía del barrio de Liniers." *Revista de Historia Bonaerense* 12:28 (2005): 55–59.
Bossio, Jorge A. *Los cafés de Buenos Aires*. Buenos Aires: Schapire, 1968.
Botana, Natalio. *El orden conservador: La política argentina entre 1880–1916*. Buenos Aires: Editorial Sudamericana, 1977.
Bourdé, Guy. *Buenos Aires: Urbanización e inmigración*. Buenos Aires: Ediciones Huemul, 1977.
Brennan, James P., and Marcelo Rougier. *The Politics of National Capitalism: Peronism and the Argentine Bourgeoisie, 1946–1976*. University Park: Pennsylvania State University Press, 2009.
Brock, Herman G. *Boots and Shoes: Leather and Supplies in Argentina, Uruguay, and Paraguay*. Washington, DC: Government Printing Office, 1919.
Brugnara, Juan A. *Universidades populares*. Buenos Aires: Editorial Tor, 1941.
Bruno, Paula, ed. *Sociabilidades y vida cultural: Buenos Aires, 1860–1930*. Bernal, Buenos Aires: Editorial Universidad Nacional de Quilmes, 2014.
Bucich, Antonio J. *La Boca del Riachuelo en la historia*. Buenos Aires: Asociación Amigos de la Escuela-Museo de Bellas Artes de La Boca, 1971.
———. "Ubicación boquense de Dr. Tomás A. Le Breton." *Cuadernos de la Boca del Riachuelo* 25 (1967).
Bunge, Alejandro E. *Una nueva Argentina*. Buenos Aires: Editorial Guillermo Kraft, 1940.
Busich Escobar, Ismael. "D. José Luis Cantilo." In *Buenos Aires: La gran provincia, 1880–1930*. https://bibliomoron.webcindario.com/cantilo1.html.
Caimari, Lila. *Apenas un delincuente: Castigo y cultura en la Argentina, 1880–1955*. Buenos Aires: Siglo Veintiuno, 2004.
———. *While the City Sleeps: A History of Pistoleros, Policemen and the Crime Beat in Buenos Aires before Perón*. Berkeley: University of California Press, 2017.
Calhoun, Craig, ed. *Habermas and the Public Sphere*. Cambridge, MA: MIT Press, 1992.
Calvino, Italo. *Invisible Cities*. Translated by William Weaver. New York: Harcourt, 1974.
Camarero, Hernán. *A la conquista obrera: Los comunistas y el mundo del trabajo en la

Argentina, 1920–1935. Buenos Aires: Siglo Veintiuno/Editora Iberoamericana, 2007.
Campione, Daniel, Mercedes López Cantera, and Bárbara Maier. "La cuestión Penelón: División en el comunismo argentino a fines de la década del '20." Paper presented at the XI Jornadas Interescuelas/Departamentos de Historia, 2007. http://cdsa.aacademica.org/000-108/534.pdf.
Cane, James. *The Fourth Enemy: Journalism and Power in the Making of Peronist Argentina, 1930–1955*. University Park: Pennsylvania State University Press, 2011.
Canop, Santiago. *Obra y acción de las universidades populares argentinas*. Buenos Aires: Macagno Hnos. y Landa, 1941.
Cascante, Edgardo. *Barracas al sud: Vida cotidiana 1870–1970*. Buenos Aires: Editorial Dunken, 2006.
Cattaruzza, Alejandro, ed. *Crisis económica, avance del estado e incertidumbre política (1930–1943)*. Volume 7 of *Nueva historia argentina*. Buenos Aires: Editorial Sudamericana, 2001.
Cecchi, Alfredo Luis. *Sinopsis histórica del Partido Socialista*. 2 vols. Santa Fe, Argentina: Fundación Casa del Pueblo, 2008, 2011.
Cedro, Juliana. "El negocio de la edición: Claridad, 1922–1937." Paper presented at the Primer Coloquio Argentina de Estudios sobre el Libro y la Editorial, 2012. www.memoria.fahce.unlp.edu.ar/trab_eventos/ev.1923/ev.1923.pdf.
Centro para la Investigación de la Historia del Fútbol. "Fundación del Club Atlético River Plate." *Boletín CIHF* 2:21 (May 13, 2004). https://fdocuments.net/document/river-plate-100.html.
Chiti, Juan B., and Francisco Agnelli. *Cincuentenario de "La Fraternidad."* Buenos Aires: Revishino Hnos., 1937.
Cisneros, Luis Fernán. *Historia de la ciudad de Avellaneda*. Buenos Aires: Ediciones Argentinas, 1926.
Clemenceau, Georges. *South America Today*. London: T. Fisher Unwin, 1911.
Club Atlético Chacarita Juniors. *Memoria y balance general correspondiente al ejercicio administrativo de año*. Buenos Aires, 1930–1941.
Club Atlético Estudiantes de La Plata. *Memoria*. La Plata, Buenos Aires, 1930–1942.
Club Atlético Lanús. *Memoria y balance general*. Lanús, Buenos Aires, 1932–1943.
Club Atlético River Plate. *Memoria y balance*. Buenos Aires, 1922–1932.
Club Atlético San Lorenzo de Almagro. *Memoria y balance general*. Buenos Aires, 1924–1930.
Club Atlético Vélez Sarsfield. *Memoria y balance general ejercicio, 1940*. Buenos Aires, 1941.
Comisión de Asuntos Históricos, Club Atlético Vélez Sarsfield. *La historia de Vélez Sarsfield (1910–1980)*. Buenos Aires: Comisión de Asuntos Históricos, 1980.
Comisión Nacional del Censo. *Tercer censo nacional, levantado el 1° de junio de 1914*. 10 vols. Buenos Aires: Talleres Gráfico de L. J. Rosso, 1916–1919.
CONABIP. *Ley, decreto, reglamento e instrucciones para bibliotecas populares*. Buenos Aires, 1942.

———. *Memoria correspondiente a los años*. Buenos Aires, 1917, 1936, 1937.

———. *Nómina de las bibliotecas populares protegidas*. Buenos Aires, 1933, 1938.

Concejo Deliberante de la Ciudad de Buenos Aires. *Ordenanzas, resoluciones y minutas de comunicación sancionadas en el periodo de sesiones de 1927*. Buenos Aires: Edición Oficial, 1928.

———. *Ordenanzas, resoluciones y minutas de comunicaciones sancionadas sesiones de 1939*. Buenos Aires: Edición Oficial, 1940.

Confederación Nacional de Juntas Vecinales. *El movimiento vecinal en Bolivia: I seminario regional*. Ouro, Bolivia: Quelco, 1991.

Consejo Nacional de Educación. *Escuelas primarias de la capital*. Buenos Aires, 1917.

Contarelli, Luis, hijo. *Acción de las entidades de bien público cultural y deportiva*. La Plata, Buenos Aires, 1953.

Córdoba, Alberto Octavio. *El barrio de Belgrano*. Buenos Aires: Municipalidad de la Ciudad de Buenos Aires, 1968.

Cortés Conde, Roberto. *The Political Economy of Argentina in the Twentieth Century*. Cambridge: Cambridge University Press, 2009.

Cubilla, Érica Elizabeth. "Sociabilidad y cultura de la clase media en Buenos Aires de 1930: El barrio de Villa Devoto." Master's thesis, IDES/Universidad Nacional de General Sarmiento, 2017.

Cutolo, Vicente Osvaldo. *Historia de los barrios de Buenos Aires*. 2 vols. 2nd ed. Buenos Aires: Editorial ELCHE, 1998.

Dagnino Pastore, José María, ed. *Casi un siglo: Lorenzo Dagnino Pastore*. Buenos Aires: Editorial Dunken, 2000.

Daskal, Rodrigo. *Los clubes en la ciudad de Buenos Aires (1932–1945)*. Buenos Aires: Editorial Teseo, 2013.

Deán, Alberto. *San Lorenzo querido: 100 años de pasión*. Buenos Aires: Dos Tintas, 2008.

Del Pino, Diego. *El barrio de Villa Crespo*. Buenos Aires: Municipalidad de la Ciudad de Buenos Aires, 1974.

———. "Un buen caudillo del barrio de Villa Crespo: Don Salvador Benedit." *Boletín del Instituto Histórico de la Ciudad de Buenos Aires* 7:13 (1989): 89–101.

Departamento Nacional del Trabajo, División de Estadística. *Condiciones de vida de la familia obrera*. Buenos Aires, 1937.

———. *Investigaciones sociales, 1938*. Buenos Aires, 1938.

Devoto, Fernando. *Historia de la inmigración en la Argentina*. Buenos Aires: Editorial Sudamericana, 2003.

Diego, José Luis de. *La otra cara de Jano: Una mirada crítica sobre el libro y la edición*. Buenos Aires: Colección Scripta Manent, 2015.

Di Stefano, Roberto, et al. *De las cofradías a las organizaciones de la sociedad civil*. Buenos Aires: Gadis, 2002.

Di Tella, Torcuato S. *Perón y los sindicatos: El inicio de una relación conflictiva*. Buenos Aires: Ariel, 2003.

Domínguez Rubio, Lucas. *El anarquismo argentino: Bibliografías, hemerografías y fundos de archivo.* Buenos Aires: Libros de Anarres, 2018.
"¿Dónde anida la democracia?" *Punta de Vista* 15 (1982): 6–10.
Duffau Soto, Nicolás. *De urgencias y necesidades: Los sectores populares montevideanos a través de la documentación de una asociación vecinal: El caso de la Comisión Fomento Aires Puros (1938–1955).* Montevideo, Uruguay: Abrelabios, 2009.
Dujovne, Alejandro. *Una historia del libro judío: La cultura judía argentina a través de sus editores, libreros, traductores, imprentas y bibliotecas.* Buenos Aires: Siglo Veintiuno, 2014.
Duke, Vic, and Liz Crolley. "Fútbol, Politicians and People: Populism and Politics in Argentina." *International Journal of the History of Sport* 18:3 (Sept. 2001): 93–116.
Elsey, Brenda. *Citizens and Sportsmen: Fútbol and Politics in 20th-Century Chile.* Austin: University of Texas Press, 2011.
Elsey, Brenda, and Joshua Nadel. *Futbolera: A History of Women and Sports in Latin America.* Austin: University of Texas Press, 2019.
Fabbri, Alejandro. *El nacimiento de una pasión: Historia de los clubes de fútbol.* Buenos Aires: Capital Intelectual, 2006.
Falcón, Ricardo, ed. *Democracia, conflicto social y renovación de ideas (1916–1930).* Volume 6 of *Nueva historia argentina.* Buenos Aires: Editorial Sudamericana, 2000.
Felsenstein, Frank, and James J. Connolly. *What Middletown Read: Print Cultural in an American Small City.* Amherst: University of Massachusetts Press, 2015.
Fernández, Manuel F. *La Unión Ferroviaria a través del tiempo.* Buenos Aires: Unión Ferroviaria, 1948.
Fernández Hirsuta, Pablo. "Alberto Barceló: Políticas públicas y caudillismo conservador en Avellaneda, 1909–1930." PhD diss., Universidad Nacional del Quilmes, 2009.
Ferrera, Carlos. "Vivir en Soldati." In *Buenos Aires voces al sur: Construcción de identidades barriales,* ed. Lidia González, 121–28. Buenos Aires: Instituto Histórico de la Ciudad de Buenos Aires, 2006.
Ferreres, Orlando J., ed. *Dos siglos de economía argentina (1810–2004).* Buenos Aires: Fundación Norte y Sur, 2005.
Fiorucci, Flavia. "La cultura, el libro y la lectura bajo el peronismo: El caso de la Comisión de Bibliotecas Populares." *Desarrollo Económico* 48:192 (2009): 543–56.
Folino, Norberto. *Barceló, Ruggierito y el populismo oligárquico.* Buenos Aires: Ediciones de la Flor, 1983.
Forment, Carlos A. *Democracy in Latin America, 1760–1900, Vol. 1: Civic Selfhood and Public Life in Mexico and Peru.* Chicago, IL: University of Chicago Press, 2003.
Fraga, Rosendo. *El general Justo.* Buenos Aires: Emecé, 1993.
Francavilla, Cayetano. *Historia de Villa Crespo.* Buenos Aires: Del Autor, 1978.
Francos Rodríguez, José. *Huellas españolas: Impresiones de un viaje por América.* Madrid: Editorial América, 1921(?).
Frydenberg, Julio D. "Espacio urbano y práctica del fútbol, Buenos Aires 1900–1915." *Revista Digital,* www.efdeportes.com/efd13/juliof.htm.

———. *Historia social del fútbol: Del amateurismo a la profesionalización.* Buenos Aires: Siglo Veintiuno, 2011.

———. "Los nombres de los clubes de fútbol, Buenos Aires 1880–1930." *Revista Digital,* www.efdeportes.com/efd2/22jdf11.htm.

———. "Redefinición del fútbol aficionado y del fútbol oficial: Buenos Aires, 1912." In *Deporte y sociedad,* ed. Pablo Alabarces, Roberto Di Giano, and Julio Frydenberg, 51–65. Buenos Aires: EUDEBA, 1998.

Función social de la escuela. Reseña de la obra educacional realizada en la jurisdicción del Concejo Escolar IV (Boca). Presidencia de Agustín R. Caffarena. Buenos Aires: El Comercio, 1908.

Gaffney, Christopher T. *Temples of the Earthbound Gods.* Austin: University of Texas Press, 2008.

Gallardo, Angel. *Memorias de Angel Gallardo.* Buenos Aires: El Elefante Blanco, 2003.

Gálvez, Eduardo. "El tango en su época de gloria: Ni prostibulario, ni orillero. Los bailes en los clubes sociales y deportivos de Buenos Aires 1938–1959." *Nuevo Mundo, Mundos Nuevos* (2009). doi.org/10.4000/nuevomundo.55183.

García, Eustasio A. "Historia de la empresa editorial en Argentina, siglo XX." In *Historia de las empresas editoriales de América Latina. Siglo XX,* ed. Juan Gustavo Cobo Borda, 15–104. Bogotá: CERLALC, 2000.

García, Natalia. *El caso Vigil: Historia sociocultural, política y educativa de la Biblioteca Vigil (1933–1981).* Rosario, Santa Fe, Argentina: Humanidades y Artes Ediciones, 2014.

García Heras, Raúl. *Transportes, negocios y política.* Buenos Aires: Sudamericana, 1994.

García Puertas, Yulima D., and Mirta C. Botana Rodríguez. "Las bibliotecas públicas cubanas en la etapa prerrevolucionaria." *Revista Cubana de Información en Ciencias de la Salud* 13:6 (2006). http://scielo.sld.cu/scielo.php?script=sci_arttext&pid=S1024-94352005000600012.

Gayol, Sandra. *Sociabilidad en Buenos Aires: Hombres, honor y cafés, 1862–1910.* Buenos Aires: Signo, 2000.

Gerchunoff, Pablo. *El eslabón perdido: La economía política de los gobiernos radicales (1916–1930).* Buenos Aires: Edhasa, 2016.

Germani, Gino. *Estructura social de la Argentina.* Buenos Aires: Raigal, 1955.

Giménez, Ángel. "Que hacer de las horas libres: Una actividad útil para la mujer: Su colaboración en las bibliotecas populares." *Vida Femenina* 16 (Aug. 15, 1938): 6–7.

González, Ricardo. "Lo propio y lo ajeno: Actividades culturales y fomentismo en una asociación vecinal, Barrio Nazca." In *Mundo urbano y cultura popular,* ed. Diego Armus, 91–128. Buenos Aires: Editorial Sudamericana, 1990.

Gorelik, Adrián. "El color del barrio: Mitología barrial y conflicto cultural en la Buenos Aires de los años veinte." *Variaciones Borges* 8 (1999): 36–68.

———. "Ensayo introductorio: *Terra Incognito*: Para una comprensión del Gran Buenos Aires como Gran Buenos Aires." In *El gran Buenos Aires.* Volume. 6 of *Historia de la provincia de Buenos Aires,* ed. Gabriel Kessler, 21–69. Buenos Aires: Edhasa/UNIPE, 2015.

———. *La grilla y el parque: Espacio público y cultura urbana en Buenos Aires, 1887–1936*. Bernal, Buenos Aires: Universidad Nacional del Quilmes, 2004.
Graciano, Osvaldo. "Entre cultura y política: La Universidad Popular Alejandro Korn, 1937–1950." *Trabajos y Comunicaciones* (Universidad Nacional de La Plata) 25 (1999): 71–120.
———. *Entre la torre de marfil y el compromiso político: Intelectuales de izquierda en la Argentina, 1918–1955*. Bernal, Buenos Aires: Universidad de Quilmes, 2008.
Gravano, Ariel. *Antropología de lo barrial: Estudios sobre producción simbólica de la vida urbana*. Buenos Aires: Espacio Editorial, 2003.
———. *El barrio en la teoría social*. Buenos Aires: Espacio Editorial, 2005.
Gruschetsky, Mariano. "Fútbol y clubes en tierras socialistas: El Club Talleres de Remedios de Escalada durante el primer peronismo." In *La cancha peronista: Fútbol y política (1946–1955)*, ed. Ranaan Rein, 221–40. San Martín, Buenos Aires: UNSAM Edita, 2015.
Guía de planos: Ciudad de Buenos Aires y suburbanos. 28th ed. Buenos Aires: Editorial Filcar, 1976.
Gutiérrez, Leandro, and Luis Alberto Romero. *Sectores populares, cultura política: Buenos Aires en la entreguerra*. Buenos Aires: Sudamericana, 1995.
Gutman, Margarita, and Jorge Enrique Hardoy. *Buenos Aires, 1536–2006: Historia urbana del área metropolitana*. Buenos Aires: Ediciones Infinito, 2007.
Halperín Donghi, Tulio. *La Argentina y la tormenta del mundo: Ideas e ideologías entre 1930 y 1945*. Buenos Aires: Siglo Veintiuno, 2003.
———. "Una ciudad entra en el siglo XX." In *Buenos Aires: El imaginario para un gran capital*, ed. Margarita Gutman and Thomas Reese, 55–66. Buenos Aires: Eudeba, 1999.
———. *La república imposible (1930–1945)*. Buenos Aires: Ariel, 2004.
———. *Vida y muerte de la república verdadera (1910–1930)*. Buenos Aires: Ariel, 1999.
Harris, Michael H. *History of Libraries in the Western World*. 4th ed. Lanham, MD: Scarecrow, 1995.
Hora, Roy. *Historia económica de la Argentina en el siglo XIX*. Buenos Aires: Siglo Veintiuno, 2010.
———. *Historia del turf argentino*. Buenos Aires: Siglo Veintiuno, 2014.
———. "Izquierda y clases populares en la Argentina, 1880–1945." *Prismas* 23 (2019): 53–75.
———. *The Landowners of the Argentine Pampas: A Social and Political History, 1860–1945*. Oxford: Oxford University Press, 2001.
Horowitz, Joel. *Argentina's Radical Party and Popular Mobilization, 1916–1930*. University Park: Pennsylvania State University Press, 2008.
———. *Argentine Unions, the State, and the Rise of Perón, 1930–1945*. Berkeley: Institute of International Studies, University of California, 1990.
———. "Football Clubs and Neighbourhoods in Buenos Aires before 1943: The Role of Political Linkages and Personal Influence." *Journal of Latin American Studies* 46:3 (Aug. 2014): 557–87.

———. "Occupational Community and the Creation of a Self-Styled Elite: Railroad Workers in Argentina." *Americas* 42:1 (July 1985): 55–81.
———. "Patrones y clientes: El empleo municipal en el Buenos Aires de los primeros gobiernos radicales (1916–1930)." *Desarrollo Económico* 46:184 (Jan.–Mar. 2007): 569–96.
Iñigo Carrera, Nicolás. *La estrategia de la clase obrera 1936*. Buenos Aires: La Rosa Blindada, 2000.
Iwanczuk, Jorge. *Historia de fútbol amateur en la Argentina*. Buenos Aires: Centro de Investigación de la Historia del Fútbol, 1992.
Jablonsky, Thomas J. *Pride in the Jungle: Community and Everyday Life in the Back of the Yards Chicago*. Baltimore, MD: Johns Hopkins University Press, 1993.
Klaiber, Jeffrey. "The Popular University and the Origins of Aprismo, 1921–1924." *Hispanic American Historical Review* 55:4 (Nov. 1975): 693–715.
Klineberg, Eric. *Palaces for the People*. New York: Broadway Books, 2018.
Korn, Francis. *Buenos Aires: Los huéspedes del 20*. Buenos Aires: Editorial Sudamericana, 1974.
Landau, Matías. *Gobernar Buenos Aires: Ciudad, política y sociedad, del siglo XIX a nuestros días*. Buenos Aires: Prometeo Libros, 2018.
Landenburger, Jorge W., and Francisco M. Conte, eds. *La Unión Cívica: Su origen, organización y tendencias*. Buenos Aires, 1890.
Lentini, Emilio. *Crónica de un milagro: Nueva Chicago, una pasión nacional*. Buenos Aires: Corregidor, 2012.
Lever, Janet. *Soccer Madness*. Chicago, IL: University of Chicago Press, 1983.
Levitsky, Steven. *Transforming Labor-Based Parties in Latin America: Argentine Peronism in Comparative Perspective*. Cambridge: Cambridge University Press, 2003.
Llanes, Ricardo M. *El barrio de Almagro*. Buenos Aires: Municipalidad de la Ciudad de Buenos Aires, 1968.
Lobato, Mirta Zaida, ed. *El progreso, la modernización y sus límites (1888–1916)*. Volume 5 of *Nueva historia argentina*. Buenos Aires: Editorial Sudamericana, 2000.
Lorenzo, Ricardo (Borocotó). *Historia del fútbol argentino*. 3 vols. Buenos Aires: Editorial Eiffel, 1955.
Luna, Félix. *Ortiz: Reportaje a la Argentina opulenta*. Buenos Aires: Editorial Sudamericana, 1978.
Lupano, María M. *La gran familia industrial: Espacio urbano, prácticas sociales e ideología (1870–1945)*. Buenos Aires: Santiago Arcos Editor, 2009.
Lyons, Martyn. "New Readers in the Nineteenth Century: Women, Children, Workers." In *A History of Reading in the West*, ed. Giglielmo Cavallo and Roger Chartier, 313–44. Amherst: University of Massachusetts Press, 1999.
Magnani, Rómulo. *El agitador comunista no debe ser amparado por la ley de despido*. Buenos Aires: Rol, 1942.
Martín Yaverovski, Alejandro. "Francia, Brasil, México y Argentina: Una propuesta de historia comparada para las Universidades Populares decimonónicas." Paper

presented at the VI Jornadas Nacionales y IV Latinoamericanas de Investigadores/as en Formación en Educación, 2018. http://eventosacademicos.filo.uba.ar/index.php/JIFIICE/VI-IV/paper/viewFile/3950/2426.

———. "Tres repúblicas barriales y sus universidades: Las universidades populares en la ciudad de Buenos Aires en periodo de entreguerras: Un esquema preliminar." *Historia Caribe* 16:38 (Jan.–June 2021): 35–80.

Mateu, Cristina. "Política e ideología de la Federación Deportiva Obrera, 1924–1929." In *Deporte y sociedad*, ed. Pablo Alabarces, Roberto Di Giano, and Julio Frydenberg, 67–86. Buenos Aires: EUDEBA, 1998.

Medina Espada, Felipe. *De la universidad popular a la facultad técnica*. Sucre, Bolivia: Universidad Mayor de San Francisco Xavier de Chuquisaca, 1999.

Ministerio de Gobierno de la Provincia de Buenos Aires. *Fomento y protección de las bibliotecas populares en el año 1914*. La Plata, Buenos Aires: Talleres de Impresiones Oficiales, 1915.

Ministerio de Justicia e Instrucción Pública. *Estadística (anexo a la memoria del ministerio), año 1927*. Buenos Aires: Talleres Gráficos de la Penitenciaría Nacional, 1928.

Miranda, Arnaldo Ignacio Adolfo. *Las bibliotecas públicas municipales de la ciudad de Buenos Aires*. Buenos Aires: Cuadernos de Buenos Aires, 1996.

Mora y Araujo, Manuel, and Ignacio Llorente, eds. *El voto peronista: Ensayos de sociología electoral argentina*. Buenos Aires: Editorial Sudamericana, 1980.

Morales, Andrés. *Fútbol, identidad y poder, 1916–1930*. Montevideo, Uruguay: Fin de Siglo, 2013.

Municipalidad de la Ciudad de Buenos Aires. *Censo de personal administrativo y obreros de la Municipalidad de Buenos Aires*. Buenos Aires, 1928.

———. *Memoria del Departamento Ejecutivo de la Municipalidad de Buenos Aires, años 1933 y 1934*. Buenos Aires: Guillermo Kraft, 1935.

———. *Memoria del Departamento Ejecutivo de la Municipalidad de Buenos Aires, año 1935*. Buenos Aires: Guillermo Kraft, 1936.

———. *Memoria del Departamento Ejecutivo de la Municipalidad de Buenos Aires, año 1936*. 3 vols. Buenos Aires, 1937.

Navarro, Marysa. *Evita*. Buenos Aires: Corregidor, 1981.

Newton, Jorge. *Historia del Club Atlético Huracán, 1908–1968*. Buenos Aires, 1968.

Obras Sanitarias de la Nación. *Memoria del directorio correspondiente al año*. Buenos Aires: Imprenta OSN, 1924, 1942.

Pan-American Union. *Cuban Books and Libraries*. Washington, DC: US Government Printing Office, 1930.

Panfichi, Aldo, and Jorge Theroldt. "Identity and Rivalry: The Football Clubs and *Barras Bravas* of Peru." In *Football in the Americas: Fútbol, Futebol, Soccer*, ed. Rory M. Miller and Liz Crolley, 143–57. London: Institute for the Study of the Americas, 2007.

Panzeri, Dante. *Burguesía y "gangsterismo" en el deporte*. Buenos Aires: Ediciones Líbera, 1974.

Parker, William Belmont, ed. *Argentines of To-Day*. 2 vols. New York: Hispanic Society of America, 1920.
Pastoriza, Elisa, and Juan Carlos Torre. *Mar del Plata: Un sueño de los argentinos*. Buenos Aires: Edhasa, 2019.
Petra, Adriana. "Hacia una historia del mundo impresa del comunismo: La Editorial Problemas (1939–1948)." In *Prácticas editoriales y cultura empresa entre los intelectuales latinoamericanos de siglo XX*, ed. Aimer Granados and Sebastián Rivera Mir, 99–126. Mexico: El Colegio Mexiquense, 2018.
Pignatelli, Adrián. *Ruggierito: Política y negocios sucios en la Avellaneda violenta de 1920 y 1930*. Buenos Aires: Editorial Nueva Mayoría, 2005.
Piñeiro, Alberto Gabriel. *Las calles de Buenos Aires: Sus nombres desde la fundación hasta nuestros días*. Buenos Aires: Instituto Histórico de la Ciudad de Buenos Aires, 2003.
Plotkin, Mariano Ben. *Mañana es San Perón*. Buenos Aires: Ariel, 1993.
Prignano, Angel Oscar. *Barriología y diversidad cultural*. Buenos Aires: Ciccus, 2008.
———. "Seis clubes de fútbol del Bajo Flores." In *San José de Flores: Las instituciones del barrio 1880–1990*, ed. Eduardo Mario Favier-Dubois, 23–36. Buenos Aires: Junta de Estudios Históricos de San José de Flores, 1993.
Privitellio, Luciano de. "Inventar el barrio: Boedo 1936–1942." *Cuadernos de Ciesal* 2:2–3 (1994): 113–28.
———. "¿Qué reforma la reforma? La quimera contra la máquina y el voto secreto y obligatorio." *Estudios Sociales* 43 (segundo semestre 2012): 29–58.
———. *Vecinos y ciudadanos: Política y sociedad en la Buenos Aires de entreguerra*. Buenos Aires: Siglo Veintiuno, 2003.
Privitellio, Luciano de, and Luis Alberto Romero. "Organizaciones de la sociedad civil, tradiciones cívicas y cultura política democrática: El caso de Buenos Aires, 1912–1976." *Revista de Historia* 1:1 (2005): 1–34.
Putnam, Robert D. *Bowling Alone: The Collapse and Revival of American Community*. New York: Touchstone, 2000.
———. *Making Democracy Work: Civic Traditions in Modern Italy*. Princeton, NJ: Princeton University Press, 1993.
Quién es quién en la Argentina. Buenos Aires: Editorial Guillermo Kraft, 1939.
Quién es quién en la Argentina. 2nd ed. Buenos Aires: Editorial Guillermo Kraft, 1941.
Quién es quién, 1943. Buenos Aires: Editorial Guillermo Kraft, 1943.
Raga, Adriana Beatriz. "Workers, Neighbors and Citizens: A Study of an Argentine Industrial Town, 1930–1950." PhD diss., Yale University, 1988.
Ramírez, Pablo. "Política y fútbol." *Todo es Historia* 206 (Feb. 1988): 34–43.
Rao, Osvaldo Christian. "José Amalfitani: El hombre que le dio vida a la leyenda." In *Los presidentes de clubes que hicieron historia*, ed. Néstor Vicente, 9–28. Buenos Aires: Alarco Ediciones, 2018.
Razori, Amílcar. *La obra de la intendencia municipal en los barrios suburbanos*. Buenos Aires: Jacobo Peuser, 1935.

Recchini de Lattes, Zulma. "La populación: Crecimiento explosivo y desaceleración." In *Buenos Aires: Historia de cuatro siglos*, 2nd ed., vol. 2, ed. José Luis Romero and Luis Alberto Romero, 225–38. Buenos Aires: Altamira, 2000.

Rein, Mónica Esti. *Politics and Education in Argentina, 1946–1962*. Armonk, NY: Sharpe, 1998.

Rein, Raanan. *Los bohemios de Villa Crespo: Judíos y fútbol en Argentina*. Buenos Aires: Sudamericana, 2012.

———, ed. *La cancha peronista: Fútbol y política (1946–1955)*. San Martín, Buenos Aires: UNSAM Edita, 2015.

Reyna, Franco D. *Cuando éramos footballers: Una historia sociocultural del surgimiento y difusión del fútbol en Córdoba (1900–1920)*. Córdoba, Argentina: Centro de Estudios Históricos Prof. Carlos S. A. Segreti, 2011.

Riley, Dylan. *The Civic Foundations of Fascism in Europe: Italy, Spain and Romania, 1870–1914*. Baltimore, MD: Johns Hopkins University Press, 2010.

Rocchi, Fernando. *Chimneys in the Desert: Industrialization in Argentina during the Export Boom Years, 1870–1930*. Stanford, CA: Stanford University Press, 2006.

———. "Industria y metrópolis: el sueño de un gran mercado." In *Buenos Aires: El imaginario para un gran capital*, ed. Magarita Gutman and Thomas Reese, 269–80. Buenos Aires: Eudeba, 1999.

Rock, David. "Machine Politics in Buenos Aires and the Argentine Radical Party, 1912–1930." *Journal of Latin American Studies* 4:2 (Nov. 1972): 233–56.

Rodríguez, Adolfo Enrique. *Historia de la policía federal argentina*, Vol. 7: *1916–1944*. Buenos Aires: Editorial Policial, 1978.

Rodríguez, Alicia N. "Club Social Mariano Boedo." Paper presented at the Primero y Segundo Congreso de Historia del Barrio de Boedo, Mar. 26, 2012. http://2congresodehistoriadelbarriodeboedo.blogspot.com/2012/03/club-social-mariano-boedo.html.

Romero, Luis Alberto. "La política en los barrios y en el centro: Parroquias, bibliotecas populares y politización antes del peronismo." In *Buenos Aires/entreguerras: La callada transformación, 1914–1945*, ed. Francis Korn and Luis Alberto Romero, 33–57. Buenos Aires: Editorial Alianza, 2006.

Rosatti, Horacio. *Cien años de multitud: Historia de Boca Juniors, una pasión argentina*. 3 vols. Buenos Aires: Galerna, 2008–2012.

Roth, Guenther. *The Social Democrats in Imperial Germany: A Study in Working-Class Isolation and National Integration*. Totowa, NJ: Bedminster, 1963.

Rovere y Oddino, Liberia, and Edgardo Cocchi. *Aspiración: Libro de lectura para primer grado inferior*. Buenos Aires: Kapelusz, 1934.

Sabato, Hilda. *The Many and the Few: Political Participation in Republican Buenos Aires*. Stanford, CA: Stanford University Press, 2001.

———. *Republics of the New World: The Revolutionary Political Experiment in 19th-Century Latin America*. Princeton, NJ: Princeton University Press, 2018.

Saítta, Sylvia. "El periodismo popular en los años veinte." In *Democracia, conflicto social y renovación de ideas (1916–1930)*, ed. Ricardo Falcón, 435–71. Buenos Aires: Editorial Sudamericana, 2000.

———. *Recuerdos de tinta: El diario "Crítica" en la década de 1920*. Buenos Aires: Editorial Sudamericana, 1998.

Salvatore, Ricardo D. *Wandering Paysanos, State Order and Subaltern Experience in Buenos Aires during the Rosas Era*. Durham, NC: Duke University Press, 2003.

Sanguinetti, Horacio. *Los socialistas independientes*. Buenos Aires: Editorial Belgrano, 1981.

Sargent, Charles S. *The Spatial Evolution of Greater Buenos Aires, Argentina, 1870–1930*. Tempe: Center for Latin American Studies, Arizona State University, 1974.

Sarlo, Beatriz. *Una modernidad periférica: Buenos Aires 1920 y 1930*. Buenos Aires: Nueva Visión, 2003.

Scher, Ariel. *La patria deportista*. Buenos Aires: Planeta, 1996.

Scher, Ariel, and Héctor Palomino. *Fútbol: Pasión de multitudes y de elites*. Buenos Aires: CISEA, 1988.

Scobie, James R. *Buenos Aires: Plaza to Suburb, 1870–1914*. New York: Oxford University Press, 1974.

Seligman, Amanda I. *Chicago's Block Clubs: How Neighbors Shape the City*. Chicago, IL: University of Chicago Press, 2016.

Sierra, Luis M. *La Paz's Colonial Specters: Urbanization, Migration, and Indigenous Political Participation, 1900–1952*. New York: Bloomsbury Academic, 2021.

Sikkink, Kathryn. "Las capacidades y la autonomía del estado en Brasil y la Argentina: Un enfoque neoinstitucionalista." *Desarrollo Económico* 23:128 (Jan.–Mar. 1993): 543–74.

Silvestre, Arturo. *Como se llega: Nuestros self-made men*. Buenos Aires: F. A. Colombo, 1931.

Sirvent, María Teresa. *Cultura popular y participación social: Una investigación en el barrio de Mataderos*. Buenos Aires: Miño y Dávila Editores, 1999.

Small, Mario Luis. *Unanticipated Gains: Origins of Network Inequality in Everyday Life*. New York: Oxford University Press, 2009.

Sociedad de Fomento Flores Sud. *Memoria y balance correspondiente al ejercicio del último año desde el 1 de julio de 1918 a junio 30 de 1919*. Buenos Aires, 1919.

Sociedad de Fomento General Benito Nazar. *Memoria y balance general correspondiente al ejercicio del año mayo 1929–abril 1930*. Buenos Aires: Talleres Gráfico Cappellano Hnos., 1930.

Sociedad de Fomento de Versailles. *Memoria y balance, 1 de abril de 1927–31 marzo de 1928*. Buenos Aires: Talleres Gráficos Pfeifer, 1928.

Stearns, Peter N. *Lives of Labor: Work in a Maturing Industrial Society*. New York: Holmes and Meier, 1975.

Stein, Steve J. "The Case of Soccer in Early Twentieth-Century Lima." In *Sport in Latin America and the Caribbean*, ed. Joseph L. Arbena and David G. LaFrance, 9–31. Wilmington, DE: Scholarly Resources, 2002.

Stokes, Susan C., et al. *Brokers, Voters, and Clientelism: The Puzzle of Distributive Politics*. New York: Cambridge University Press, 2013.
Suriano, Juan. *Anarquistas: Cultura y política libertaria en Buenos Aires, 1890–1910*. Buenos Aires: Manantial, 2001.
———. *Auge y caída del anarquismo argentina, 1880–1930*. Buenos Aires: Capital Intelectual, 2009.
Szwarcberg, Mariela. "Building a Following: Local Candidates' Political Career and Clientelism in Argentine Municipalities." *Latin American Politics and Society* 55:3 (Fall 2013): 1–18.
———. "The Micro Foundations of Political Clientelism: Lessons from the Argentine Case." *Latin American Research Review* 48:2 (2013): 32–54.
Tarcus, Horacio, ed. *Diccionario biográfico de la izquierda Argentina*. Buenos Aires: Emecé, 2007.
Tocqueville, Alexis de. *Democracy in America*. Translated by Henry Reeve. New York: Bantam Classics, 2000.
Torre, Juan Carlos, ed. *Los años peronistas (1943–1955)*. Volume 8 of *Nueva historia argentina*. Buenos Aires: Editorial Sudamericana, 2002.
Torre, Juan Carlos, and Elisa Pastoriza. "La democratización del bienestar." In *Los años peronistas*, ed. Juan Carlos Torre, 257–312. Buenos Aires: Editorial Sudamericana, 2002.
Torres, Horacio. "Evolución de los procesos de estructuración especial urbana. El caso de Buenos Aires." *Desarrollo Económico* 15:58 (July–Sept. 1975): 281–306.
Torres Aguilar, Morelos. *Cultura y revolución: La Universidad Popular Mexicana (ciudad de México, 1912–1920)*. Mexico: Universidad Nacional Autónoma de México, 2009.
Tripaldi, Nicolás. "Origen e inserción de las bibliotecas obreras en el entorno bibliotecario argentino." *Libraría* 1:1 (1997): 22–37.
Unión Ferroviaria. *Memoria y balance correspondiente al año 1936*. Buenos Aires, 1937.
Universidades Populares Florentino Ameghino. *Memoria del consejo directivo y de las rectorías*. Buenos Aires, 1938, 1939.
Universidades Populares Florentino Ameghino y Femenina de Palermo. *Memoria, 1935*. Buenos Aires, 1935.
Universidad Popular Bernardino Rivadavia. *Memoria, condiciones de ingreso y programa de cursos*. Buenos Aires, 1926.
Universidad Popular de Boedo. *Memoria del ejercicio*. Buenos Aires, 1937–1941.
Universidad Popular Florentino Ameghino. *Estatutos*. Buenos Aires, 1929.
———. *Informe del consejo directivo: Rectoría y balance general, 1933*. Buenos Aires, 1933.
———. *Memoria, 1934*. Buenos Aires, 1934.
———. *La Universidad Popular Florentino Ameghino en su XV aniversario*. Buenos Aires: Universidad Popular Florentino Ameghino, 1941.
Universidad Popular de Flores Sud. *Memoria, balance e inventario, 1934–1935*. Buenos Aires, 1935.
Universidad Popular de La Boca. *Memoria y balance del ejercicio*. Buenos Aires, 1941–1942.

———. *XL año lectivo*. Buenos Aires, 1956.
Universidad Popular de Villa del Parque. *Memoria del consejo directivo*. Buenos Aires, 1937, 1940.
Valdez, María José. "Algunas hipótesis sobre los mecanismos de financiamiento político de la Unión Cívica Radical: Las campañas electorales de 1928 y 1930 en la ciudad de Buenos Aires." In *Los costos de la política: Del centenario al primer peronismo*, ed. Diego A. Mauro and Leandro Lichtmajer, 41–57. Buenos Aires: Imago Mundi, 2014.
———. "Prácticas electorales en Buenos Aires, 1912–1930." http://historiapolitica.com/datos/biblioteca/valdez.pdf.
Vargas Llosa, Mario. *A Fish in the Water: A Memoir*. Translated by Helen Lane. London: Faber and Faber, 1994.
Vecchio, Ofelio. *Aquí entre nosotros*. Buenos Aires: EDG Ediciones, 1994.
———. *Mataderos, mi barrio*. Buenos Aires: Editora Nueva Lugano, 1981.
Ventieri, Marcelo Horacio. *Historia del Club Atlético Temperley*. Buenos Aires: Editorial de los Cuatro Vientos, 2006.
Verbitsky, Bernardo. "Grandeza y decadencia de 'Estrella del Sur.'" In *El fútbol*, ed. Jean Cau et al., 65–87. Buenos Aires: Editorial Jorge Álvarez, 1967.
Vicente, Ricardo. *La Avellaneda de Barceló en la década infame, 1932–1943*. Buenos Aires: Ediciones Cooperativas, 2011.
Viguera, Aníbal. "Participación electoral y prácticas políticas de los sectores populares en Buenos Aires, 1912–1922." *Entrepasados* 1:1 (1991): 5–33.
Walter, Richard J. *Politics and Urban Growth in Buenos Aires, 1910–1942*. Cambridge: Cambridge University Press, 1993.
———. *The Province of Buenos Aires and Argentine Politics, 1912–1943*. Cambridge: Cambridge University Press, 1985.
———. *The Socialist Party of Argentina, 1890–1930*. Austin: University of Texas Press, 1977.
Weitz-Shapiro, Rebecca. *Curbing Clientelism in Argentina: Politics, Power, and Social Policy*. New York: Cambridge University Press, 2014.
Yablon, Ariel. "Patronage and Party System in Buenos Aires, 1880–1886." Paper delivered at the Conference of Latin American History, 2005. In possession of author.
Zarazaga, Rodrigo. "Brokers beyond Clientelism: A New Perspective through the Argentine Case." *Latin American Politics and Society* 56:3 (Fall 2014): 23–45.
Ziperstein, Ernesto. *Tango y fútbol: Dos pasiones argentinas*. Buenos Aires: Instituto Movilizador de Fondos Cooperativos, 2006.

Index

acculturation, civic associations and, 18
adult education, 14, 119–20, 122–24
Agnelli, Francisco, 52
Almagro (barrio), 56–59
Almagro football club, 9, 155n24; political capital and, 38–40
Alvear, Marcelo T. de, 23–24, 57, 114, 126, 137
Alvear, Regina P. de, 132
Amalfitani, José, 52
Los Amigos de la Ciudad, 108, 113
anarchists, 24–25, 79, 82, 110, 122
Anastasi, Leonidas, 126
Anastasi, Manilo, 51
Antipersonalist Radicals, 24, 32, 35, 109, 126, 128, 140; Larrandart and, 57, 59
Argentina: clientelism in, 144–45; Consejo Nacional de Educación, 119, 124, 126–27, 136; democracy in, 4–5, 145–46; economy of, 13, 23, 135, 146–47; education in, 121–23; football in, 42–46; government of, 9–10, 25–26, 52, 94; immigration in, 13, 17–18, 22; libraries and, 68–69, 91–92; politics in, 8, 14, 22–25; publishing industry in, 71, 73; sports in, 42. *See also* Buenos Aires
Argentinos Juniors football club, 52
Arias, Florencio, 33
Arias, Pedro F., 136
Asociación de Fomento 12 de Octubre, 106, 115
Asociación de Fomento y Biblioteca Popular Cornelio Saavedra, 70, 88, 148
Asociación de Fomento y Biblioteca Popular Emilio Mitre de Caballito Sud, 98–101, 111
Asociación de Fomento y Cultura Los Olivos, 101, 116
Asociación de Fomento y Cultural Unión de Vélez Sarsfield Sud, 96
Asociación de Fomento Defensa Vecinal, 36
Asociación de Fomento Edilicio, Cultural y Biblioteca Popular Villa Luro Norte, 103, 106
Asociación de Fomento Santiago de Liniers, 101
Asociación de Fomento de Villa Devoto, 70, 96, 104, 107
Asociaciones Vecinales de Fomento de la Ciudad de Buenos Aires, 117
Asociación Fomento y Cultura Flores Sud, 72, 86, 116
Asociación General Alvear de Fomento Edilicio, 107–8
Atlanta football club, 44, 46–47, 64
atmosphere, of libraries, 89, 166n63
Avellaneda (barrio), 26–27, 80–82; Barceló and, 59–64

Bacigaluppi, José, 66
Barceló, Alberto: Avellaneda and, 59–64; Gardel and, 27
Bard, Leopoldo, 19, 65–66
Barracas (barrio), 26, 136
barrio identities, 2–3, 21–22, 147; civic associations and, 5–6, 12; football clubs and, 46–49, 67; sociedades de fomento and, 98, 102
barrio improvements, 9, 95–96; infrastructure and, 171n69; politicians and, 32, 94, 114–17; publicity and, 32, 103–4; sociedades de fomento and, 102–4, 111
Barrio Norte, 16, 152n13
barrios, *xii*, 19; bibliotecas populares and, 91–93; civic associations and, 1, 8; class and, 15–16, 45, 97; conditions in, 94, 97–98, 102–4; flooding in, 17, 97, 102, 107, 112; football clubs and, 2, 45, 49; micro, 20–21, 49, 97; needs of, 17, 106–7; parks in, 17, 42–43, 53, 98, 101–2, 105, 111; paved streets in, 17, 32, 94, 98, 145; politicians and, 6, 32; pride in, 9, 22, 147; problems in, 14, 16–18; recognition of, 20, 152n9, 152n13, 152n27; running water in, 17, 25–26, 103, 105, 111; sewer system in, 17, 103, 105; store owners in, 15, 55, 94–95, 97, 128; in tangos, 1, 11–12; universidades populares and, 134. *See also specific barrios*
Bavastro, Francisco L., 81–82
Belgrano (barrio), 50, 135
Benedit, Salvador, 36, 81
Biblioteca Almirante Brown, 79
Biblioteca Obrera, 79, 90
Biblioteca Popular Alberdi (Gerli), 78, 80–81
Biblioteca Popular Alberdi (Villa Crespo), 36, 77, 81–82, 132, 148
Biblioteca Popular Bartolomé Mitre, 77
Biblioteca Popular Belgrano, 82–83
Biblioteca Popular Carlos Mauli, 78
Biblioteca Popular Cornelio Saavedra, 69–70, 88, 148
Biblioteca Popular Democracia y Progreso, 72, 79, 84–85
Biblioteca Popular Emilio Mitre de Caballito Sud, 98–101, 111
Biblioteca Popular General Juan Martín de Pueyrredón, 72, 78, 86–88, 90
Biblioteca Popular Iberoamericana, 73
Biblioteca Popular Juan N. Madero, 86
Biblioteca Popular Nueva Chicago, 74–75, 163n24
Biblioteca Popular Sarmiento, 83–84
bibliotecas populares (popular libraries), 7, 147; barrios and, 91–93; city council and, 74, 82–83; Communist Party and, 79, 82; community and, 78–79, 81, 92; CONABIP and, 73–74, 80, 84; democracy and, 69; elites and, 81–82; governance of, 72–75; government support for, 74, 76–77, 82–84, 91–93; Great Depression and, 74, 87; ideologies and, 71, 79–80, 82; membership of, 72, 77–78, 80–81, 86–88, 91; needs of, 69, 92; political capital and, 81–82; politicians and, 68–69, 91–92; problems of, 86–88; Radical Party and, 71, 74, 79–80, 82–85, 88; readership of, 69, 72–73, 83, 85, 88–91; recognition of, 73–75, 78–79, 148; role of, 75–77; sociability and, 77–79, 92–93; Socialist Party and, 75, 79–81, 83, 90; social mobility and, 69–70, 93; sociedades de fomento and, 84–85, 101–2, 163n24; students and, 69, 82, 88–93, 166n61; subsidies for, 73–75, 84–88, 92; in

suburbs, 78, 86; subventions for, 74, 82, 86; unions and, 70, 79, 81
Bidegain, Pedro, 49, 129; Larrandart and, 56–59
Big Five football clubs, 37, 46
La Boca (barrio), 49, 53, 125–28; Elena and, 35–36; River Plate football club and, 65–67
Boca Alumni football club, 35
Boca Juniors football club, 1, 20, 46–50, 66, 127–28, 146, 157n39; class and, 44; Elena and, 35–36; Justo and, 51–52; Macri and, 41, 146; stadium for, 53
Boedo (barrio), 21, 41–42, 147
Boffi, Luis L., 37–38, 59, 144
Boloque, Carlos, 50
Boloque, Leandro, 59, 62–63
books: as entertainment, 88–89, 91; income and, 71–72; languages of, 69, 89; porteños and, 68–69, 91–93, 148
Bourdeu, Julián, 81
bourgeoisie, 44, 80–81, 97
Braylan, Bernardo, 70
Brugnara, Juan, 120–21, 137, 139–40
Buenos Aires, Argentina, 7, 29–30; Asociaciones Vecinales de Fomento de la Ciudad, 117; cafés in, 20–21, 44, 49, 57, 65, 71, 100; city council of, 26; civic associations and, 2, 149; class in, 152n22; diversity and, 27, 45; economy of, 17–18, 119, 140–41; geography of, *xii*, 12; growth of, 3, 12, 16–19, 94, 143; intendente of, 25–26; literacy in, 15; mortality rate in, 18; politics in, 25–26; University of, 37. *See also specific topics*
businesses, local, 97, 100–101, 117
businessmen, 117; football and, 52, 67; Nueva Chicago football club and, 55; politics and, 29

bus lines, 19, 58, 105

Caballito (barrio), 107, 126, 131
cafés, 20–21, 44, 49, 57, 65, 71, 100
Calvete, Adolfo, 83, 88
campaigns, 42, 49, 108–9, 149; in football clubs, 62, 64; political parties and, 30–32
Canaveri, Pedro, 63–64
Cantilo, José Luis, 84, 105, 107
Caras y Caretas (magazine), 42, 57
Carbone, Luis, 61–63
Castillo, Ramón, 25, 139
Centro Social Nueva Chicago, 34, 54–55
Chacarita Juniors football club, 47–48, 51
Cichero, Camilo, 20, 49
city council, 26; Almagro football club and, 39; barrio conditions and, 102; bibliotecas populares and, 74, 82–83; football clubs and, 35–36; sociedades de fomento and, 102–11, 113–14
civic associations, 7, 9, 41, 151n10; acculturation and, 18; barrio identities and, 5–6, 12; barrios and, 1, 8; Buenos Aires and, 2, 149; clientelism and, 3, 28–29, 142–44, 149; colonization of, 14; courses of, 36, 47–48, 61, 63, 66, 83, 101–2; democracy and, 2, 4–5, 14, 143–46; leisure time and, 3, 6, 15, 68, 144; in Mataderos, 54–55; needs of, 6, 14, 28–29; police and, 29–30; political capital and, 28–40; politicians and, 13, 32–33, 143, 149; politics and, 8, 30–33, 38–40; porteños and, 29, 143, 146; problems of, 146–49; sociability and, 20–21, 143–44. *See also* bibliotecas populares; football clubs; sociedades de fomento; universidades populares

class, 19; barrios and, 15–16, 45, 97; bibliotecas populares and, 91; in Buenos Aires, 152n22; football clubs and, 44, 59; universidades populares and, 120–21, 127, 131–34
Clemenceau, Georges, 12
clientelism: in Argentina, 144–45; civic associations and, 3, 28–29, 142–44, 149; politics and, 3, 6, 28–29, 31–32, 146
colectivos, 18–19
Colombo, Raúl H., 39–40
Colón (barrio), 100–101
colonization, of civic associations, 14. *See also* influence
comisarios, police, 29–30, 81, 107, 132
Comisión Protectora de Bibliotecas Populares (CONABIP), 73–75, 78–80, 84–89
Communist Party: bibliotecas populares and, 79, 82; football clubs and, 44–45; sociedades de fomento and, 110–11, 116; universidades populares and, 122
community: barrios and, 12; bibliotecas populares and, 78–79, 81, 92; football clubs and, 47, 49, 54–55, 63; politics and, 56–59; respectability and, 21, 95
CONABIP. *See* Comisión Protectora de Bibliotecas Populares
Concentración Obrera, 104, 110
conditions, in barrios, 94, 97–98, 102–4
Congress, of Argentina, 26, 74, 77, 82; sociedades de fomento and, 105–6, 109, 112, 117; universidades populares and, 126, 129, 131, 135, 138
congresses, of sociedades de fomento, 112–13
Consejo Nacional de Educación (National Council of Education), 119, 124, 126–27, 136
Conservative Party, 27, 38; football clubs and, 53–54, 59–60, 62–63, 66; sociedades de fomento, 107, 109, 116
consortium, of universidades populares, 121, 137–41
coronavirus pandemic, football clubs and, 156n9
courses: of civic associations, 36, 47–48, 61, 63, 66, 83, 101–2; of universidades populares, 127–28, 130–31, 135–36
Crítica (newspaper), 34, 38, 50–51, 56
Cullen, Tomás R., 109

Dagnino family, 107–8
Defensores de Belgrano football club, 50
Della Latta, Jerónimo, 62–63
democracy, 27; in Argentina, 4–5, 145–46; bibliotecas populares and, 69; civic associations and, 2, 4–5, 14, 143–46
development societies. *See* sociedades de fomento
diversity, 133; barrios and, 15, 17, 27; Buenos Aires and, 27, 45
Duarte de Perón, Eva, 85

economy: of Argentina, 13, 23, 135, 146–47; of Buenos Aires, 17–18, 119, 140–41
education, 10, 15; adult, 14, 119–20, 122–24; in Argentina, 121–23; practical, 119, 123, 133; sociedades de fomento and, 101–2
elections, for football clubs, 41–43, 49; manipulation in, 61–64
Elena, Reinaldo, 35–36, 51, 144
elites, 45, 55, 117; bibliotecas populares and, 81–82; football clubs and,

50; politics and, 84; sociedades de fomento and, 100
enrollment, of universidades populares, 127, 130–31
entertainment: books as, 88–89, 91; politics and, 30; sociedades de fomento and, 101
Estudiantes de La Plata football club, 48–49

facilities: for bibliotecas populares, 77; for football, 53–54, 63–64; for universidades populares, 123, 129, 135–36, 138, 141–42
factions, in political parties, 57–59
families, universidades populares and, 120–21, 131, 133–34, 174n43
Ferrocarril Oeste, 66, 84–85
Ferrocarril Pacífico, 106
Ferrocarril Sud, 51–52, 59
flooding, in barrios, 17, 97, 102, 107, 112
Flores (barrio), 132
Flores Sud (barrio), 111
football, 47–49; in Argentina, 42–46; businessmen and, 52, 67; facilities for, 53–54, 63–64; influence and, 53–54, 57–58; passion for, 7, 32, 41; professionalization of, 50–51, 61; schools and, 42–43
football clubs, 7, 9; barrio identities and, 46–49, 67; barrios and, 2, 45, 49; Big Five, 37, 46; city council and, 35–36; class and, 44, 59; community and, 47, 49, 54–55, 63; Conservative Party and, 53–54, 59–60, 62–63, 66; coronavirus pandemic and, 156n9; elections for, 41–43, 49; electoral manipulation in, 61–64; governance of, 43–44; *El Gráfico* and, 44, 49, 51; Justo and, 51–52; politicians and, 32, 50–51, 53–55, 146–47;

politics and, 1, 67, 146; popularity of, 46, 49, 65; problems in, 61–64; Radical Party and, 50–51, 56–61, 63–65; rivalry and, 57–59; sociability and, 43, 47–48, 64, 67; Socialist Party and, 44–45, 50–51, 54–55, 58–59, 62, 66; subsidies for, 39, 58; in suburbs, 52–53; tangos and, 48–49. *See also* stadiums, for football clubs
football fields, 46, 51–53; of Nueva Chicago, 55; River Plate and, 65–66
Fouiller, Félix O., 83–84
Francis (pope), 147
fraud, in politics, 23, 25, 27
Frondizi, Arturo, 39
funding, 9–10, 52; universidades populares and, 120–21, 125–31, 135–36, 138, 141
fundraising: bibliotecas populares and, 74; sociedades de fomento and, 98–99, 101

Gallardo, Angel, 126–27, 132
Gandulfo, Petrona de, 61, 66
Gardel, Carlos, 27
gender, 32, 144; bibliotecas populares and, 72–73; football clubs and, 48–49; politics and, 14–15, 23; readership and, 69, 72–73, 89; universidades populares and, 124–25, 139–40. *See also* women
geography, of Buenos Aires, xii, 12
Ghio, Fernando, 33–34, 54–55, 75, 104
González, Elpidio, 29
González, Lidia, 70
Gorelik, Adrián, 20, 26, 114
governance: of bibliotecas populares, 72–75; CONABIP and, 73–74; of football clubs, 43–44; of sociedades de fomento, 98–100; of universidades populares, 123–25, 139

government, of Argentina, 9–10, 25–26, 52; lobbying of, 94
government support, 9–10, 52, 145; for bibliotecas populares, 74, 76–77, 82–84, 91–93; of universidades populares, 127–30, 132–33, 135–38. *See also* subsidies; subventions
Goyeneche, Arturo, 51, 126
El Gráfico (magazine), 44, 49, 51
Great Depression, 13, 24–25; bibliotecas populares and, 74, 87; universidades populares and, 135, 137
Groppo, Pedro, 61
growth: of barrios, 16; of bibliotecas populares, 73; of Buenos Aires, 3, 12, 16–19, 94, 143; of sociedades de fomento, 97–98; of suburbs, 27–28
Guereño, Juan, 85, 132
Guerrico, Federico, 51
Guerrico, José, 109

Hermelo, Ricardo, 79, 132
honorary commissions, 33, 54–55, 84, 88, 129
Huracán football club, 53–54; rivalry and, 57

identities, 20; politicians and, 31. *See also* barrio identities
ideologies: bibliotecas populares and, 71, 79–80, 82; of universidades populares, 123–25
immigration, in Argentina, 13, 17–18, 22; politics and, 23
income, of porteños, 13, 52; books and, 71–72; families and, 120–21, 134; for teachers, 120, 137–38, 141
Independent Socialists, 24, 107
Independiente football club, 45, 53, 60–61, 63–64, 146
industry: publishing, 71, 73; railroads and, 13, 18, 51–52, 79, 84, 106, 110; in suburbs, 26–27; universidades populares and, 125–26
influence: football and, 53–54, 57–58; of politicians, 57–58, 106–7; sociedades de fomento and, 96–97. *See also* political capital
infrastructure, 7, 9, 102–5, 114–15; growth and, 16–17; improvements to, 171n69
inspections, of universidades populares, 124
intendente (mayor): of Buenos Aires, 25–26; sociedades de fomento and, 104–7, 114–17; Vedia y Mitre, 36, 115
Iriondo, Remigio, 36–37, 82, 137

Justo, Augustín, 24–25, 132, 136; football clubs and, 51–52

land, subdivision of, 16, 102, 109
languages, of books, 69, 89
Lanús football club, 48
Larrandart, Eduardo, 49; Bidegain and, 56–59
Latin America: football clubs and, 45; libraries in, 76; sociedades de fomento in, 95; universidades populares in, 122
Le Breton, Tomás, 126–27
leisure time, civic associations and, 3, 6, 15, 68, 144
Levitsky, Steven, 145
libraries, 72–74; Argentina and, 68–69, 91–92; atmosphere of, 89, 166n63; public, 75–76; schools and, 76–77, 92–93
Liga de Fomento de Villa General Mitre, 72–73
Liga de Fomento Federico Lacroze, 100
Liniers (barrio), 84–85

literacy, 34, 68; in Buenos Aires, 15
lobbying, government, 94; sociedades de fomento and, 104–8, 118
local businesses, 97, 100–101, 117

Macri, Mauricio, 1, 146, 171n69; Boca Juniors and, 41, 146
Magnani, Rómulo, 82, 131–32
Malbec, Ernesto, 62
Manuel Belgrano (sociedad de fomento), 101–2, 104, 115–17
Marechal, Leopoldo, 82
Massa, Lorenzo, 56
Mataderos (barrio), 20, 33–34, 99, 102, 124; civic associations in, 54–55
mayor. *See* intendente
media coverage, 22, 44, 65
medical services, 47, 61, 78, 140; sociedades de fomento and, 98–101
membership: of bibliotecas populares, 72, 77–78, 80–81, 87–88; of football clubs, 43–44, 46–49, 55, 58, 60–65, 67, 146; of sociedades de fomento, 96–102, 114; of universidades populares, 120, 124, 135–36, 141
membership dues: of bibliotecas populares, 72, 74–75, 80–81, 86–87, 91; sociedades de fomento and, 96, 99–100, 114; universidades populares and, 120, 124, 129–30, 136, 138, 140–41
micro barrios, 20–21, 49, 97
Mignaburu, Juan R., 63
Mohr, Alejandro, 54–55
mortality rate, in Buenos Aires, 18

La Nación, 47, 57, 85
National Council of Education. *See* Consejo Nacional de Educación
native-born residents, 18; bibliotecas populares and, 69; politics and, 31–32. *See also* porteños

needs: of barrios, 17, 106–7; of bibliotecas populares, 69, 92; of civic associations, 6, 14, 28–29; of football clubs, 50; of politicians, 28–29, 50, 69, 92; of porteños, 12–14; sociedades de fomento and, 97, 118; universidades populares and, 119–21, 141–42
Newbery, Jorge, 53
newspapers, 39; bibliotecas populares and, 71, 73; *Crítica*, 34, 38, 50–51, 56; *La Nación*, 47, 57, 85
Noel, Carlos, 114
Nueva Chicago (barrio). *See* Mataderos
Nueva Chicago football club, 33, 54–55
Núñez (barrio), 22, 67

Ortiz, Roberto M., 25, 35, 62, 126
Ortiz de Zárate, Miguel, 38–40, 155n24

Padilla, Tiburcio, 51
parks, 17, 42–43, 53, 98, 101–2, 105, 111
passion, for football, 7, 32, 41
La Paternal (barrio), 88
patronage, 109–10; bibliotecas populares and, 92; football clubs and, 43; political capital and, 31–33, 35
paved streets, in barrios, 17, 32, 94, 98, 145; sociedades de fomento and, 102–3, 105, 107, 109, 113
Penelón, José, 104, 110–11
Perón, Juan, 2, 6, 25, 144
Peronist Party, 144–46, 148–49, 151n9
Personalist Radicals, 24, 114, 129
petitions, 82, 106, 112–13, 115–17
Platense football club, 125
police, 60; civic associations and, 29–30; politics and, 82; sociedades de fomento and, 112
political capital, 6; Almagro football club and, 38–40; bibliotecas populares and, 81–82; civic associations

political capital (*continued*) and, 28–40; football clubs and, 42; patronage and, 31–33, 35; universidades populares and, 36–38
political parties, 114–17; activists and, 33–34, 38, 56–67, 69–70; campaigns and, 30–32; civic associations and, 38; Concentración Obrera, 104, 110; factions in, 57–59; football clubs and, 44–45; Peronists, 144–46, 148–49, 151n9; Progressive Democrats, 24–25, 36–37, 79, 108; scandals and, 152n5; sociedades de fomento and, 94; universidades populares and, 128; wards and, 30, 56. *See also* Communist Party; Conservative Party; Radical Party; Socialist Party
political pressure, 26, 97, 145; from sociedades de fomento, 17, 102–6
politicians, 6; barrio improvements and, 32, 94, 114–17; bibliotecas populares and, 68–69, 91–92; civic associations and, 13, 32–33, 143, 149; football clubs and, 32, 50–51, 53–55, 146–47; honorary commissions and, 33, 54–55, 84, 88, 129; influence of, 57–58, 106–7; libraries and, 76–77; needs of, 28–29, 50, 69, 92; popularity of, 31–32, 171n69; publicity and, 103–4, 108, 115; sociedades de fomento and, 108–11; universidades populares and, 135–36, 142; voter support and, 2–3, 14, 97
politics: in Argentina, 8, 14, 22–25; Buenos Aires, 25–26; civic associations and, 8, 30–33, 38–40; clientelism and, 3, 6, 28–29, 31–32, 146; community and, 56–59; *Crítica* on, 56; elites and,

84; football clubs and, 1, 67, 146; fraud in, 23, 25, 27; gender and, 14–15, 23; police and, 82; Racing football club and, 60–61; universidades populares and, 120, 127, 129, 132, 137–38, 141
popularity: of football clubs, 46, 49, 65; of politicians, 31–32, 171n69
popular libraries. *See* bibliotecas populares
popular universities. *See* universidades populares
porteños, 5, 15–16; books and, 68–69, 91–93, 148; civic associations and, 29, 143, 146; needs of, 12–14. *See also* income, of porteños
practical education, 119, 123, 133
preferences, reading and, 68, 83–86, 88–91, 166n66
pressure, political, 17, 26, 97, 102–6, 145
pride: in barrios, 9, 22, 147; football clubs and, 67
problems: in barrios, 14, 16–18; of bibliotecas populares, 86–88; of civic associations, 146–49; in football clubs, 61–64; sociedades de fomento and, 94, 103, 106–7, 111; universidades populares and, 124, 126, 136–38
professionalization, of football, 50–51, 61
Progressive Democrats, 24–25, 36–37, 79, 108
the province. *See* suburbs
publications: *Caras y Caretas*, 42, 57; *Crítica*, 34, 38, 50–51, 56; *El Gráfico*, 44, 49, 51; *La Nación*, 47, 57, 85; of sociedades de fomento, 96
publicity: barrio improvements and, 32, 103–4; media coverage and, 22, 44, 65; politicians and, 103–4, 108, 115

public libraries, 75–76
publishing industry, in Argentina, 71, 73

Racing football club, 27, 59–63, 146; sociability and, 60–61; women in, 48–49
Radical Party, 23, 25, 30–31, 37–38, 153n39, 157n39; Antipersonalists of, 24, 32, 35, 57, 59, 109, 126, 128, 140; bibliotecas populares and, 71, 74, 79–80, 82–85, 88; Bidegain in, 49, 58–59, 129; football clubs and, 50–51, 56–61, 63–65; Personalists and, 24, 114, 129; sociedades de fomento and, 99, 105, 109–10, 114–15; universidades populares and, 126–30, 132, 138–40
railroads, 13, 18, 51–52, 79, 84, 106, 110
Ravignani, Emilio, 61, 109–10
Razori, Amílcar, 101, 115–16
readership, of bibliotecas populares, 83, 85, 88, 90–91; gender and, 69, 72–73, 89
reading, 148; preferences and, 83–86, 88–91, 166n66. *See also* books
recognition: of barrios, 20, 152n9, 152n13, 152n27; of bibliotecas populares, 73–75, 78–79, 148; of sociedades de fomento, 96–99, 114
Recoleta (barrio), 152n13
reform, voting, 2, 41–42, 97
respectability, 117; community and, 21, 95; sociedades de fomento and, 103–4
Retiro (barrio), 152n13
revenue, of football clubs, 46–47
rivalry, football clubs and, 57–59
River Plate football club, 35–37, 43–44, 46, 51, 67, 146; fields and, 65–66; stadium for, 53; universidades populares and, 125, 127–28; women and, 48

Roca, Julio, 23
role: of bibliotecas populares, 75–77; of sociedades de fomento, 94–98, 117–18
Rouco Oliva, José, 107–9
Rovere y Oddino, Liberia, 73
running water, in barrios, 17, 25–26, 103, 105, 111

Sáenz Peña voting reform law, 13, 23, 28, 36, 45, 81
Sánchez, Joaquín, 81–82
Sánchez Terrero, Eduardo, 49, 52
San Lorenzo de Almagro football club, 37, 42, 56, 59, 146, 147; rivalry and, 57; stadium of, 41, 58; tangos and, 49
Santiago Diz, Domingo, 110
Sarmiento, Domingo Faustino, 71, 73
Sarobe, José María, 37
scandals, political parties and, 152n5
school boards (concejos escolares), 33, 36–37, 54, 83, 136
schools, 119, 121; football and, 42–43; libraries and, 76–77, 92–93; political capital and, 36–37; universidades populares and, 148–49
Scobie, James, 20
sewer system, in barrios, 17, 103, 105
Small, Mario, 31
sociability, 5–6, 21; bibliotecas populares and, 77–79, 92–93; Boca Juniors football club and, 47–48; civic associations and, 20–21, 143–44; football clubs and, 43, 47–48, 64, 67; Racing football club and, 59–62; River Plate football club and, 66; sociedades de fomento and, 100–102, 117; universidades populares and, 141
social capital, 31

Socialist Party, 25, 30–31; bibliotecas populares and, 75, 79–81, 83, 90; football clubs and, 44–45, 50–51, 54–55, 58–59, 62, 66; Ghio and, 33–34; Independents and, 24, 107; sociedades de fomento and, 103–4, 107, 113–16; universidades populares and, 122, 126, 136, 139–40
social mobility, 19, 120–21; bibliotecas populares and, 69–70, 93
Sociedad de Fomento Asociación Belgrano R., 100, 102–4, 109, 113
Sociedad de Fomento Democracia y Progreso, 84–85, 132, 165n50
Sociedad de Fomento Edilicio y Cultura José Enrique Rodó, 33, 84, 99, 101–2, 115
Sociedad de Fomento General Benito Nazar, 100, 105
Sociedad de Fomento of Villa Lugano, 103
Sociedad de Fomento Teniente General Luis María Campos, 110
Sociedad de Fomento de Versailles, 103, 109
sociedades de fomento (development societies), 34, 81, 148, 170n56; barrio identities and, 98, 102; barrio improvements and, 102–4, 111; bibliotecas populares and, 84–85, 101–2, 163n24; city council and, 102–11, 113–14; Communist Party and, 110–11, 116; Congress and, 105–6, 109, 112, 117; Conservative Party, 107, 109, 116; fundraising and, 98–99, 101; governance of, 98–100; influence and, 96–97; intendentes and, 104–7, 114–17; lobbying and, 104–8, 118; medical services and, 98–101; membership of, 96–102, 114; needs and, 97, 118; paved streets and, 102–3, 105, 107, 109, 113; political pressure from, 17, 102–6; politicians and, 108–11; problems and, 94, 103, 106–7, 111; Radical Party and, 99, 105, 109–10, 114–15; recognition of, 96–99, 114; respectability and, 103–4; role of, 94–98, 117–18; sociability and, 100–102, 117; Socialist Party and, 103–4, 107, 113–16
Spanish Civil War, 25, 71
sports, 42, 45, 48. See also football
stadiums, for football clubs, 35, 38, 46, 53, 66, 155n2; of Independiente, 63; of San Lorenzo de Almagro, 41, 58
store owners, 15, 55, 94–95, 97, 128. See also businessmen
strikes, of unions, 97, 116
students: bibliotecas populares and, 69, 82, 88–93, 166n61; of universidades populares, 130, 132–34, 134, 174n43
subdivision, of land, 16, 102, 109
subsidies: bibliotecas populares and, 73–75, 84–88, 92; for football clubs, 39, 58; universidades populares and, 123, 129–32, 138–40
suburbs, of Buenos Aires, 12, 28, 59–64; bibliotecas populares in, 78, 86; football clubs in, 52–53; transportation systems and, 26–27
subventions: for bibliotecas populares, 74, 82, 86; for universidades populares, 128–33, 135, 137–38, 140–41
subway, 18–19, 112–13, 116, 170n56

Talleres de Remedios de Escalada football club, 52
Tamborini, José P., 50, 88

tangos, 57; barrios in, 1, 11–12; football clubs and, 48–49
teachers, 32–33, 73, 89, 92, 125; income for, 120–21, 137–38, 141
Temperley football club, 44
Traba, Francisco, 115–16
transportation systems, 65; bus lines, 19, 58, 105; colectivos, 18–19; suburbs and, 26–27; subway, 18–19, 112–13, 116, 170n56; trolleys, 18–19, 56, 105, 116
trolley system, 18–19, 56, 105, 116
Trucco, Rómulo, 39

Unión Ferroviaria, 110, 166n61
unions, 45, 52, 113, 126; bibliotecas populares and, 70, 79, 81; strikes of, 97, 116
universidades populares (popular universities), 10; class and, 120–21, 127, 131–34; Congress and, 126, 129, 131, 135, 138; consortium of, 121, 137–41; courses of, 127–28, 130–31, 135–36; enrollment of, 127, 130–31; facilities for, 123, 129, 135–36, 138, 141–42; families and, 120–21, 131, 133–34, 174n43; funding and, 120–21, 125–31, 135–36, 138, 141; governance of, 123–25, 139; government support of, 127–30, 132–33, 135–38; ideologies of, 123–25; membership of, 120, 124, 129–30, 135–36, 138, 140–41; need for, 119–21, 141–42; political capital and, 36–38; politicians and, 135–36, 142; politics and, 120, 127, 129, 132, 137–38, 141; problems and, 124, 126, 136–38; Radical Party and, 126–30, 132, 138–40; schools and, 148–49; Socialist Party and, 122, 126, 136, 139–40; students of, 130, 132–34, 134, 174n43; subsidies and, 123, 129–32, 138–40; subventions for, 128–33, 135, 137–38, 140–41
Universidad Popular Bartolomé Mitre, 124
Universidad Popular de Belgrano, 135, 149
Universidad Popular Bernardino Rivadavia, 124, 131–32
Universidad Popular Bernardo de Irigoyen, 136
Universidad Popular de La Boca, 121–22, 125–29, 149
Universidad Popular de Boedo, 57, 125, 129–31
Universidad Popular Femenina de Palermo, 139
Universidad Popular Florentino Ameghino, 36, 124–25, 137–40
Universidad Popular de Flores Intendente Torcuato de Alvear, 132–34, 134, 138, 173n40
Universidad Popular de Flores Sud, 125
Universidad Popular Industrial de Buenos Aires, 140–41
Universidad Popular del Oeste, 126
Universidad Popular de Villa del Parque, 121, 124, 140
Universidad Popular de Villa Pueyrredón, 123–24, 139–40
University of Buenos Aires, 37
Uriburu, José F., 24

Vago, Enrique, 136, 140
Vedia y Mitre, Mariano de, 36, 115
Vélez Sarsfield (barrio), 116
Vélez Sarsfield football club, 52, 64, 85
Verbitsky, Bernardo, 50
Villa Crespo (barrio), 36–37, 81–82, 137
Villa del Parque (barrio), 109
Villa Devoto (barrio), 96, 103
Villa Lugano (barrio), 107, 110

Villa Pueyrredón (barrio), 70
Villa Urquiza (barrio), 83
Villemur, Pedro, 58–59, 129
Vinciguerra, Rómulo, 109, 140, 144, 175n63
vocational training, 14–15, 127–28, 142, 148–49
voter support, politicians and, 2–3, 14, 97
voting, 26; reform of, 2, 41–42, 97; Sáenz Peña law and, 13, 23, 28, 36, 45, 81

wards, political parties and, 30, 56
Weitz-Shapiro, Rebecca, 3
women, 15, 23, 32, 48–49, 60, 72–73, 78, 89, 125, 136, 144; in sociedades de fomento, 96; as students, 131, 133–34, 139

Yrigoyen, Hipólito, 23, 29, 58, 105, 112, 153n39

Zolezzi, Antonio, 66